THE HELM

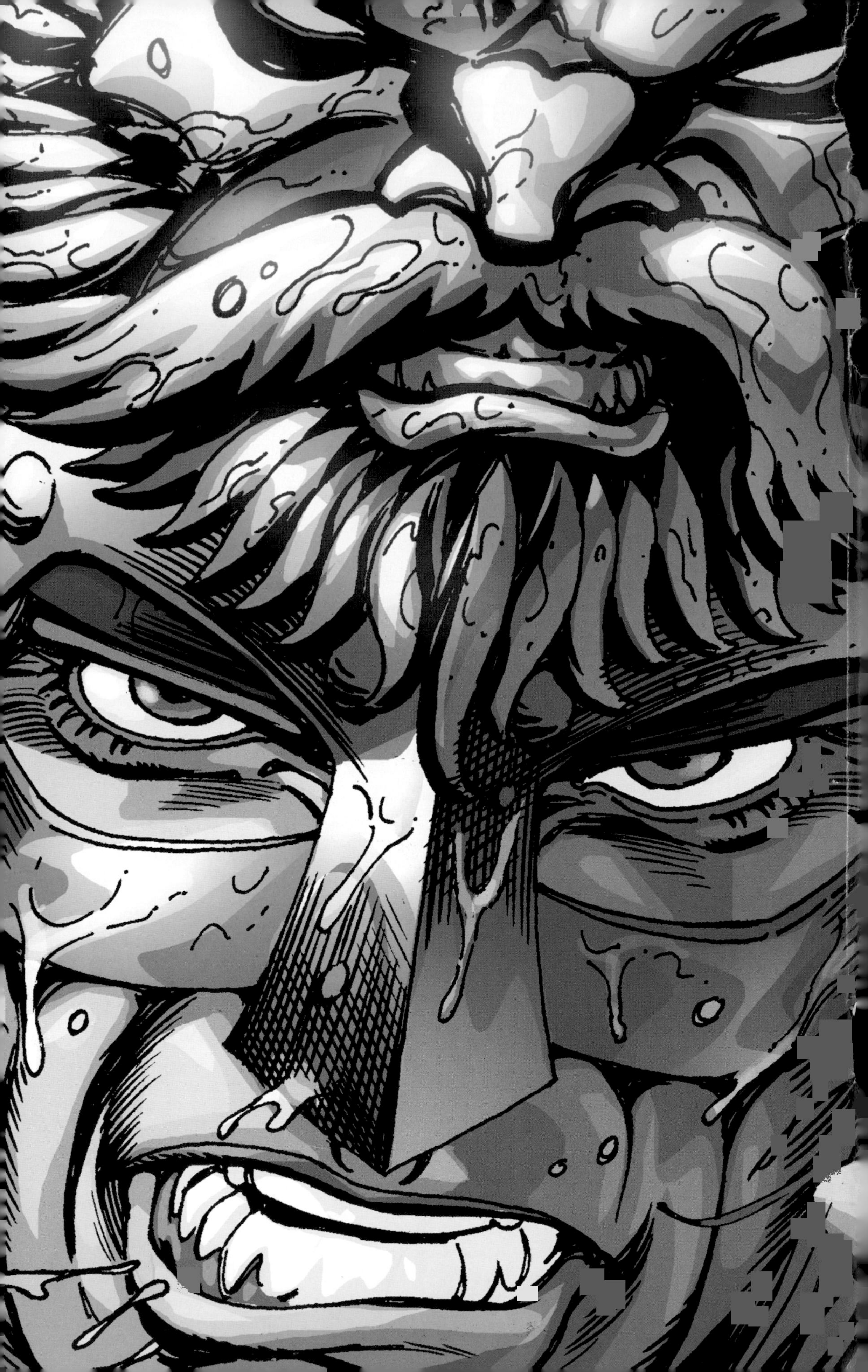

THE HELM

STORY
JIM HARDISON

COVERS AND BREAKDOWNS
BART SEARS

FINISHES
RANDY ELLIOTT

COLORS
DAN JACKSON

LETTERS
DAVE LANPHEAR

DARK HORSE BOOKS®

Publisher **MIKE RICHARDSON**
Art Director **LIA RIBACCHI**
Collection Designer **JOSH ELLIOTT**
Assistant Editor **PATRICK THORPE**
Associate Editor **KATIE MOODY**
Editor **DAVE LAND**

DARK HORSE BOOKS
A division of Dark Horse Comics, Inc.
10956 SE Main Street
Milwaukie OR 97222

darkhorse.com

To find a comic shop in your area, call the Comic Shop
Locator Service toll-free at (888) 266-4226

First edition: April 2009
ISBN 978-1-59582-261-1

3 5 7 9 10 8 6 4 2

Printed at Midas Printing International, Ltd., Huizhou, China.

THE HELM™

This book collects issues one through four of the Dark Horse comic-book series *The Helm*.

MIKE RICHARDSON President and Publisher NEIL HANKERSON Executive Vice President TOM WEDDLE Chief Financial Officer RANDY STRADLEY Vice President of
Publishing MICHAEL MARTENS Vice President of Business Development ANITA NELSON Vice President of Marketing, Sales, and Licensing DAVID SCROGGY Vice
President of Product Development DALE LAFOUNTAIN Vice President of Information Technology DARLENE VOGEL Director of Purchasing KEN LIZZI General Counsel
DAVEY ESTRADA Editorial Director SCOTT ALLIE Senior Managing Editor CHRIS WARNER Senior Books Editor, Dark Horse Books ROB SIMPSON Senior Books Editor,
M Press/DH Press DIANA SCHUTZ Executive Editor CARY GRAZZINI Director of Design and Production LIA RIBACCHI Art Director CARA NIECE Director of Scheduling

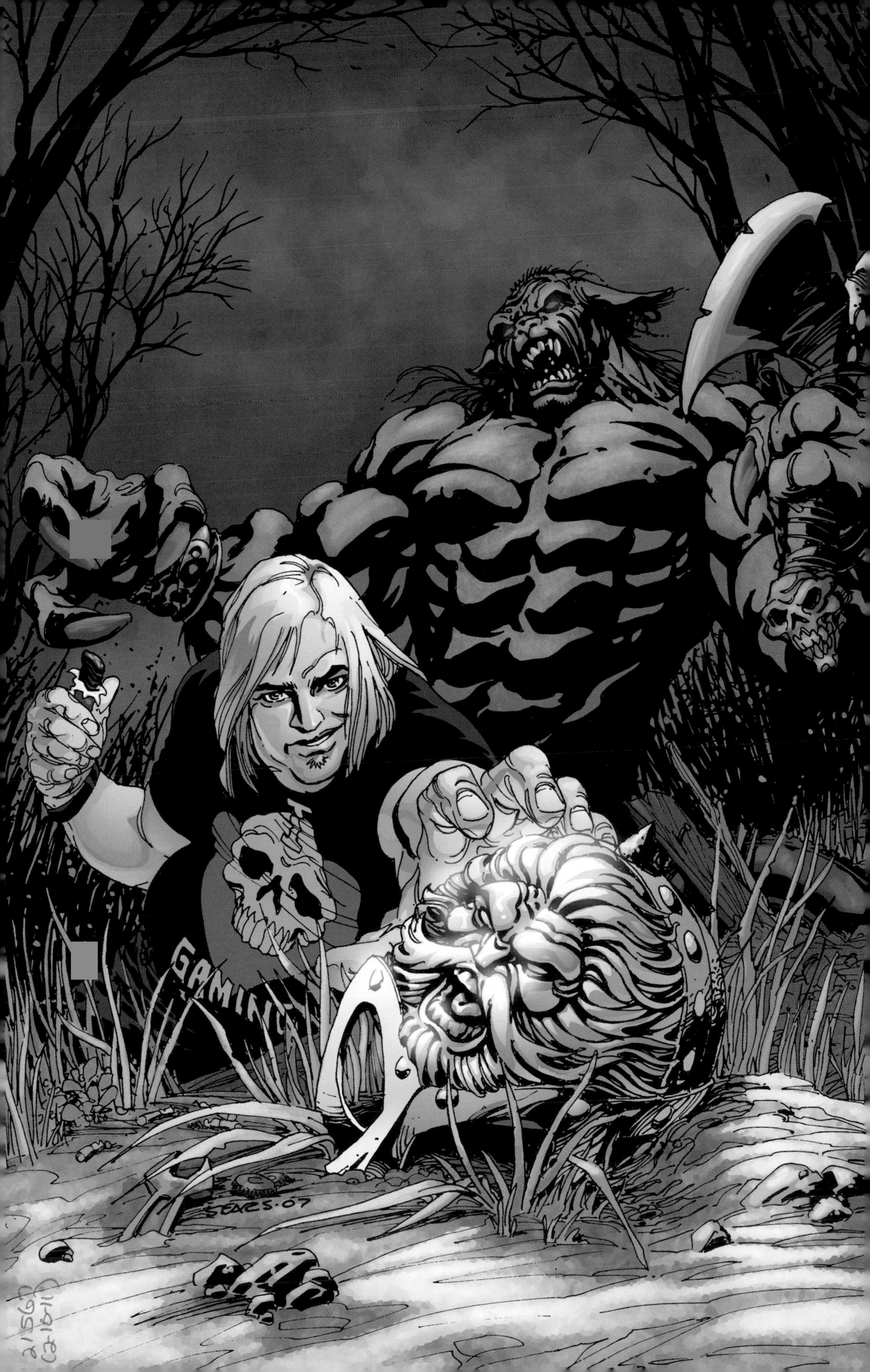

CHAPTER 1
VALHALLADRIM

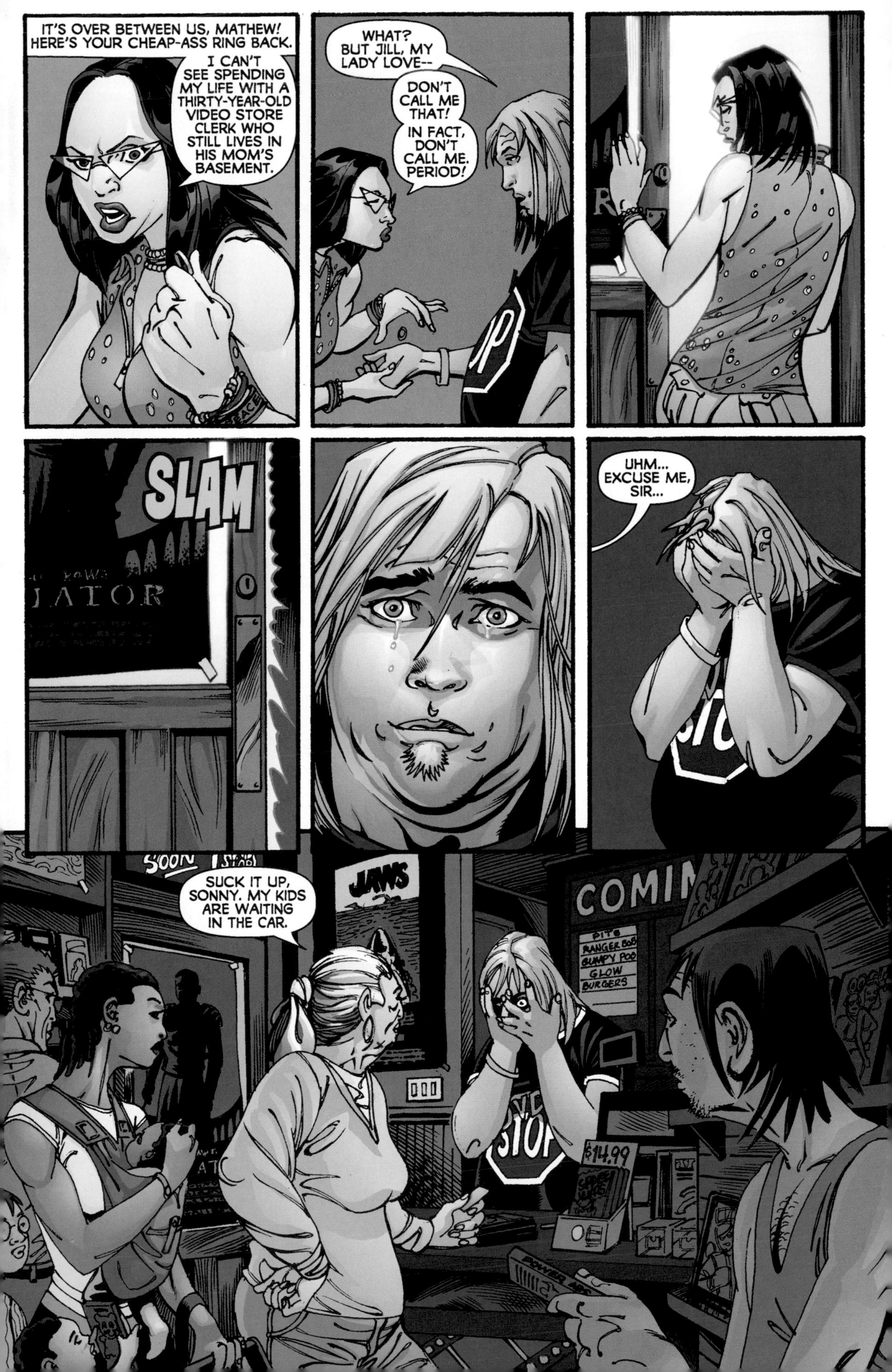
IT'S OVER BETWEEN US, MATHEW! HERE'S YOUR CHEAP-ASS RING BACK.
I CAN'T SEE SPENDING MY LIFE WITH A THIRTY-YEAR-OLD VIDEO STORE CLERK WHO STILL LIVES IN HIS MOM'S BASEMENT.
WHAT? BUT JILL, MY LADY LOVE--
DON'T CALL ME THAT!
IN FACT, DON'T CALL ME. PERIOD!
SLAM
UHM... EXCUSE ME, SIR...
SUCK IT UP, SONNY. MY KIDS ARE WAITING IN THE CAR.
JAWS
COMIN
GLOW
BURGERS
$14.99

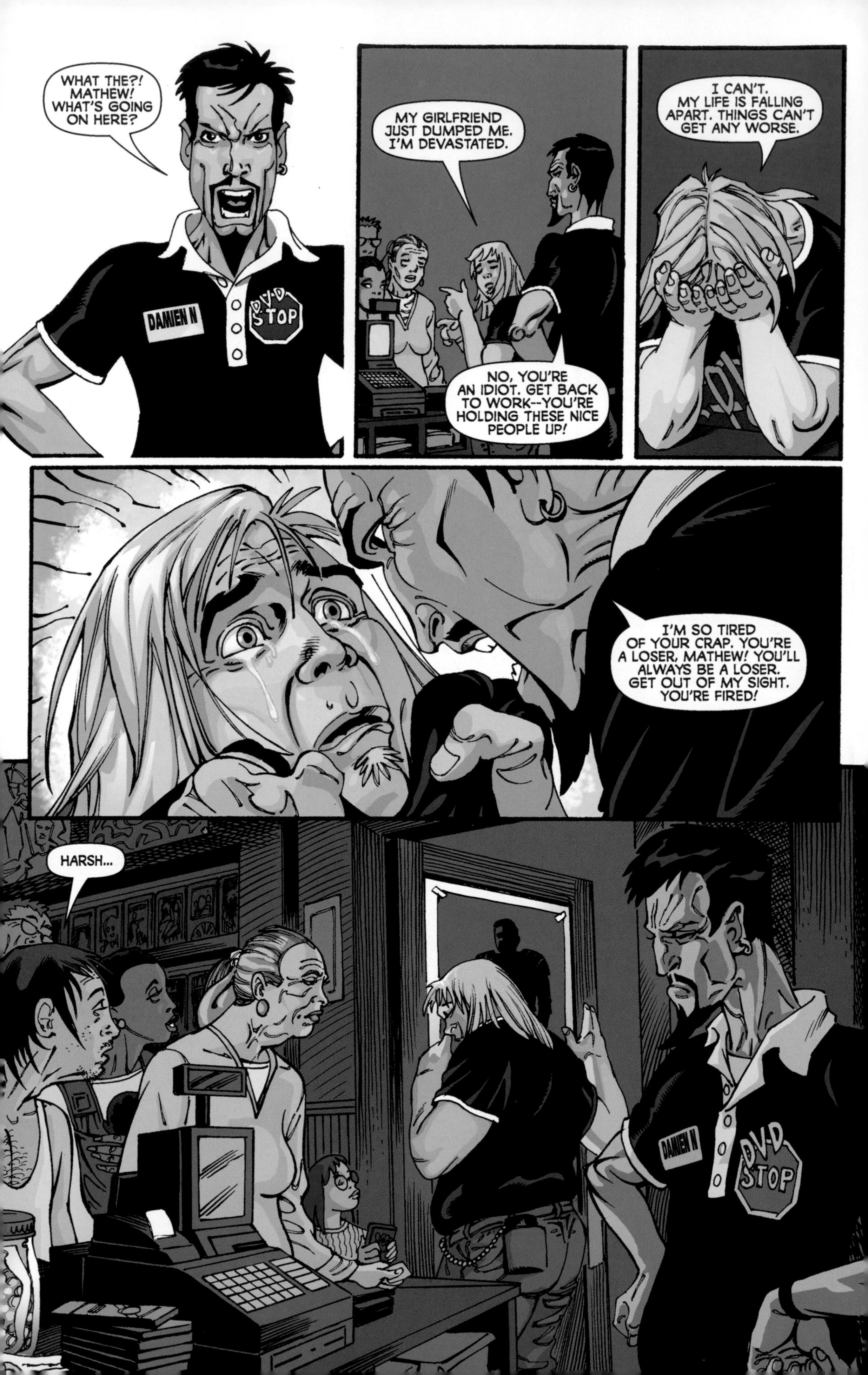
WHAT THE?! MATHEW! WHAT'S GOING ON HERE?
DAMIEN N
DVD STOP
MY GIRLFRIEND JUST DUMPED ME. I'M DEVASTATED.
NO, YOU'RE AN IDIOT. GET BACK TO WORK--YOU'RE HOLDING THESE NICE PEOPLE UP!
I CAN'T. MY LIFE IS FALLING APART. THINGS CAN'T GET ANY WORSE.
I'M SO TIRED OF YOUR CRAP. YOU'RE A LOSER, MATHEW! YOU'LL ALWAYS BE A LOSER. GET OUT OF MY SIGHT. YOU'RE FIRED!
HARSH...
DAMIEN N
DVD STOP

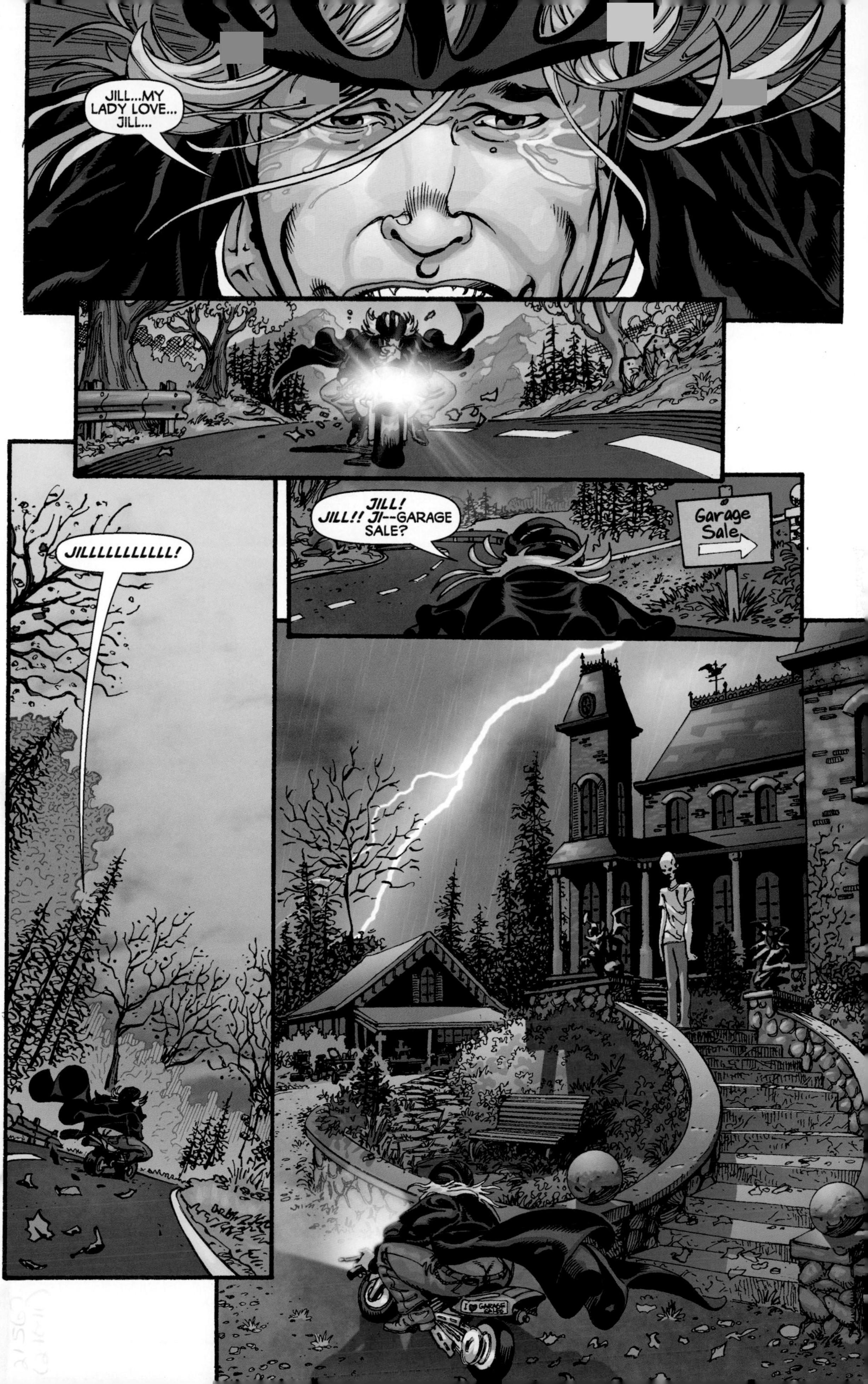
JILL...MY LADY LOVE... JILL...
JILLLLLLLLLLLL!
JILL! JILL!! JI--GARAGE SALE?
Garage Sale

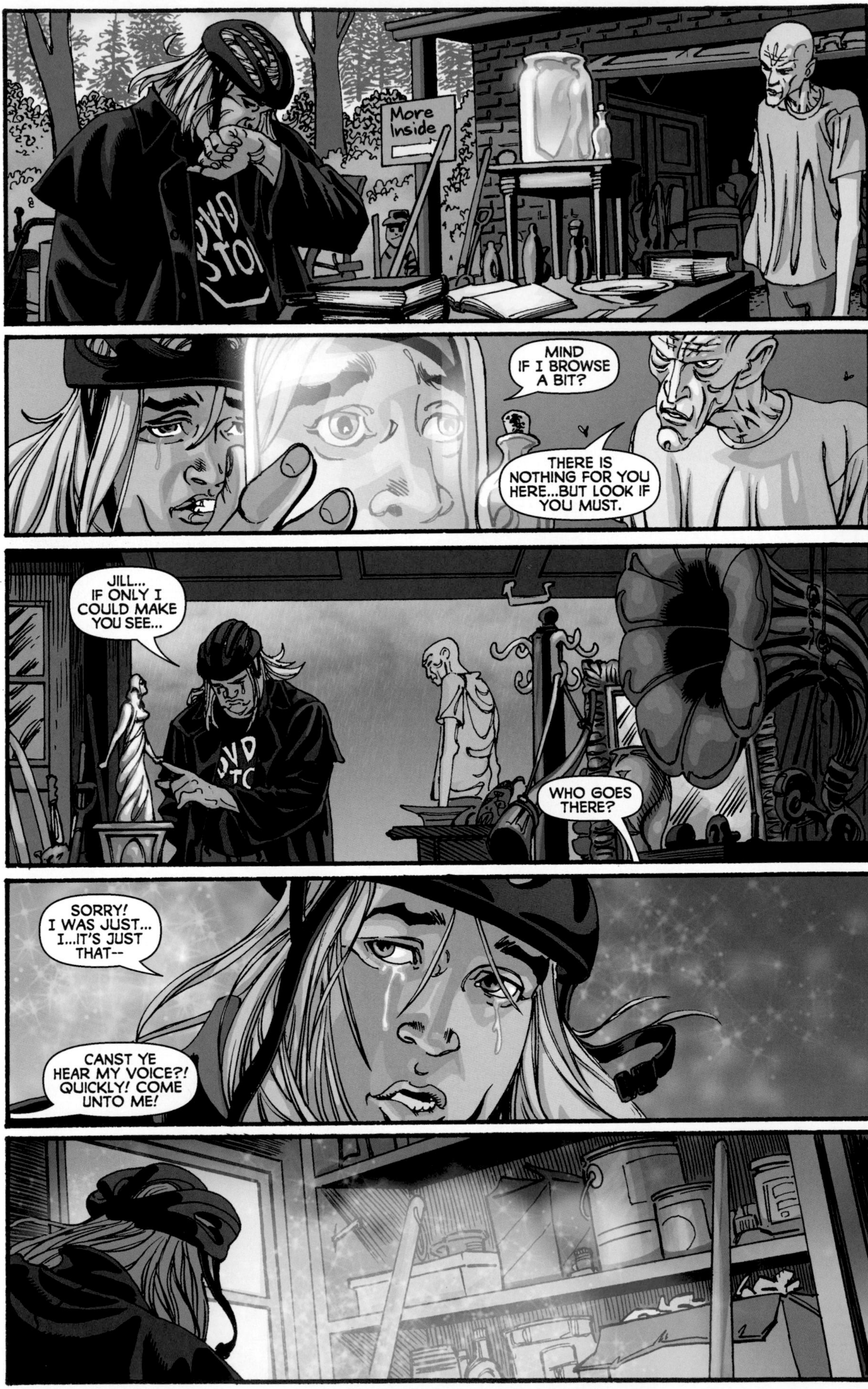
More Inside
DVD STO
MIND IF I BROWSE A BIT?
THERE IS NOTHING FOR YOU HERE...BUT LOOK IF YOU MUST.
JILL... IF ONLY I COULD MAKE YOU SEE...
WHO GOES THERE?
SORRY! I WAS JUST... I...IT'S JUST THAT--
CANST YE HEAR MY VOICE?! QUICKLY! COME UNTO ME!

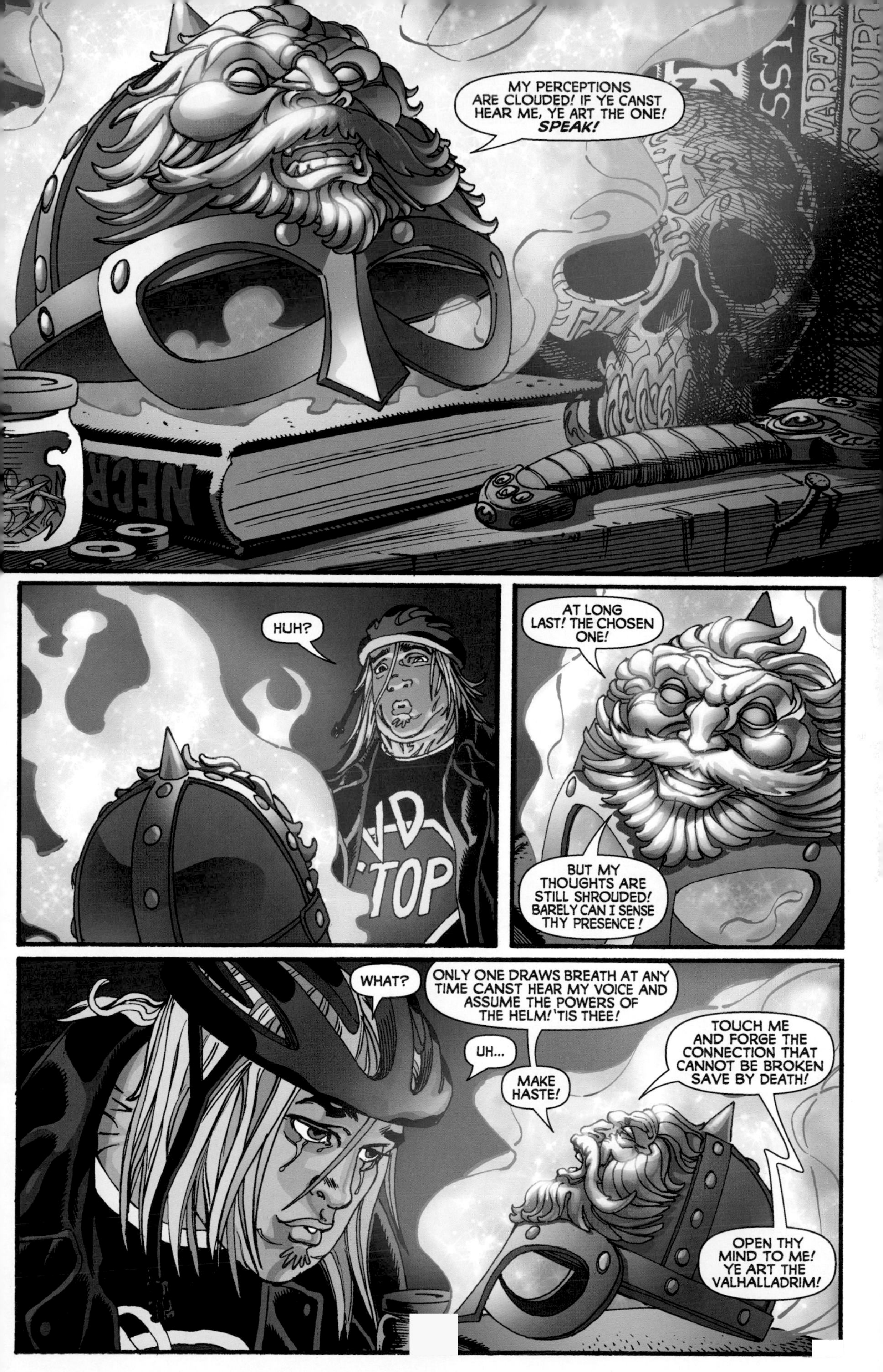
MY PERCEPTIONS ARE CLOUDED! IF YE CANST HEAR ME, YE ART THE ONE! SPEAK!
HUH?
AT LONG LAST! THE CHOSEN ONE!
BUT MY THOUGHTS ARE STILL SHROUDED! BARELY CAN I SENSE THY PRESENCE!
WHAT?
ONLY ONE DRAWS BREATH AT ANY TIME CANST HEAR MY VOICE AND ASSUME THE POWERS OF THE HELM! 'TIS THEE!
UH...
MAKE HASTE!
TOUCH ME AND FORGE THE CONNECTION THAT CANNOT BE BROKEN SAVE BY DEATH!
OPEN THY MIND TO ME! YE ART THE VALHALLADRIM!

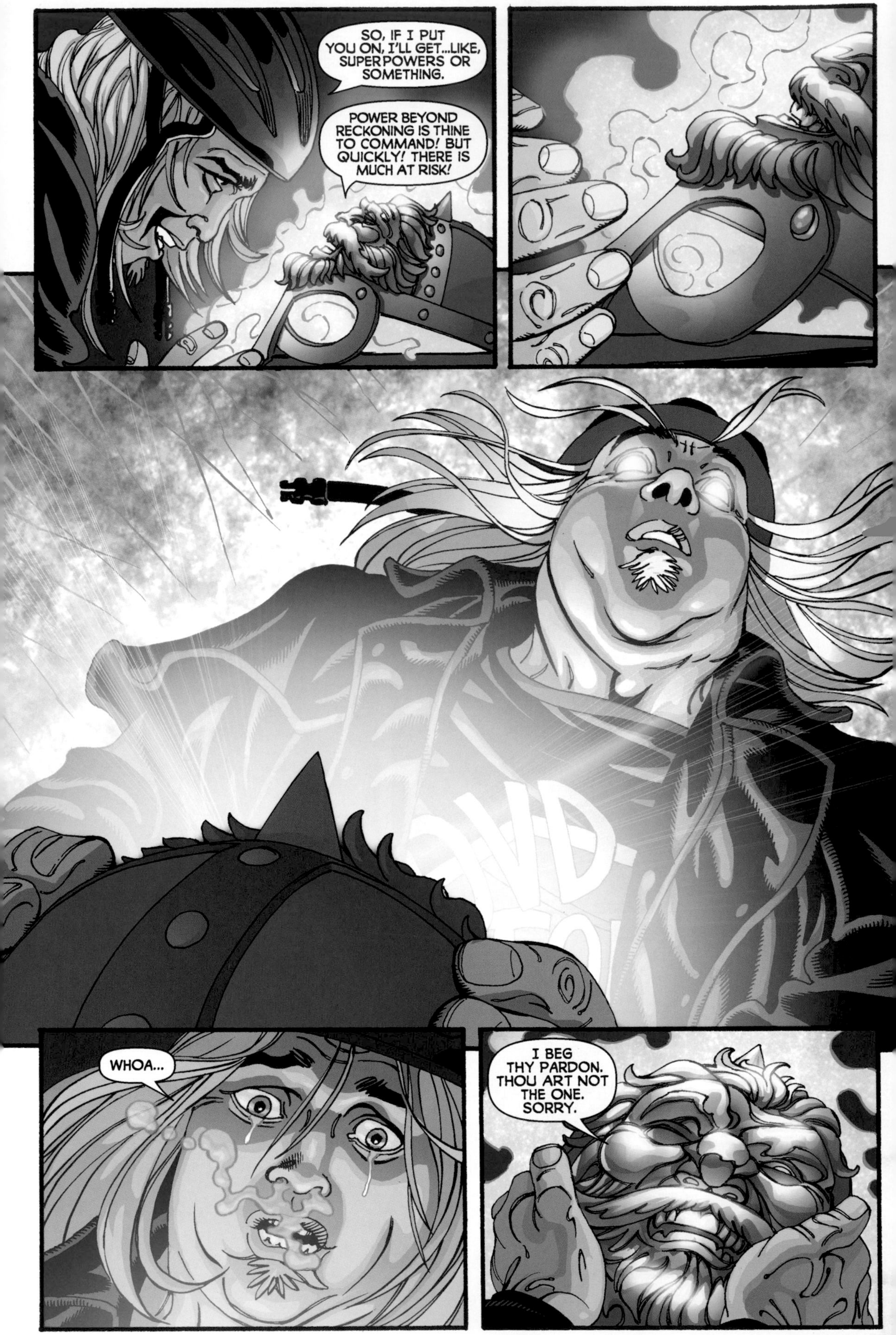
SO, IF I PUT YOU ON, I'LL GET...LIKE, SUPERPOWERS OR SOMETHING.
POWER BEYOND RECKONING IS THINE TO COMMAND! BUT QUICKLY! THERE IS MUCH AT RISK!
WHOA...
I BEG THY PARDON. THOU ART NOT THE ONE. SORRY.

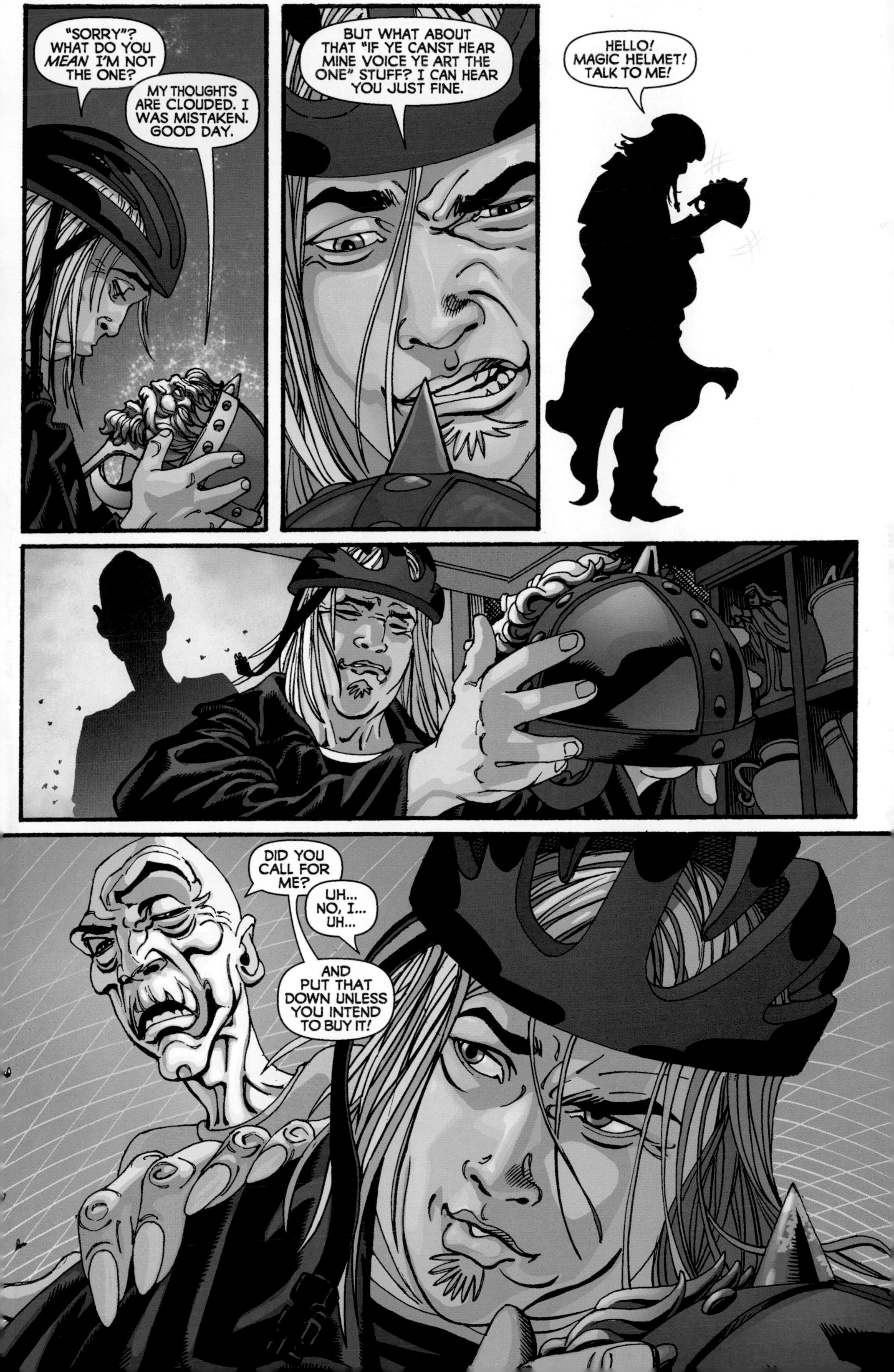
"SORRY"? WHAT DO YOU *MEAN* I'M NOT THE ONE?
MY THOUGHTS ARE CLOUDED. I WAS MISTAKEN. GOOD DAY.
BUT WHAT ABOUT THAT "IF YE CANST HEAR MINE VOICE YE ART THE ONE" STUFF? I CAN HEAR YOU JUST FINE.
HELLO! MAGIC HELMET! TALK TO ME!
DID YOU CALL FOR ME?
UH... NO, I... UH...
AND PUT THAT DOWN UNLESS YOU INTEND TO BUY IT!

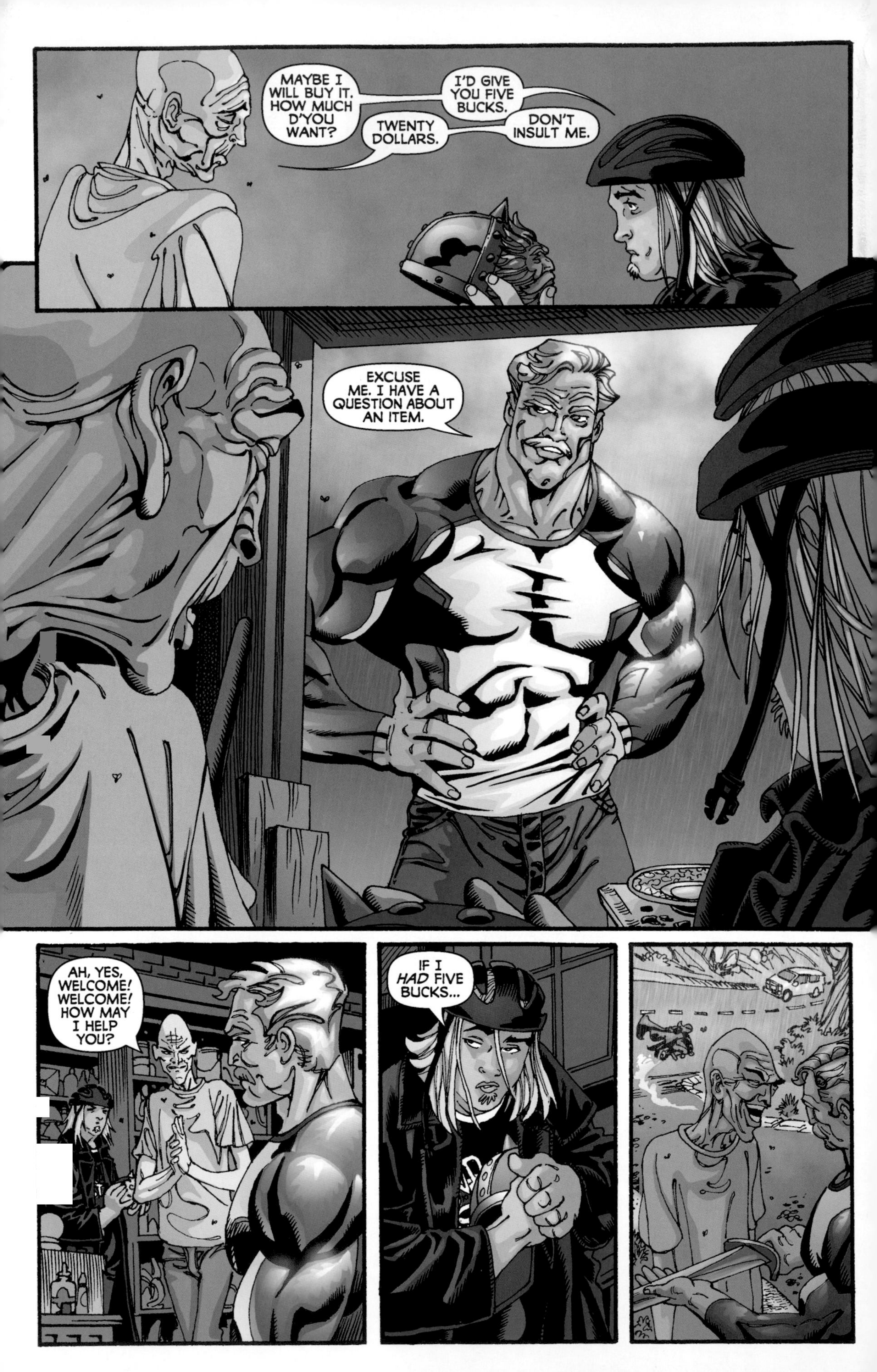
MAYBE I WILL BUY IT. HOW MUCH D'YOU WANT?
TWENTY DOLLARS.
I'D GIVE YOU FIVE BUCKS.
DON'T INSULT ME.
EXCUSE ME. I HAVE A QUESTION ABOUT AN ITEM.
AH, YES, WELCOME! WELCOME! HOW MAY I HELP YOU?
IF I *HAD* FIVE BUCKS...

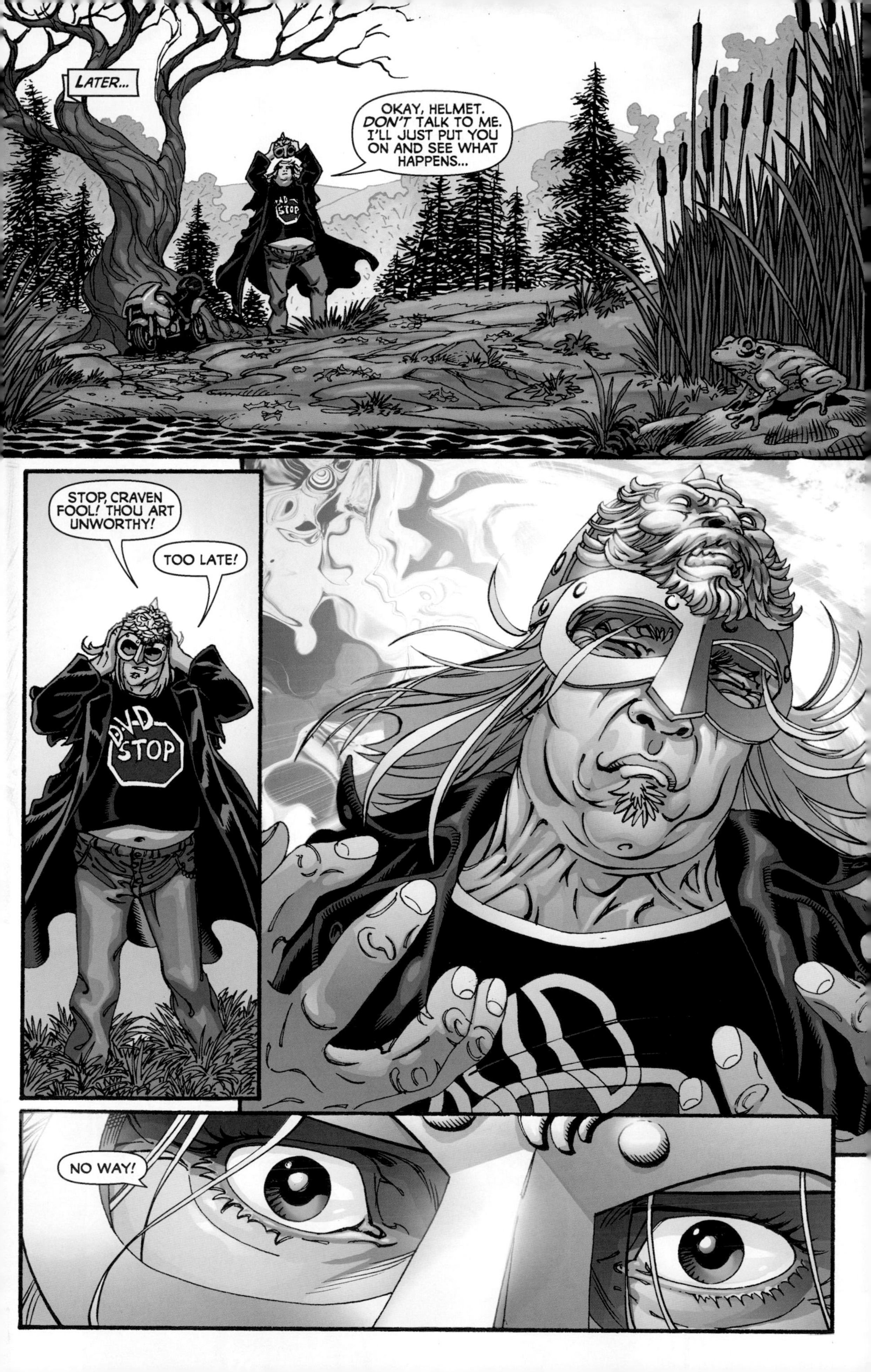
LATER...
OKAY, HELMET. DON'T TALK TO ME. I'LL JUST PUT YOU ON AND SEE WHAT HAPPENS...
D.V.D. STOP
STOP, CRAVEN FOOL! THOU ART UNWORTHY!
TOO LATE!
D.V.D. STOP
NO WAY!

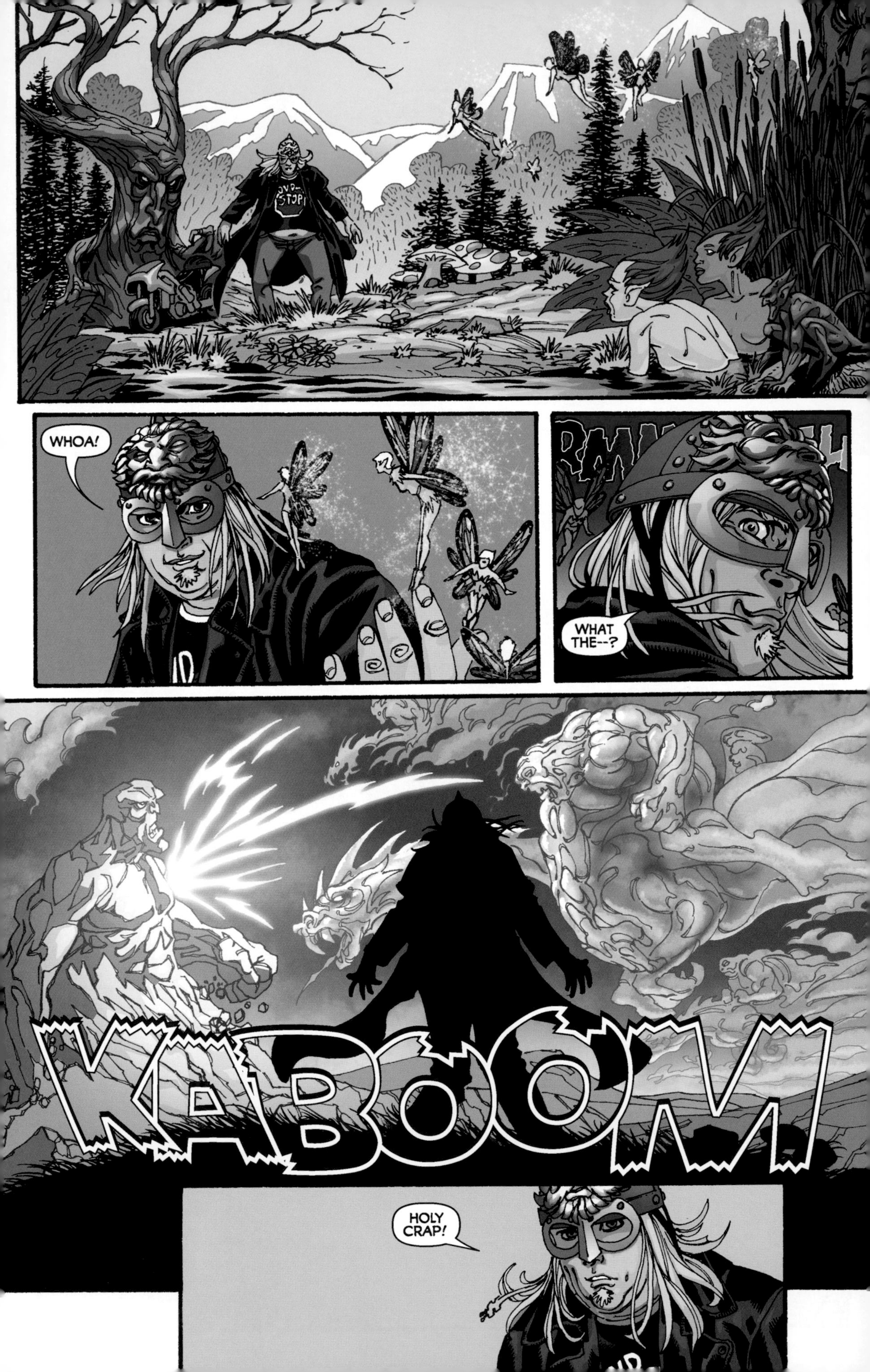
WHOA!
WHAT THE--?
KABOOM!
HOLY CRAP!

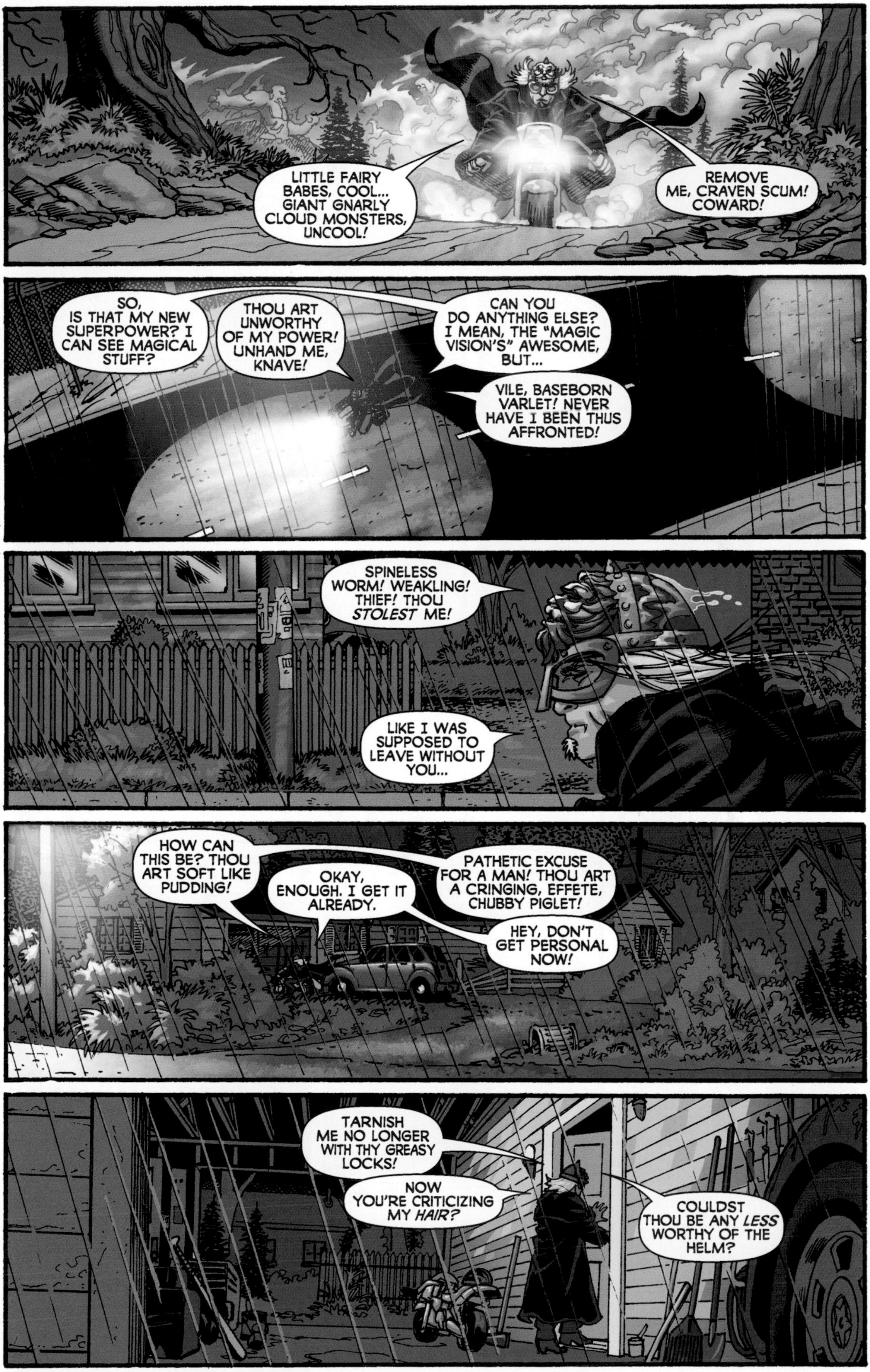
LITTLE FAIRY BABES, COOL... GIANT GNARLY CLOUD MONSTERS, UNCOOL!
REMOVE ME, CRAVEN SCUM! COWARD!
SO, IS THAT MY NEW SUPERPOWER? I CAN SEE MAGICAL STUFF?
THOU ART UNWORTHY OF MY POWER! UNHAND ME, KNAVE!
CAN YOU DO ANYTHING ELSE? I MEAN, THE "MAGIC VISION'S" AWESOME, BUT...
VILE, BASEBORN VARLET! NEVER HAVE I BEEN THUS AFFRONTED!
SPINELESS WORM! WEAKLING! THIEF! THOU STOLEST ME!
LIKE I WAS SUPPOSED TO LEAVE WITHOUT YOU...
HOW CAN THIS BE? THOU ART SOFT LIKE PUDDING!
OKAY, ENOUGH. I GET IT ALREADY.
PATHETIC EXCUSE FOR A MAN! THOU ART A CRINGING, EFFETE, CHUBBY PIGLET!
HEY, DON'T GET PERSONAL NOW!
TARNISH ME NO LONGER WITH THY GREASY LOCKS!
NOW YOU'RE CRITICIZING MY HAIR?
COULDST THOU BE ANY LESS WORTHY OF THE HELM?

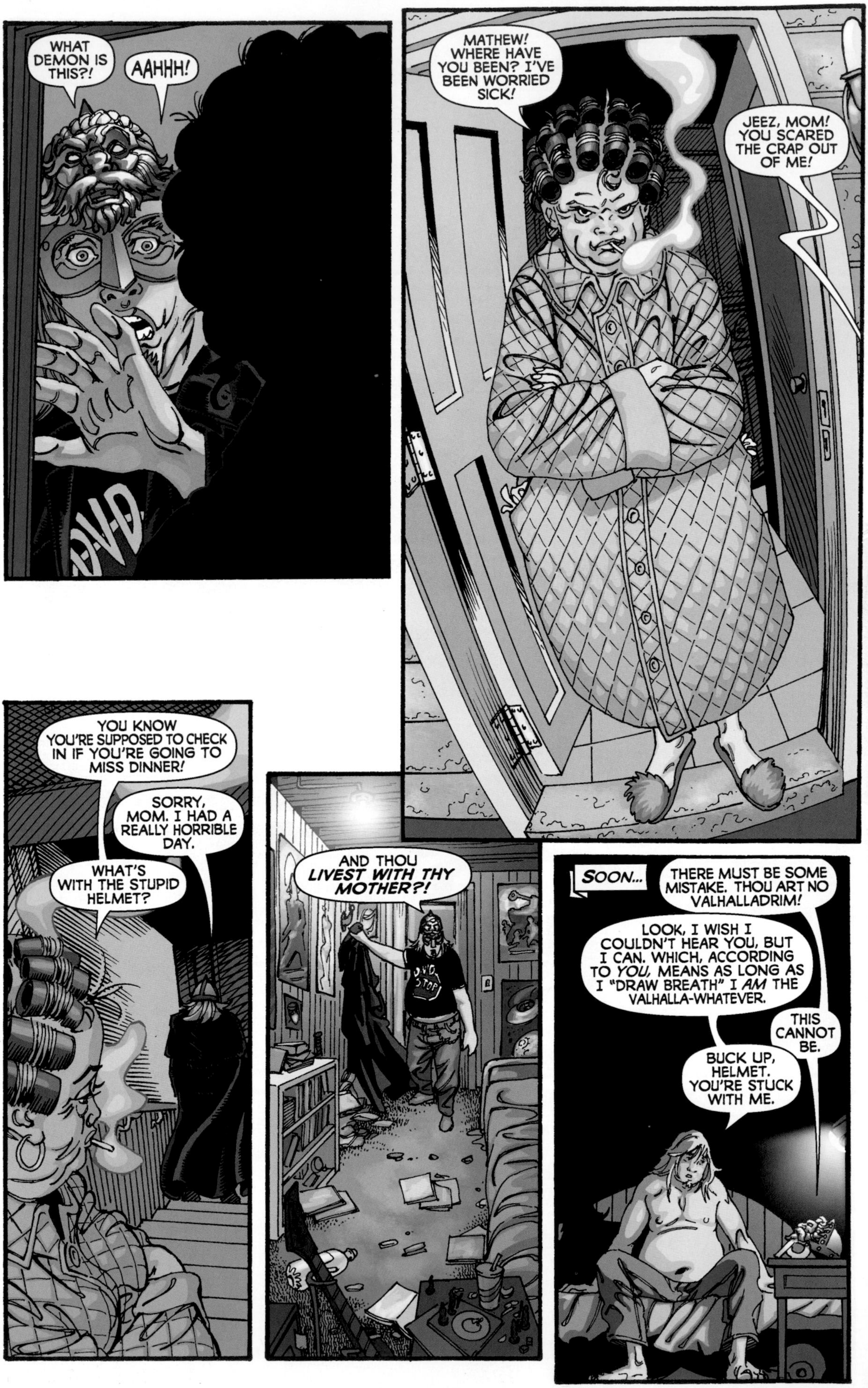
WHAT DEMON IS THIS?!
AAHHH!
MATHEW! WHERE HAVE YOU BEEN? I'VE BEEN WORRIED SICK!
JEEZ, MOM! YOU SCARED THE CRAP OUT OF ME!
YOU KNOW YOU'RE SUPPOSED TO CHECK IN IF YOU'RE GOING TO MISS DINNER!
SORRY, MOM. I HAD A REALLY HORRIBLE DAY.
WHAT'S WITH THE STUPID HELMET?
AND THOU *LIVEST WITH THY MOTHER?!*
SOON...
THERE MUST BE SOME MISTAKE. THOU ART NO VALHALLADRIM!
LOOK, I WISH I COULDN'T HEAR YOU, BUT I CAN. WHICH, ACCORDING TO *YOU,* MEANS AS LONG AS I "DRAW BREATH" I *AM* THE VALHALLA-WHATEVER.
THIS CANNOT BE.
BUCK UP, HELMET. YOU'RE STUCK WITH ME.

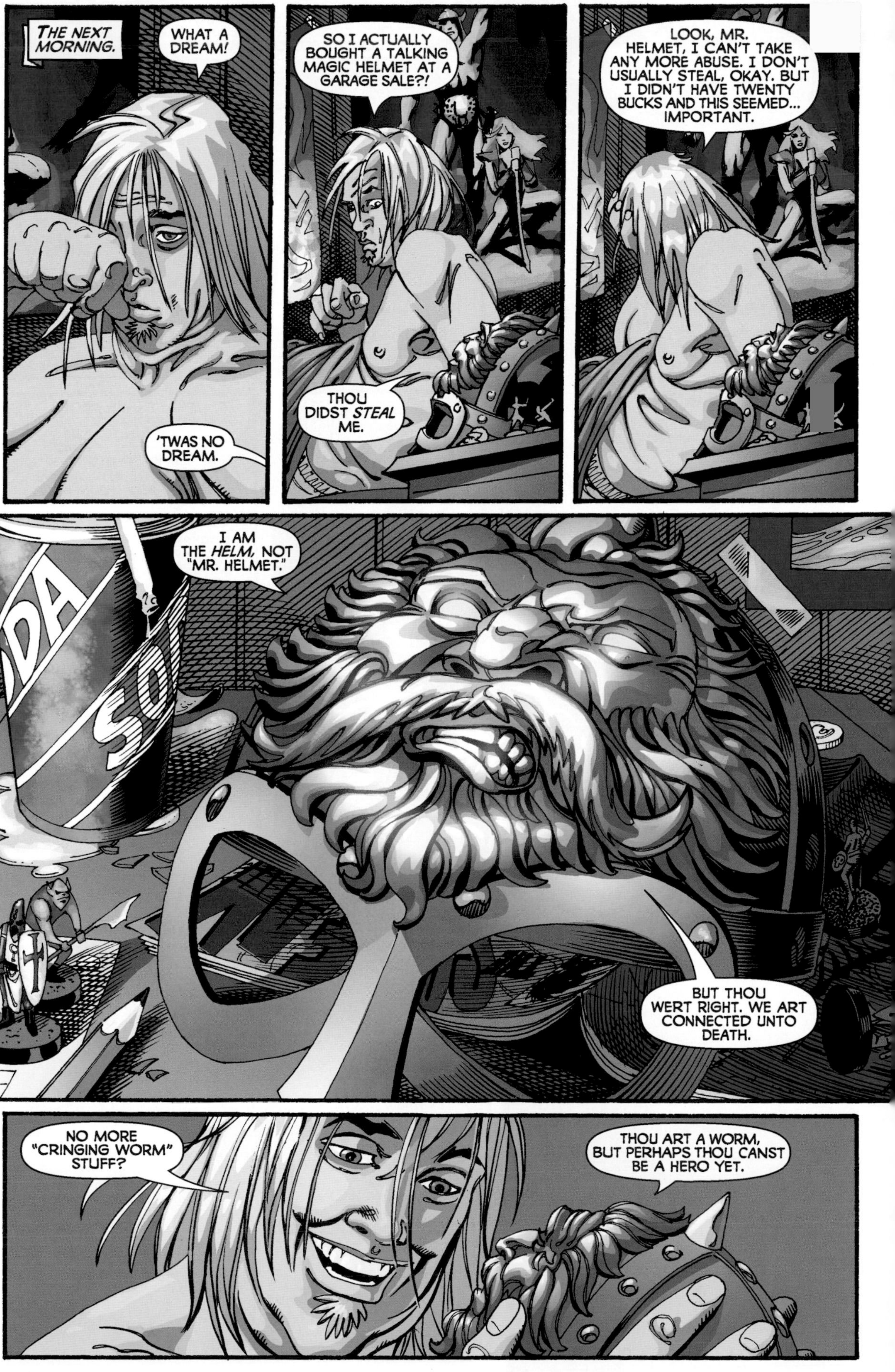
THE NEXT MORNING.
WHAT A DREAM!
'TWAS NO DREAM.
SO I ACTUALLY BOUGHT A TALKING MAGIC HELMET AT A GARAGE SALE?!
THOU DIDST STEAL ME.
LOOK, MR. HELMET, I CAN'T TAKE ANY MORE ABUSE. I DON'T USUALLY STEAL, OKAY. BUT I DIDN'T HAVE TWENTY BUCKS AND THIS SEEMED... IMPORTANT.
I AM THE HELM, NOT "MR. HELMET."
SODA
BUT THOU WERT RIGHT. WE ART CONNECTED UNTO DEATH.
NO MORE "CRINGING WORM" STUFF?
THOU ART A WORM, BUT PERHAPS THOU CANST BE A HERO YET.

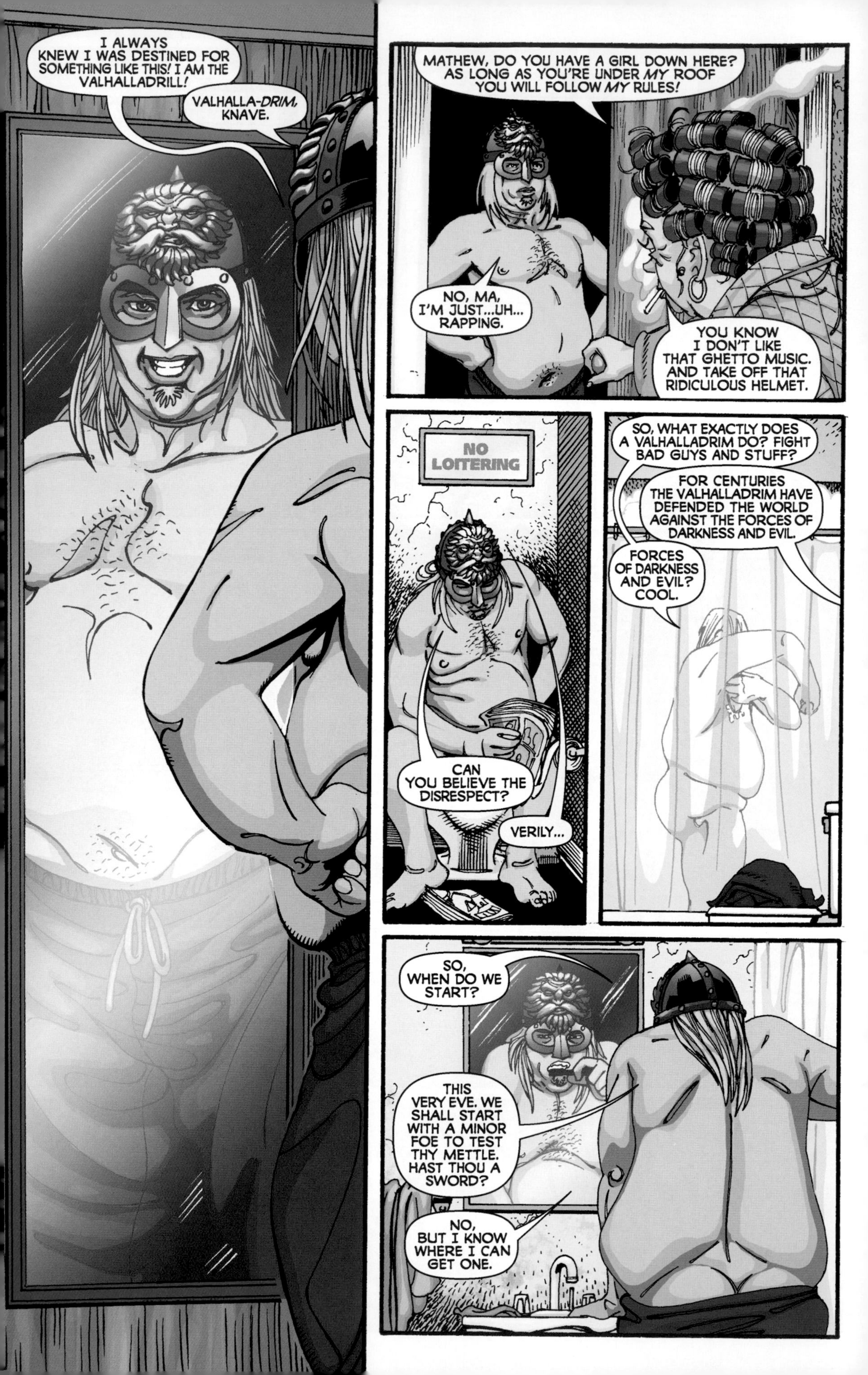

I ALWAYS KNEW I WAS DESTINED FOR SOMETHING LIKE THIS! I AM THE VALHALLADRILL!
VALHALLA-*DRIM*, KNAVE.
MATHEW, DO YOU HAVE A GIRL DOWN HERE? AS LONG AS YOU'RE UNDER *MY* ROOF YOU WILL FOLLOW *MY* RULES!
NO, MA, I'M JUST...UH... RAPPING.
YOU KNOW I DON'T LIKE THAT GHETTO MUSIC. AND TAKE OFF THAT RIDICULOUS HELMET.
NO LOITERING
CAN YOU BELIEVE THE DISRESPECT?
VERILY...
SO, WHAT EXACTLY DOES A VALHALLADRIM DO? FIGHT BAD GUYS AND STUFF?
FOR CENTURIES THE VALHALLADRIM HAVE DEFENDED THE WORLD AGAINST THE FORCES OF DARKNESS AND EVIL.
FORCES OF DARKNESS AND EVIL? COOL.
SO, WHEN DO WE START?
THIS VERY EVE. WE SHALL START WITH A MINOR FOE TO TEST THY METTLE. HAST THOU A SWORD?
NO, BUT I KNOW WHERE I CAN GET ONE.

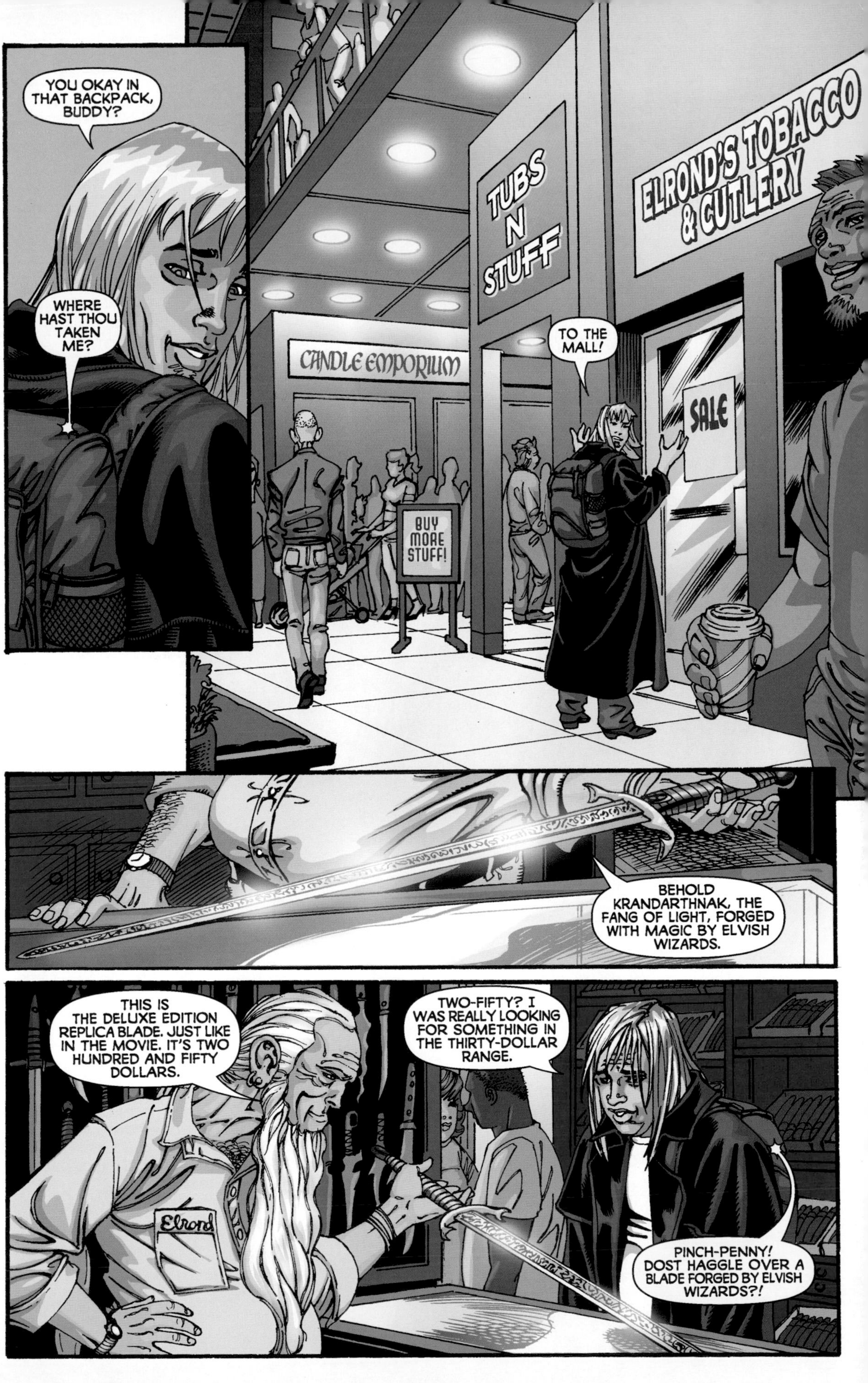
YOU OKAY IN THAT BACKPACK, BUDDY?
WHERE HAST THOU TAKEN ME?
TUBS N STUFF
ELROND'S TOBACCO & CUTLERY
CANDLE EMPORIUM
TO THE MALL!
SALE
BUY MORE STUFF!
BEHOLD KRANDARTHNAK, THE FANG OF LIGHT, FORGED WITH MAGIC BY ELVISH WIZARDS.
THIS IS THE DELUXE EDITION REPLICA BLADE. JUST LIKE IN THE MOVIE. IT'S TWO HUNDRED AND FIFTY DOLLARS.
TWO-FIFTY? I WAS REALLY LOOKING FOR SOMETHING IN THE THIRTY-DOLLAR RANGE.
Elrond
PINCH-PENNY! DOST HAGGLE OVER A BLADE FORGED BY ELVISH WIZARDS?!

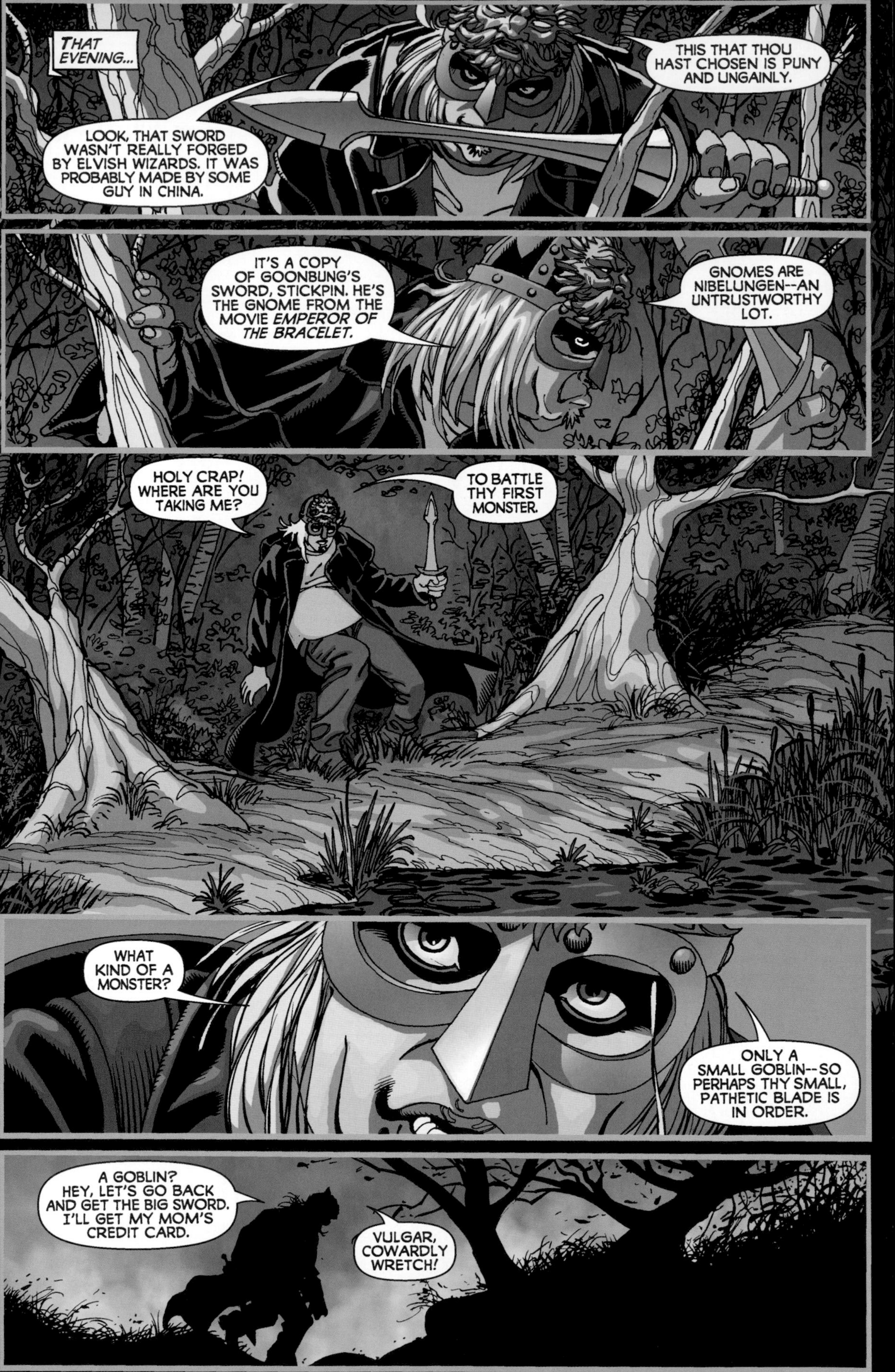
THAT EVENING...
THIS THAT THOU HAST CHOSEN IS PUNY AND UNGAINLY.
LOOK, THAT SWORD WASN'T REALLY FORGED BY ELVISH WIZARDS. IT WAS PROBABLY MADE BY SOME GUY IN CHINA.
IT'S A COPY OF GOONBUNG'S SWORD, STICKPIN. HE'S THE GNOME FROM THE MOVIE *EMPEROR OF THE BRACELET.*
GNOMES ARE NIBELUNGEN--AN UNTRUSTWORTHY LOT.
HOLY CRAP! WHERE ARE YOU TAKING ME?
TO BATTLE THY FIRST MONSTER.
WHAT KIND OF A MONSTER?
ONLY A SMALL GOBLIN--SO PERHAPS THY SMALL, PATHETIC BLADE IS IN ORDER.
A GOBLIN? HEY, LET'S GO BACK AND GET THE BIG SWORD. I'LL GET MY MOM'S CREDIT CARD.
VULGAR, COWARDLY WRETCH!

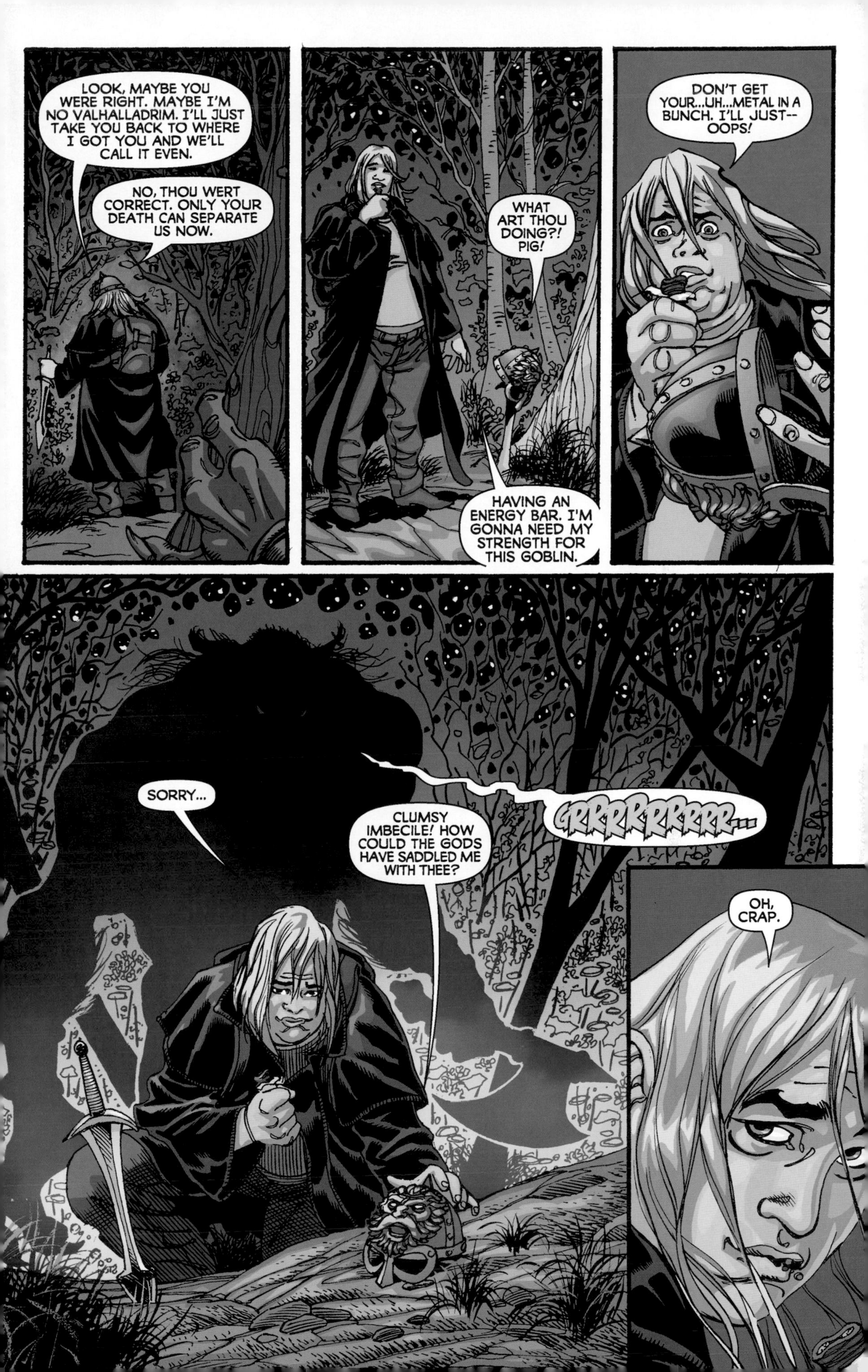
LOOK, MAYBE YOU WERE RIGHT. MAYBE I'M NO VALHALLADRIM. I'LL JUST TAKE YOU BACK TO WHERE I GOT YOU AND WE'LL CALL IT EVEN.
NO, THOU WERT CORRECT. ONLY YOUR DEATH CAN SEPARATE US NOW.
WHAT ART THOU DOING?! PIG!
HAVING AN ENERGY BAR. I'M GONNA NEED MY STRENGTH FOR THIS GOBLIN.
DON'T GET YOUR...UH...METAL IN A BUNCH. I'LL JUST--OOPS!
SORRY...
CLUMSY IMBECILE! HOW COULD THE GODS HAVE SADDLED ME WITH THEE?
GRRRRRRRRR...
OH, CRAP.

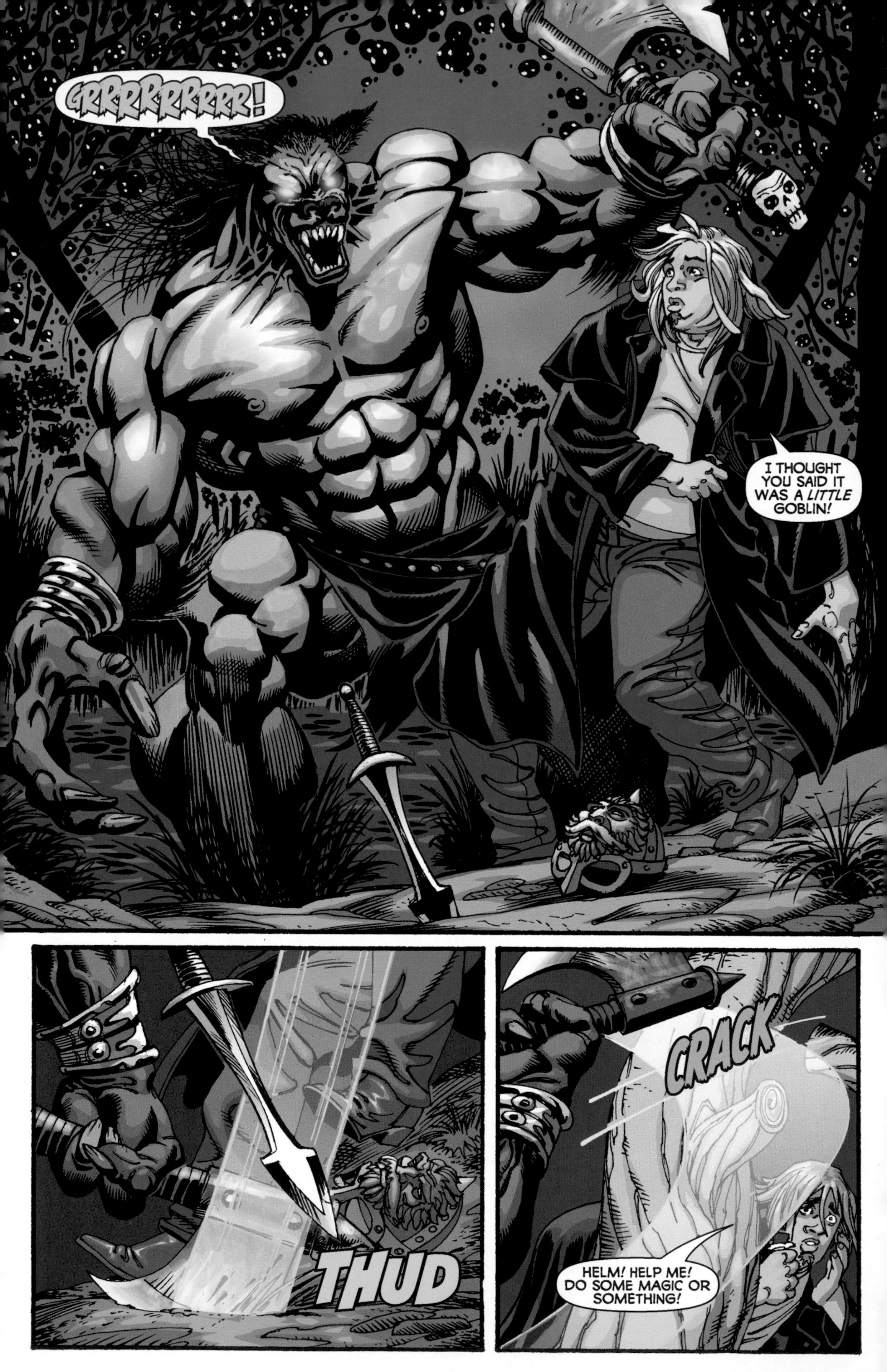
GRRRRRRRRR!
I THOUGHT YOU SAID IT WAS A *LITTLE* GOBLIN!
THUD
CRACK
HELM! HELP ME! DO SOME MAGIC OR SOMETHING!

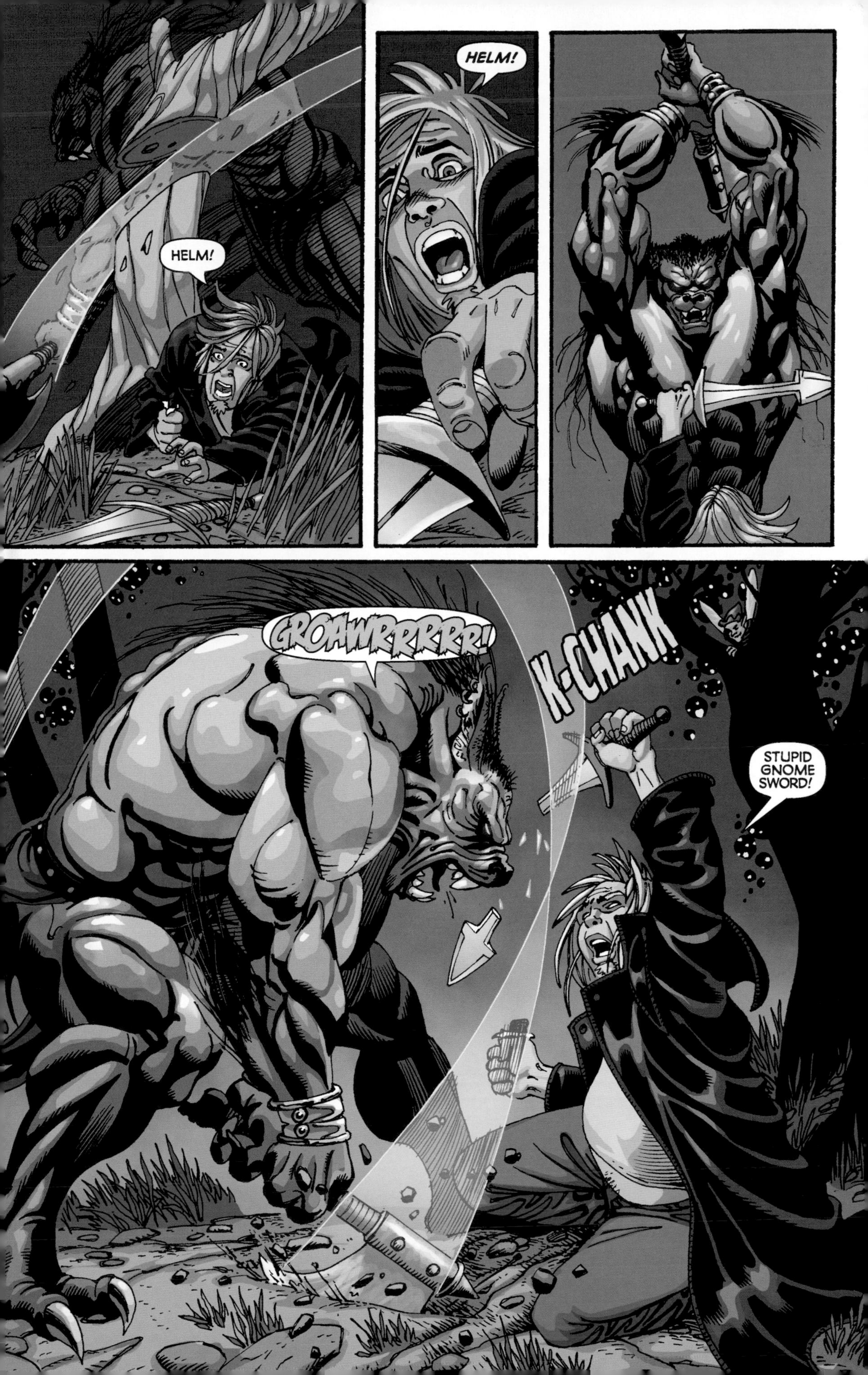
HELM!
HELM!
GROAWRRRRR!
K-CHANK
STUPID GNOME SWORD!

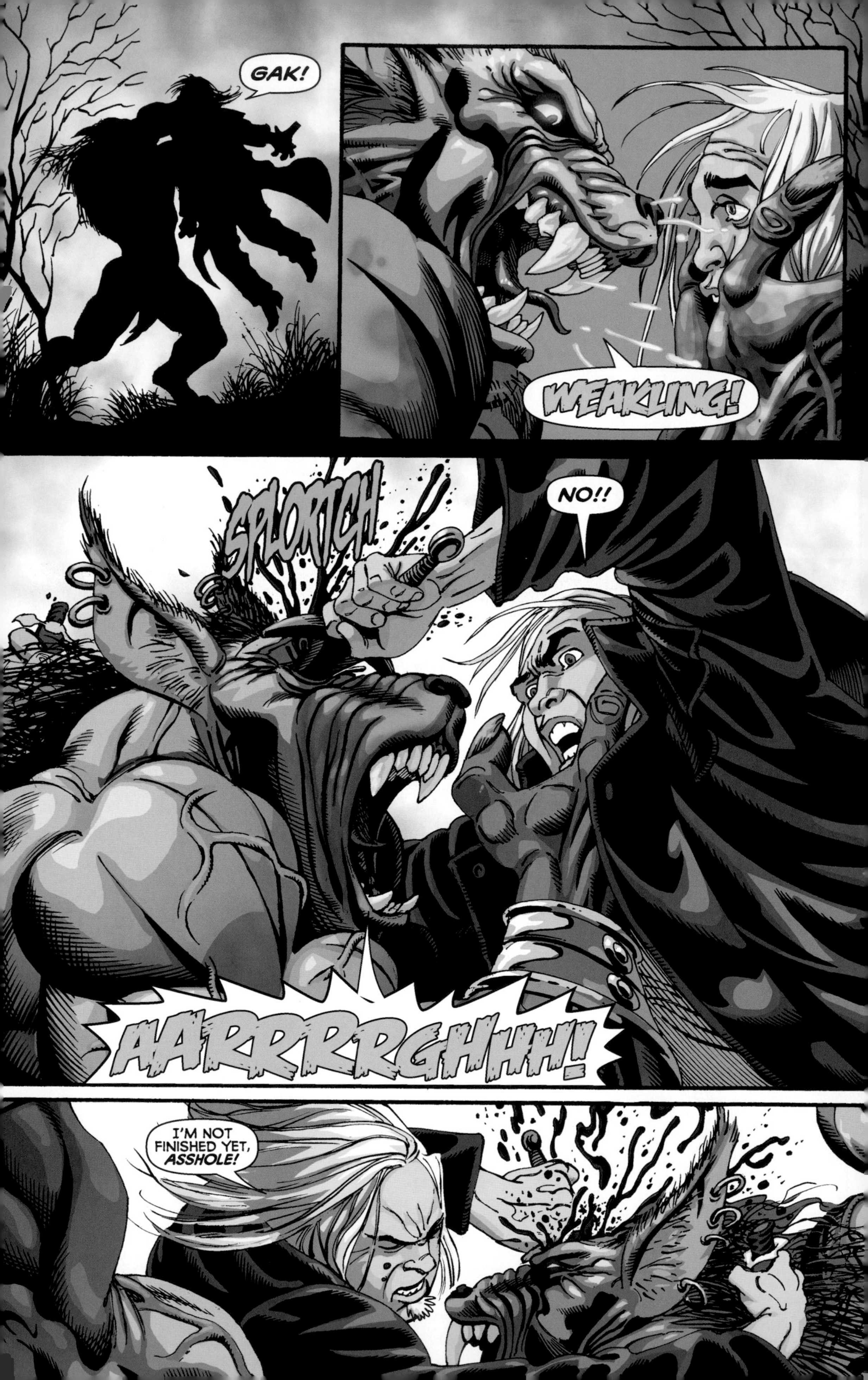
GAK!
WEAKLING!
SPLORTCH
NO!!
AARRRRGHHH!
I'M NOT FINISHED YET, ASSHOLE!

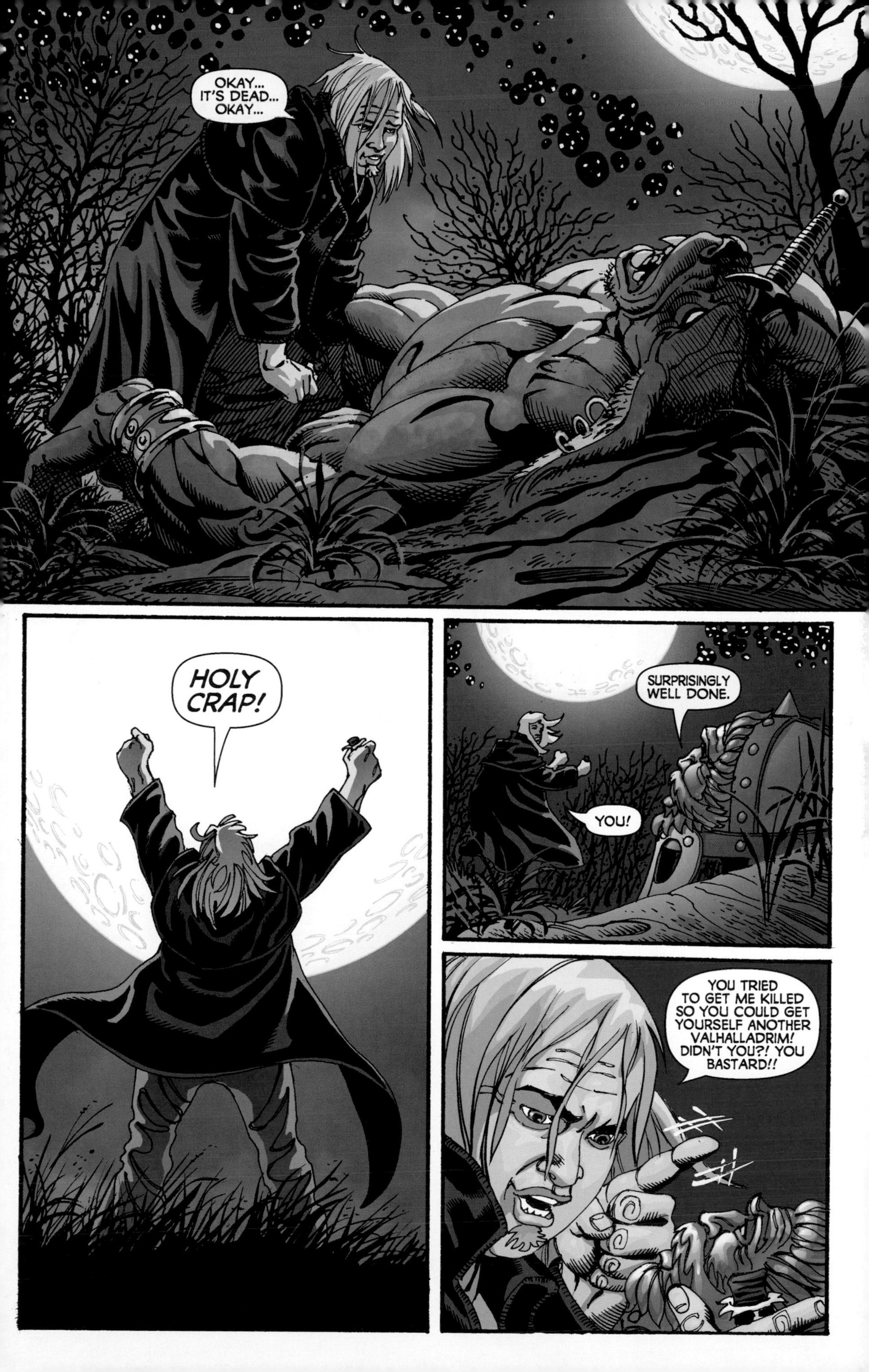
OKAY... IT'S DEAD... OKAY...
HOLY CRAP!
SURPRISINGLY WELL DONE.
YOU!
YOU TRIED TO GET ME KILLED SO YOU COULD GET YOURSELF ANOTHER VALHALLADRIM! DIDN'T YOU?! YOU BASTARD!!

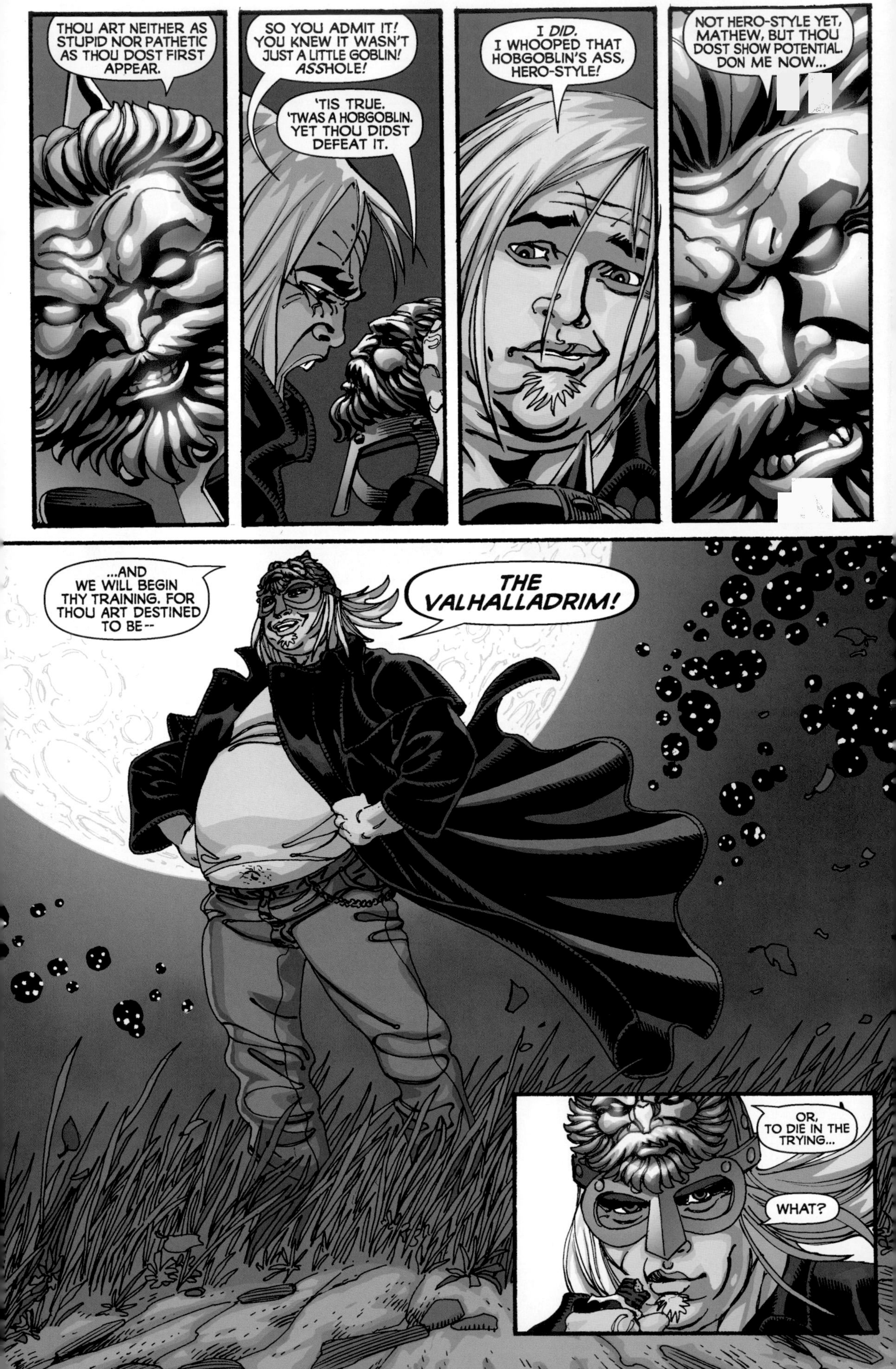
THOU ART NEITHER AS STUPID NOR PATHETIC AS THOU DOST FIRST APPEAR.
SO YOU ADMIT IT! YOU KNEW IT WASN'T JUST A LITTLE GOBLIN! ASSHOLE!
'TIS TRUE. 'TWAS A HOBGOBLIN. YET THOU DIDST DEFEAT IT.
I DID. I WHOOPED THAT HOBGOBLIN'S ASS, HERO-STYLE!
NOT HERO-STYLE YET, MATHEW, BUT THOU DOST SHOW POTENTIAL. DON ME NOW...
...AND WE WILL BEGIN THY TRAINING. FOR THOU ART DESTINED TO BE--
THE VALHALLADRIM!
OR, TO DIE IN THE TRYING...
WHAT?

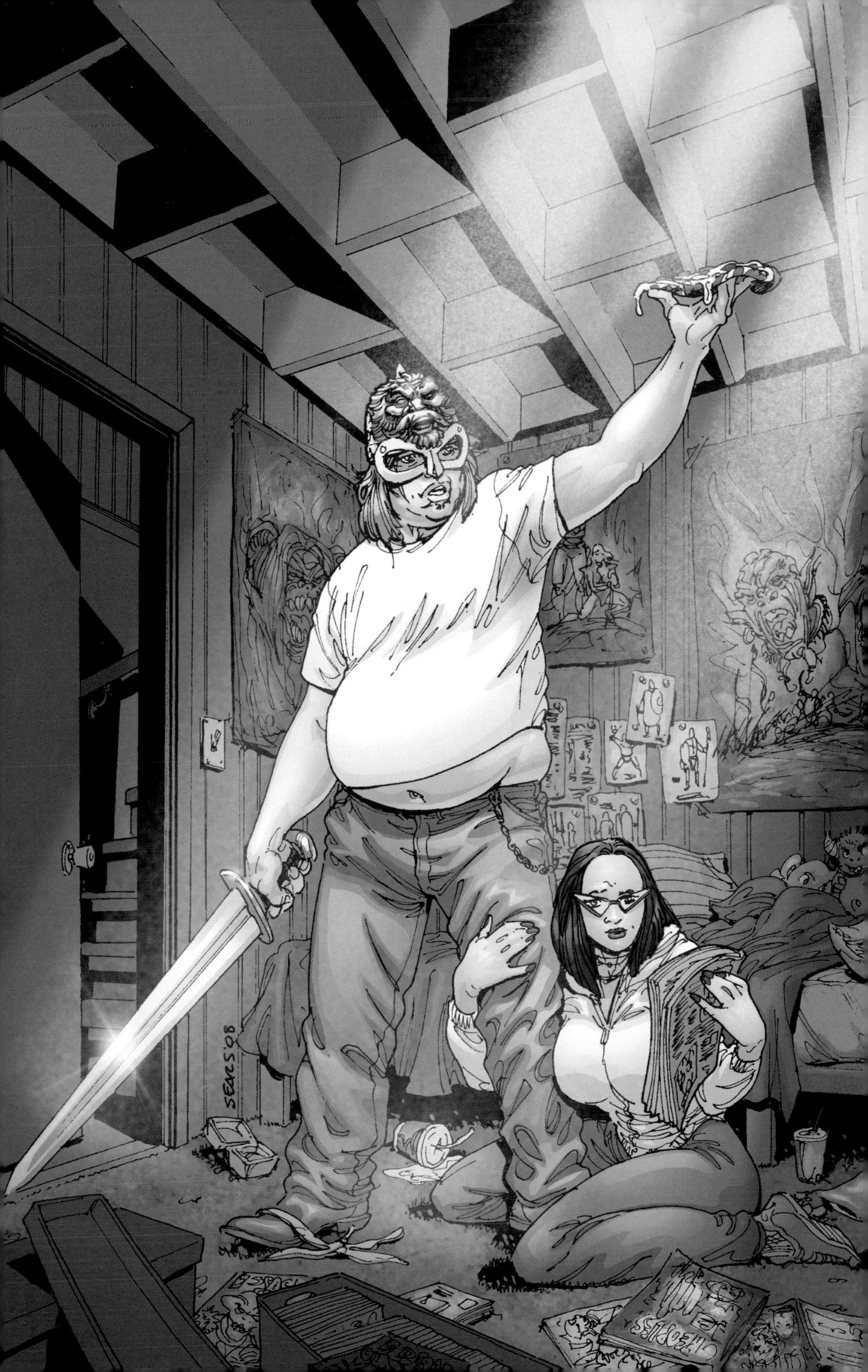
SEARS '08

CHAPTER 2
JILL

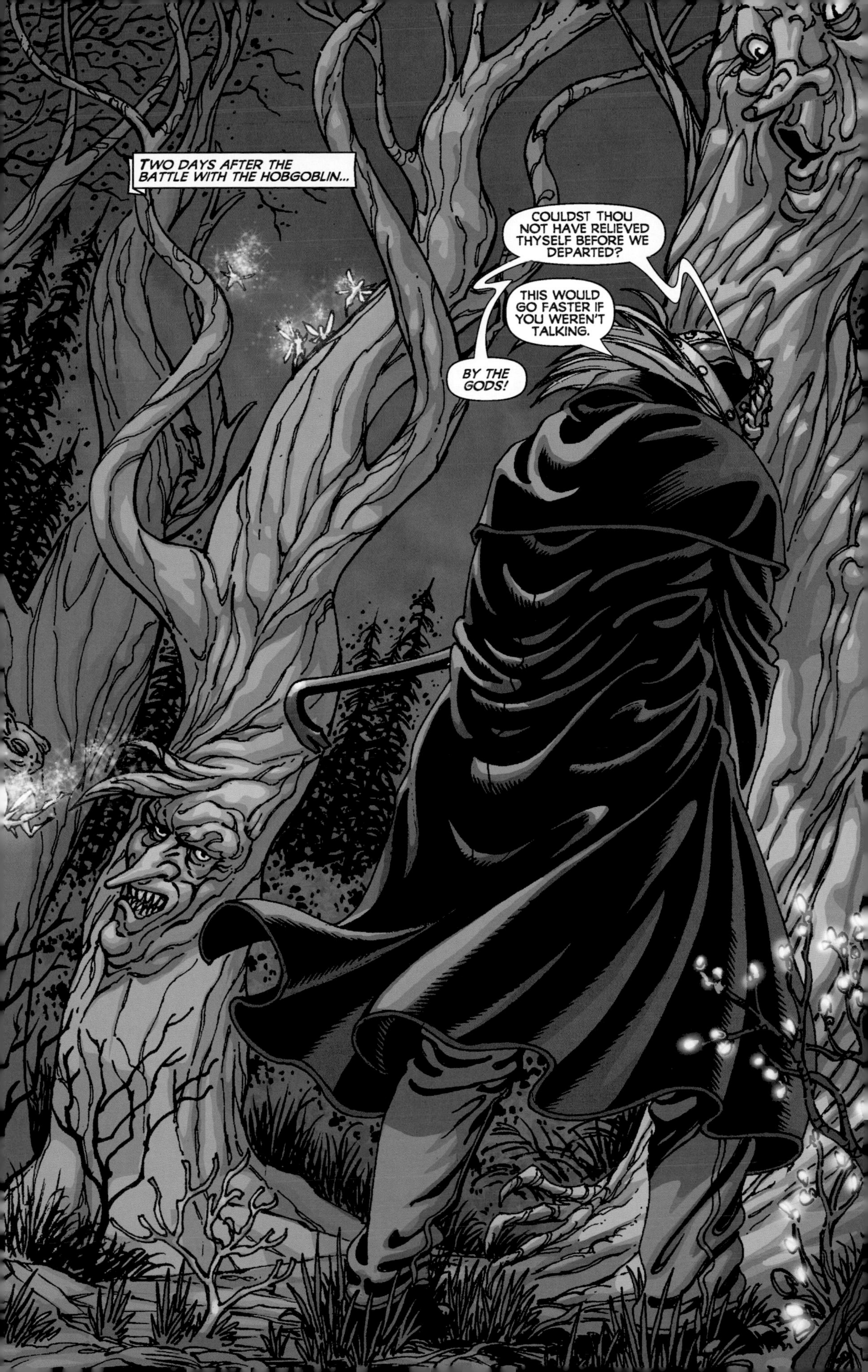
TWO DAYS AFTER THE BATTLE WITH THE HOBGOBLIN...
COULDST THOU NOT HAVE RELIEVED THYSELF BEFORE WE DEPARTED?
THIS WOULD GO FASTER IF YOU WEREN'T TALKING.
BY THE GODS!

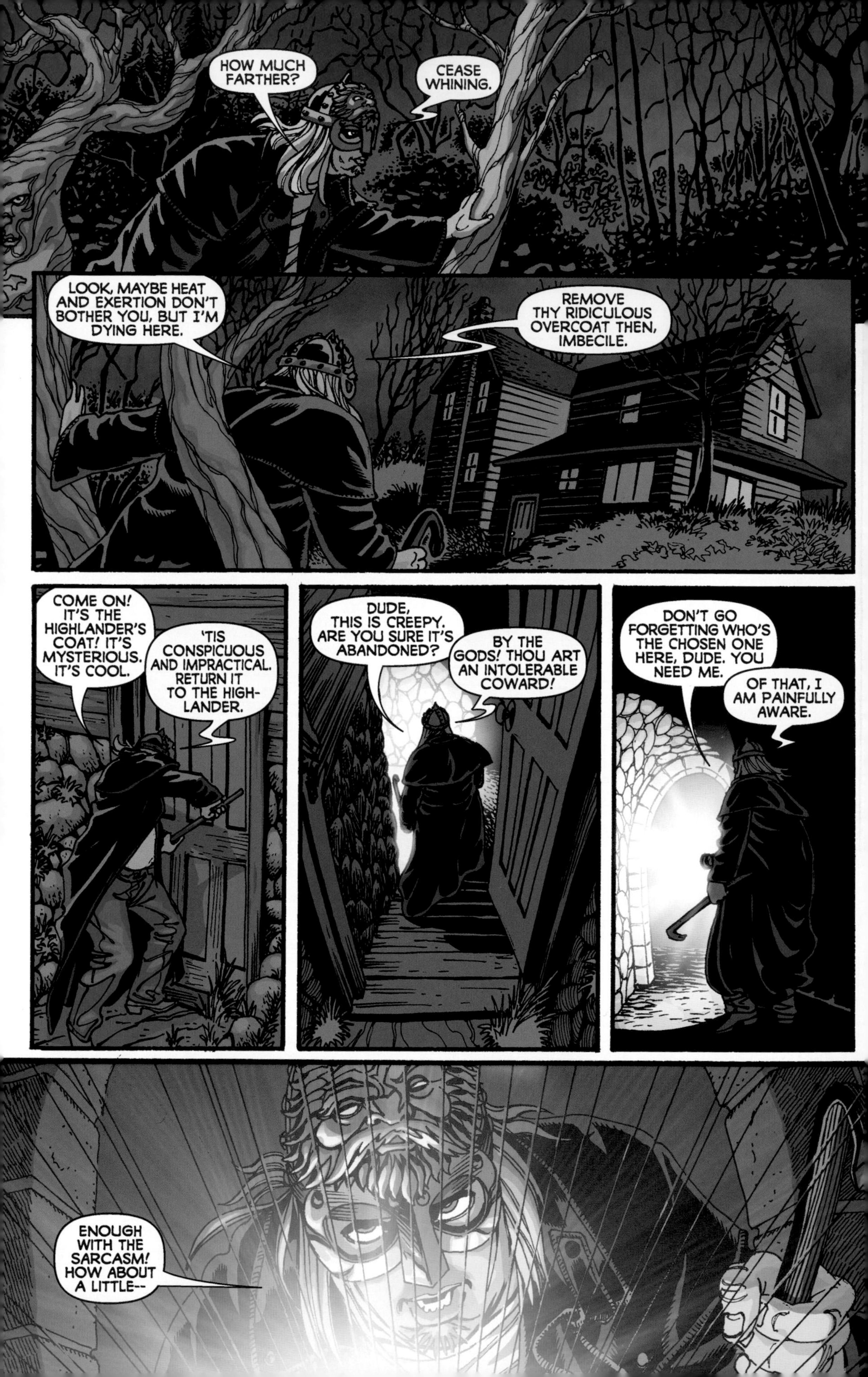
HOW MUCH FARTHER?
CEASE WHINING.
LOOK, MAYBE HEAT AND EXERTION DON'T BOTHER YOU, BUT I'M DYING HERE.
REMOVE THY RIDICULOUS OVERCOAT THEN, IMBECILE.
COME ON! IT'S THE HIGHLANDER'S COAT! IT'S MYSTERIOUS. IT'S COOL.
'TIS CONSPICUOUS AND IMPRACTICAL. RETURN IT TO THE HIGH-LANDER.
DUDE, THIS IS CREEPY. ARE YOU SURE IT'S ABANDONED?
BY THE GODS! THOU ART AN INTOLERABLE COWARD!
DON'T GO FORGETTING WHO'S THE CHOSEN ONE HERE, DUDE. YOU NEED ME.
OF THAT, I AM PAINFULLY AWARE.
ENOUGH WITH THE SARCASM! HOW ABOUT A LITTLE--

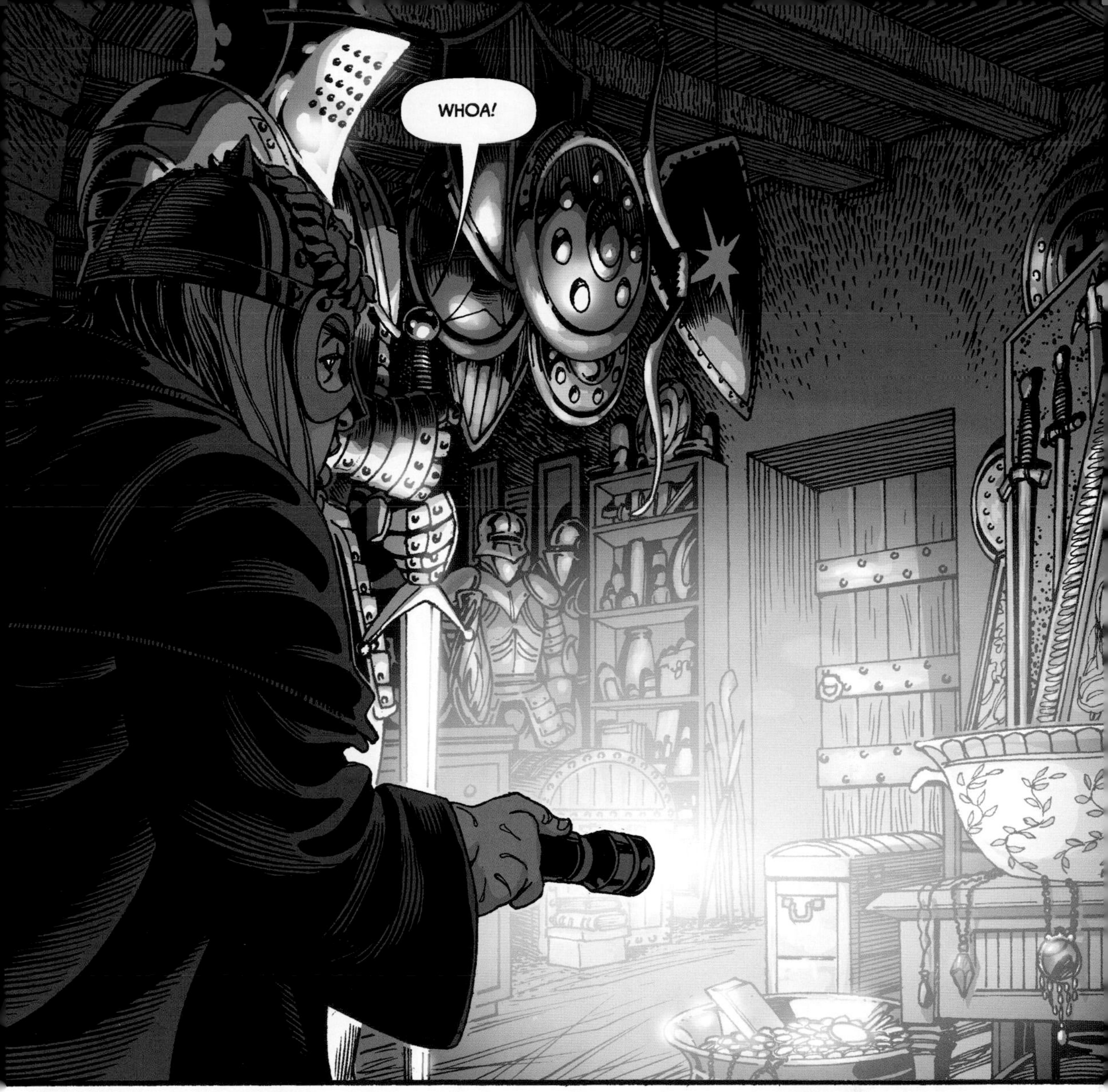
WHOA!

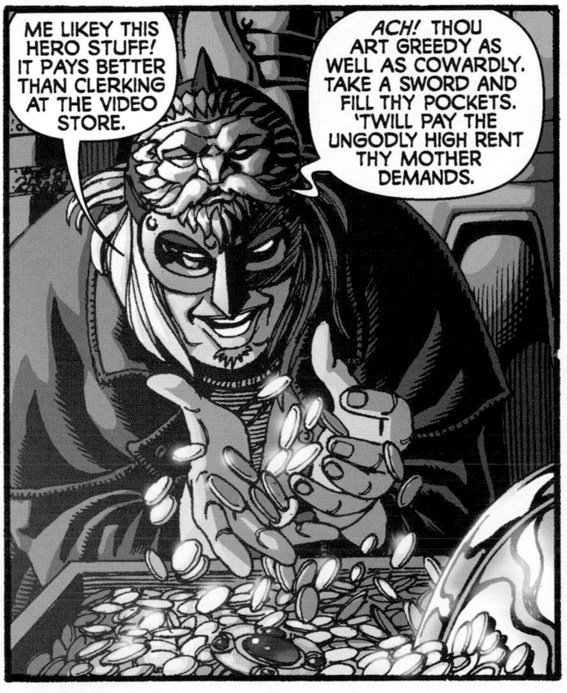
ME LIKEY THIS HERO STUFF! IT PAYS BETTER THAN CLERKING AT THE VIDEO STORE.
ACH! THOU ART GREEDY AS WELL AS COWARDLY. TAKE A SWORD AND FILL THY POCKETS. 'TWILL PAY THE UNGODLY HIGH RENT THY MOTHER DEMANDS.

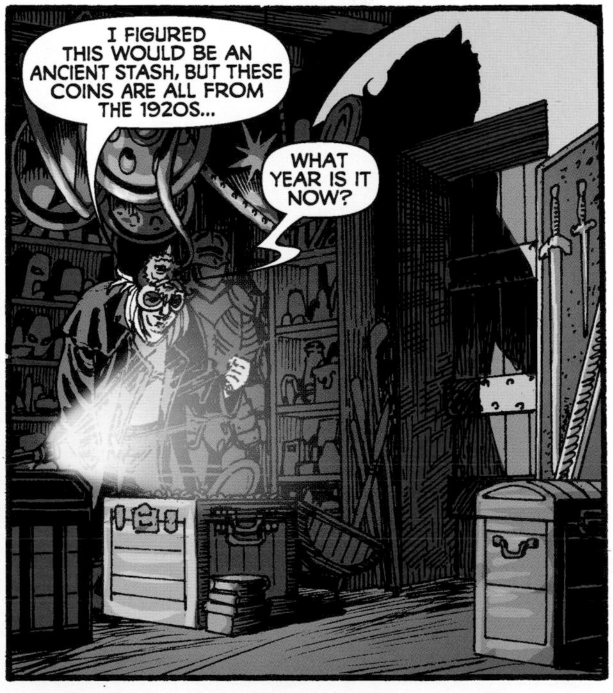
I FIGURED THIS WOULD BE AN ANCIENT STASH, BUT THESE COINS ARE ALL FROM THE 1920S...
WHAT YEAR IS IT NOW?

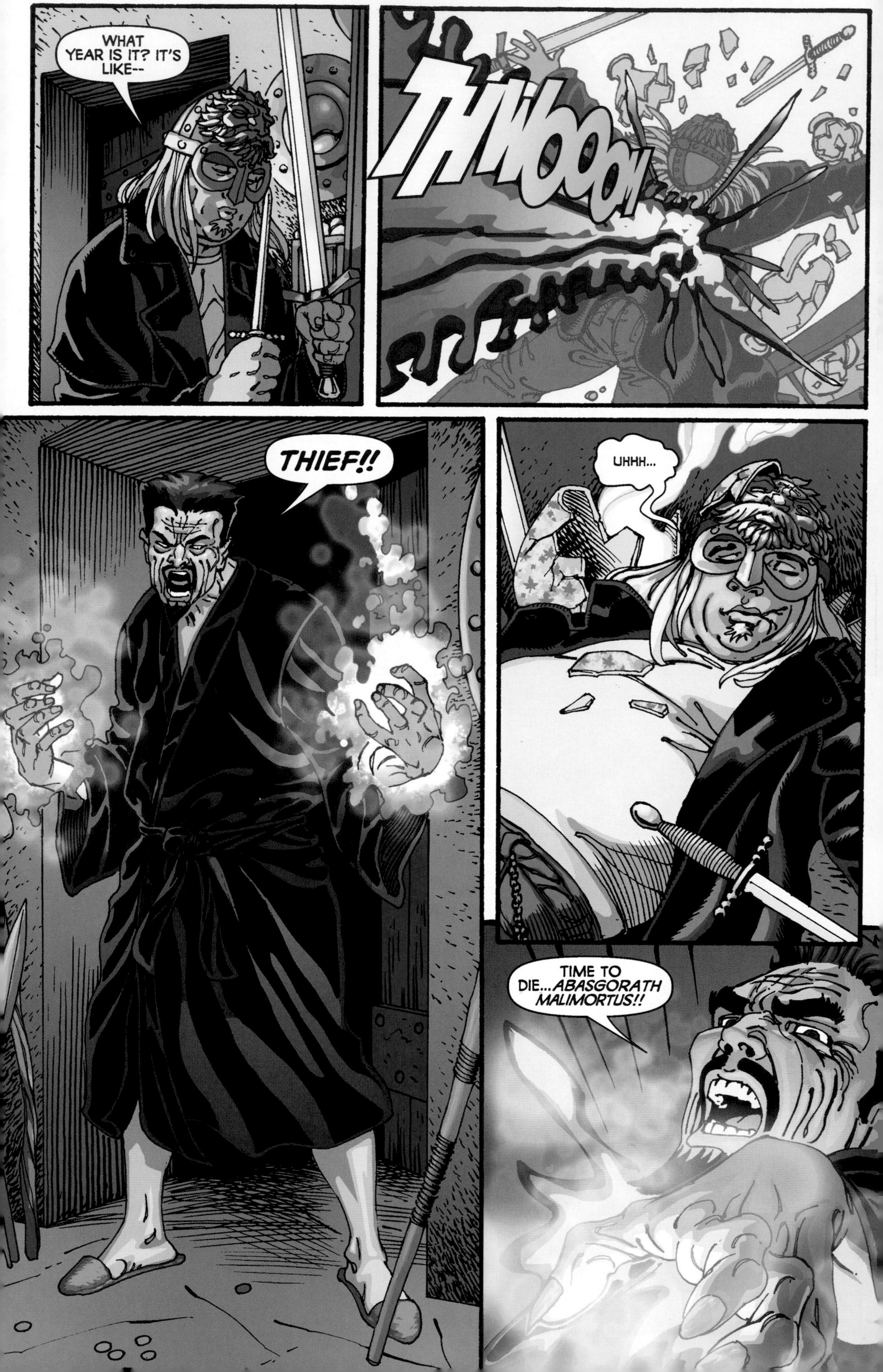
WHAT YEAR IS IT? IT'S LIKE--
THWOOOOM
THIEF!!
UHHH...
TIME TO DIE...*ABASGORATH MALIMORTUS!!*

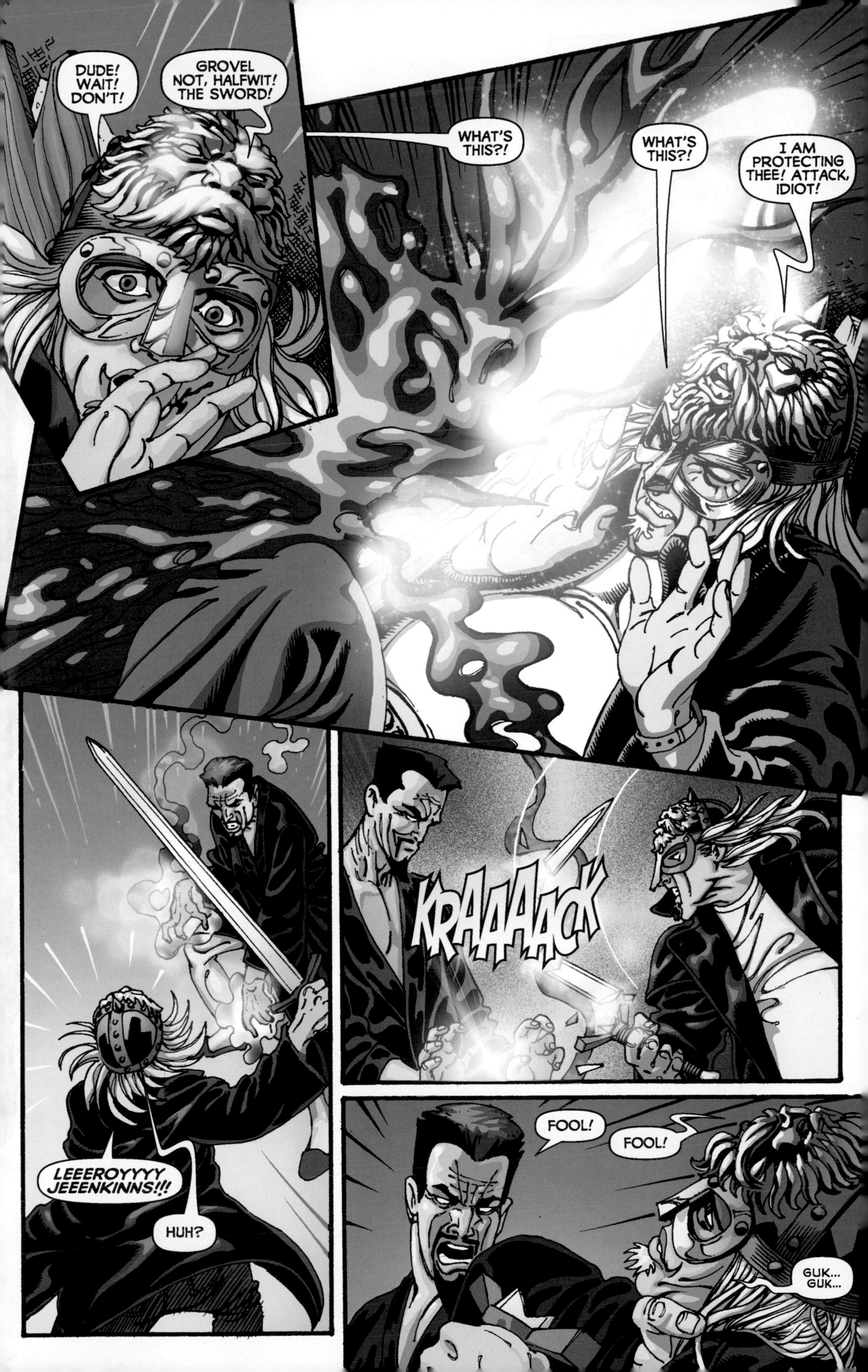
DUDE! WAIT! DON'T!
GROVEL NOT, HALFWIT! THE SWORD!
WHAT'S THIS?!
WHAT'S THIS?!
I AM PROTECTING THEE! ATTACK, IDIOT!
LEEEROYYYY JEEENKINNS!!!
HUH?
KRAAAACK
FOOL!
FOOL!
GUK... GUK...

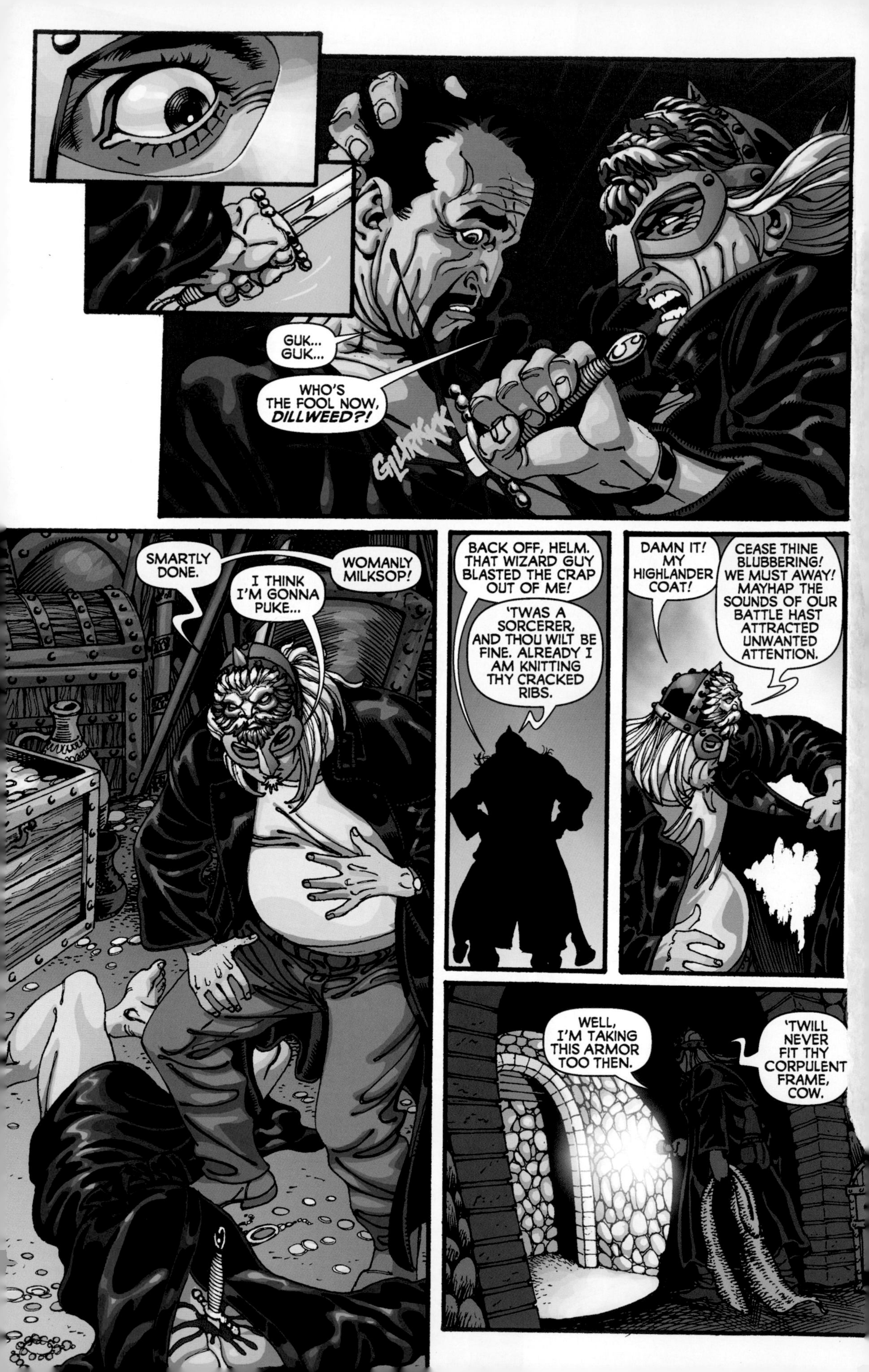
GUK... GUK...
WHO'S THE FOOL NOW, *DILLWEED?!*
GLURKKK
SMARTLY DONE.
WOMANLY MILKSOP!
I THINK I'M GONNA PUKE...
BACK OFF, HELM. THAT WIZARD GUY BLASTED THE CRAP OUT OF ME!
'TWAS A SORCERER, AND THOU WILT BE FINE. ALREADY I AM KNITTING THY CRACKED RIBS.
DAMN IT! MY HIGHLANDER COAT!
CEASE THINE BLUBBERING! WE MUST AWAY! MAYHAP THE SOUNDS OF OUR BATTLE HAST ATTRACTED UNWANTED ATTENTION.
WELL, I'M TAKING THIS ARMOR TOO THEN.
'TWILL NEVER FIT THY CORPULENT FRAME, COW.

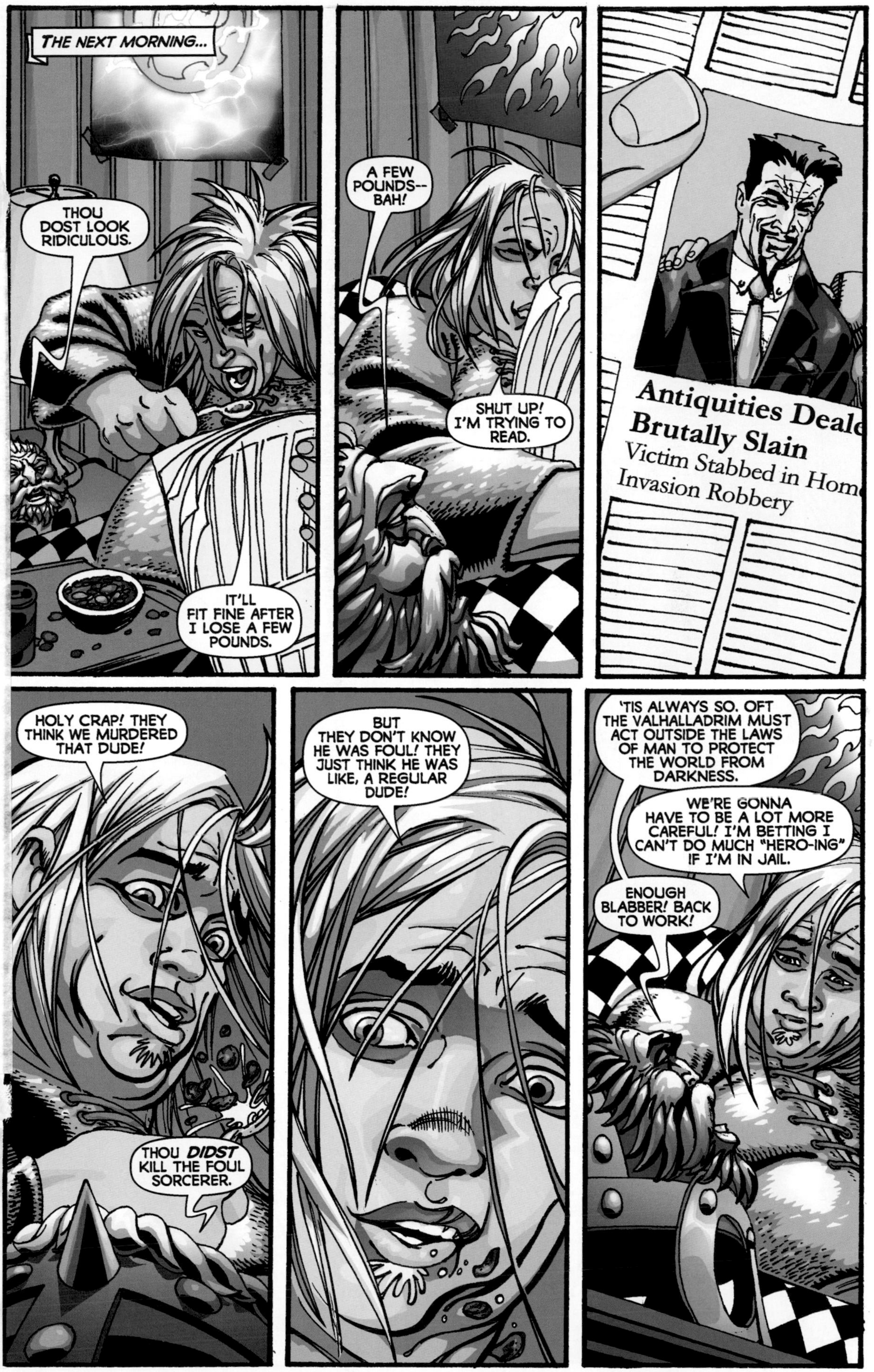
THE NEXT MORNING...
THOU DOST LOOK RIDICULOUS.
IT'LL FIT FINE AFTER I LOSE A FEW POUNDS.
A FEW POUNDS-- BAH!
SHUT UP! I'M TRYING TO READ.
Antiquities Deale
Brutally Slain
Victim Stabbed in Hom
Invasion Robbery
HOLY CRAP! THEY THINK WE MURDERED THAT DUDE!
THOU *DIDST* KILL THE FOUL SORCERER.
BUT THEY DON'T KNOW HE WAS FOUL! THEY JUST THINK HE WAS LIKE, A REGULAR DUDE!
'TIS ALWAYS SO. OFT THE VALHALLADRIM MUST ACT OUTSIDE THE LAWS OF MAN TO PROTECT THE WORLD FROM DARKNESS.
WE'RE GONNA HAVE TO BE A LOT MORE CAREFUL! I'M BETTING I CAN'T DO MUCH "HERO-ING" IF I'M IN JAIL.
ENOUGH BLABBER! BACK TO WORK!

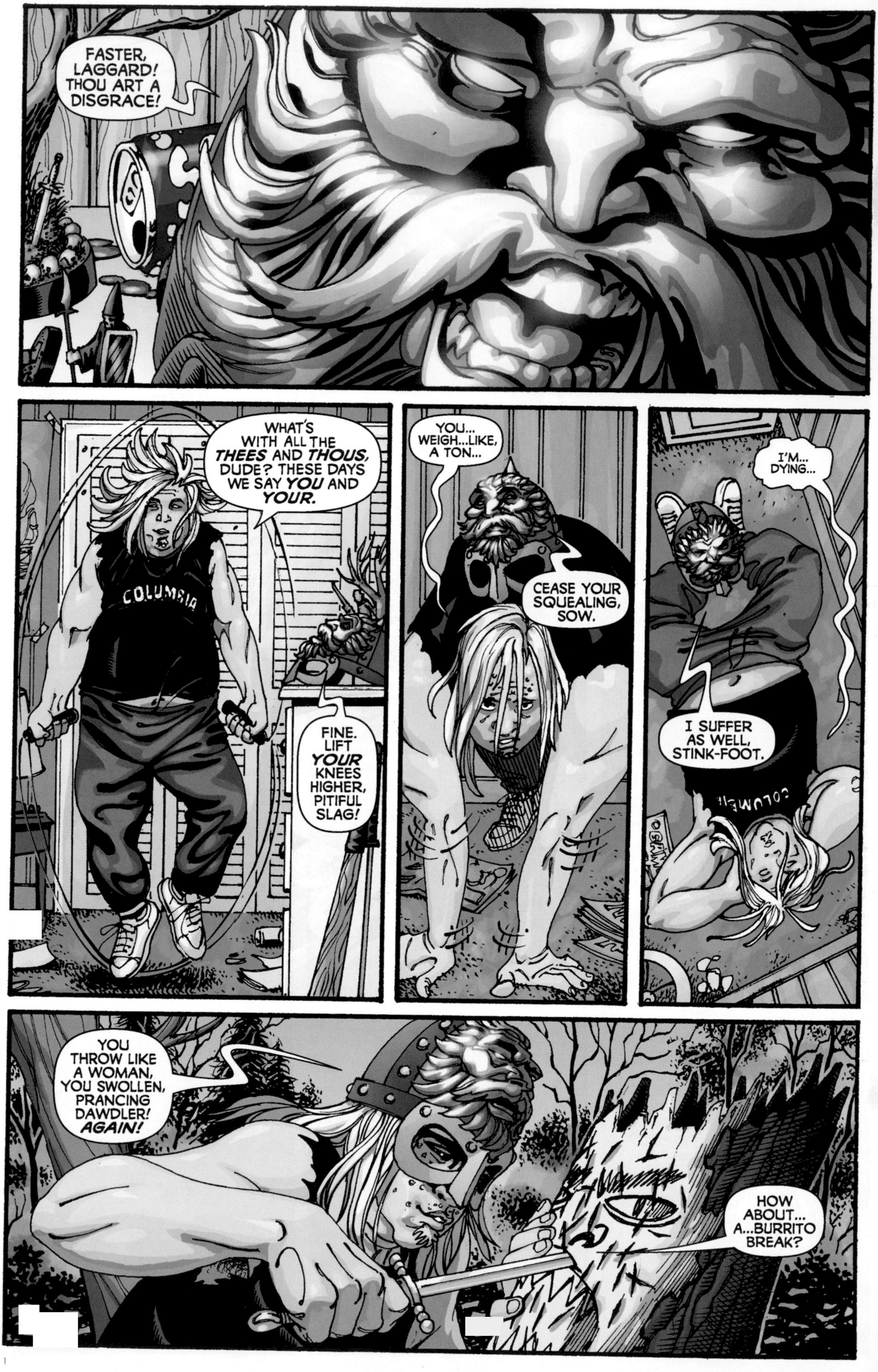
FASTER, LAGGARD! THOU ART A DISGRACE!
WHAT'S WITH ALL THE THEES AND THOUS, DUDE? THESE DAYS WE SAY YOU AND YOUR.
FINE. LIFT YOUR KNEES HIGHER, PITIFUL SLAG!
YOU... WEIGH...LIKE, A TON...
CEASE YOUR SQUEALING, SOW.
I'M... DYING...
I SUFFER AS WELL, STINK-FOOT.
YOU THROW LIKE A WOMAN, YOU SWOLLEN, PRANCING DAWDLER! AGAIN!
HOW ABOUT... A...BURRITO BREAK?

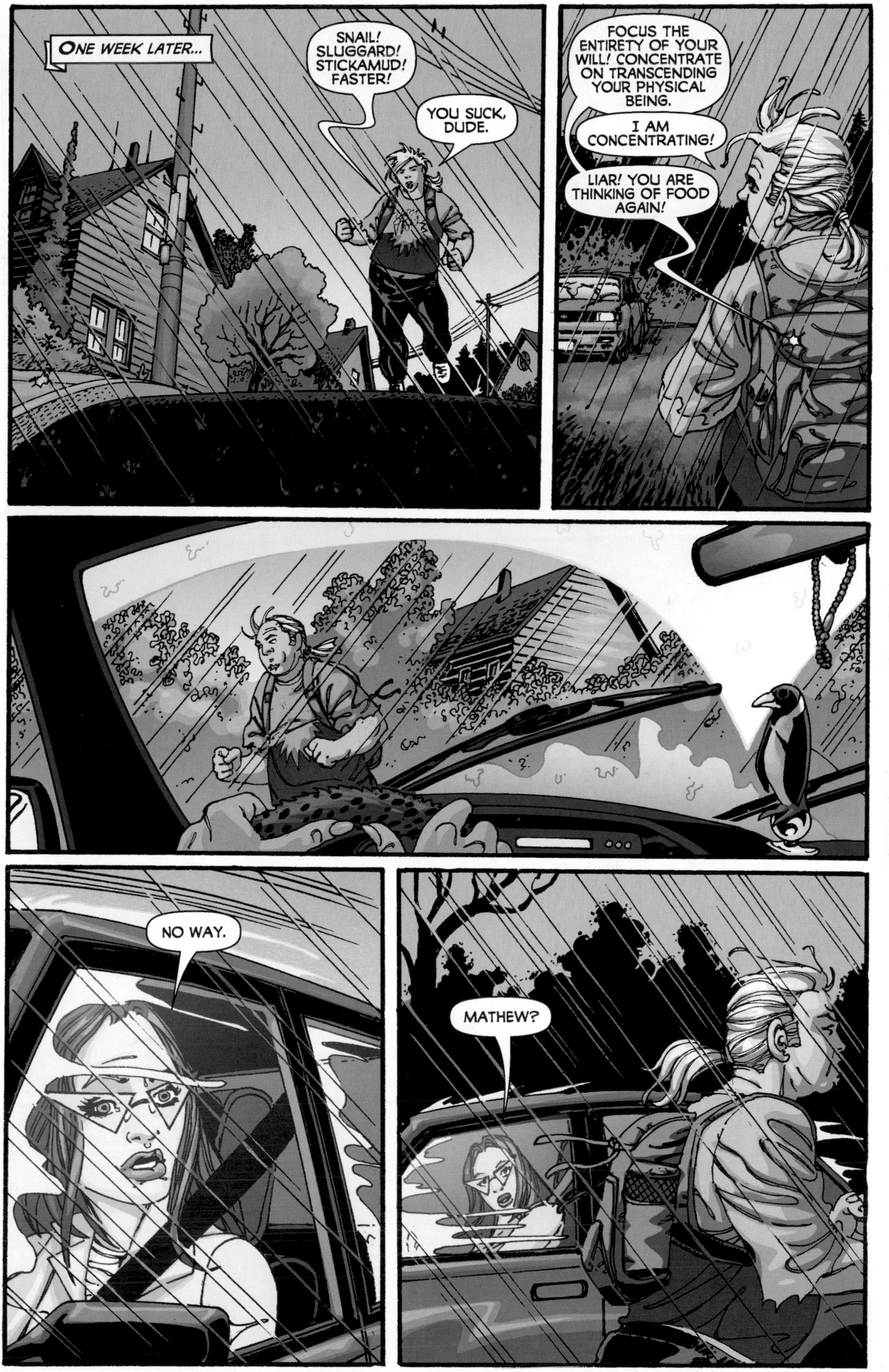
ONE WEEK LATER...
SNAIL! SLUGGARD! STICKAMUD! FASTER!
YOU SUCK, DUDE.
FOCUS THE ENTIRETY OF YOUR WILL! CONCENTRATE ON TRANSCENDING YOUR PHYSICAL BEING.
I AM CONCENTRATING!
LIAR! YOU ARE THINKING OF FOOD AGAIN!
NO WAY.
MATHEW?

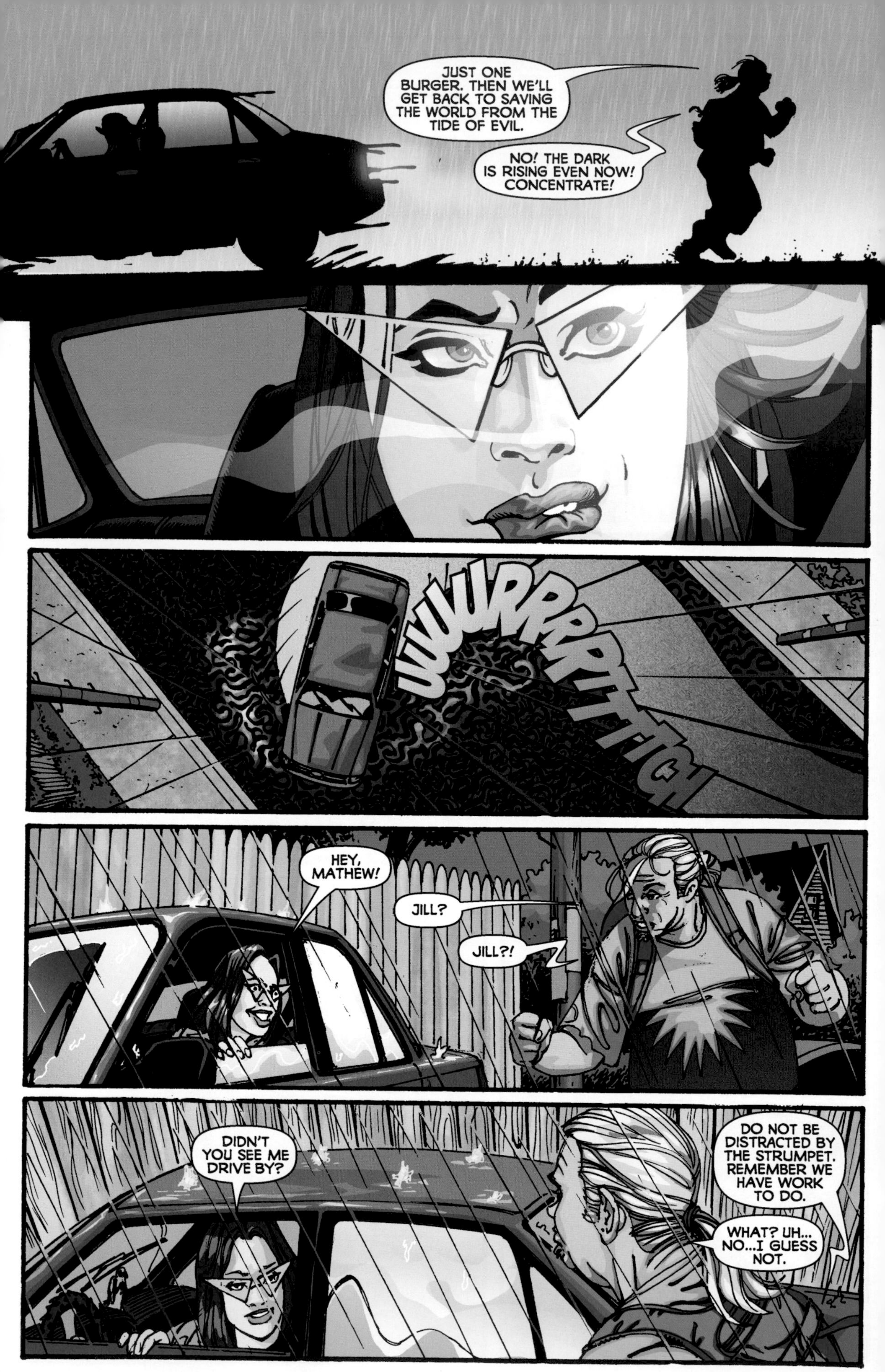
JUST ONE BURGER. THEN WE'LL GET BACK TO SAVING THE WORLD FROM THE TIDE OF EVIL.
NO! THE DARK IS RISING EVEN NOW! CONCENTRATE!
WWUURRRRTTTCH
HEY, MATHEW!
JILL?
JILL?!
DIDN'T YOU SEE ME DRIVE BY?
DO NOT BE DISTRACTED BY THE STRUMPET. REMEMBER WE HAVE WORK TO DO.
WHAT? UH... NO...I GUESS NOT.

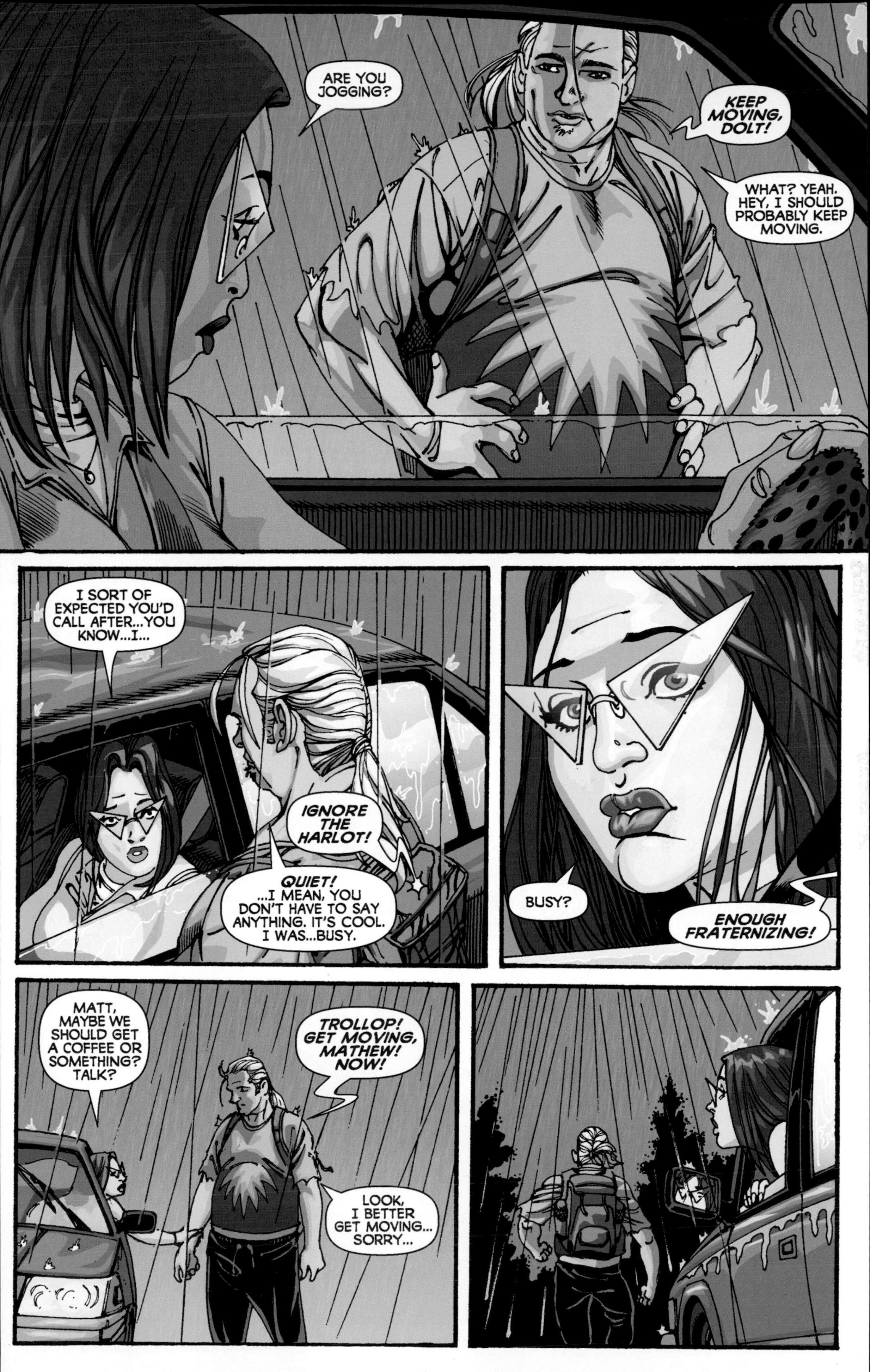
ARE YOU JOGGING?
KEEP MOVING, DOLT!
WHAT? YEAH. HEY, I SHOULD PROBABLY KEEP MOVING.
I SORT OF EXPECTED YOU'D CALL AFTER...YOU KNOW...I...
IGNORE THE HARLOT!
QUIET! ...I MEAN, YOU DON'T HAVE TO SAY ANYTHING. IT'S COOL. I WAS...BUSY.
BUSY?
ENOUGH FRATERNIZING!
MATT, MAYBE WE SHOULD GET A COFFEE OR SOMETHING? TALK?
TROLLOP! GET MOVING, MATHEW! NOW!
LOOK, I BETTER GET MOVING... SORRY...

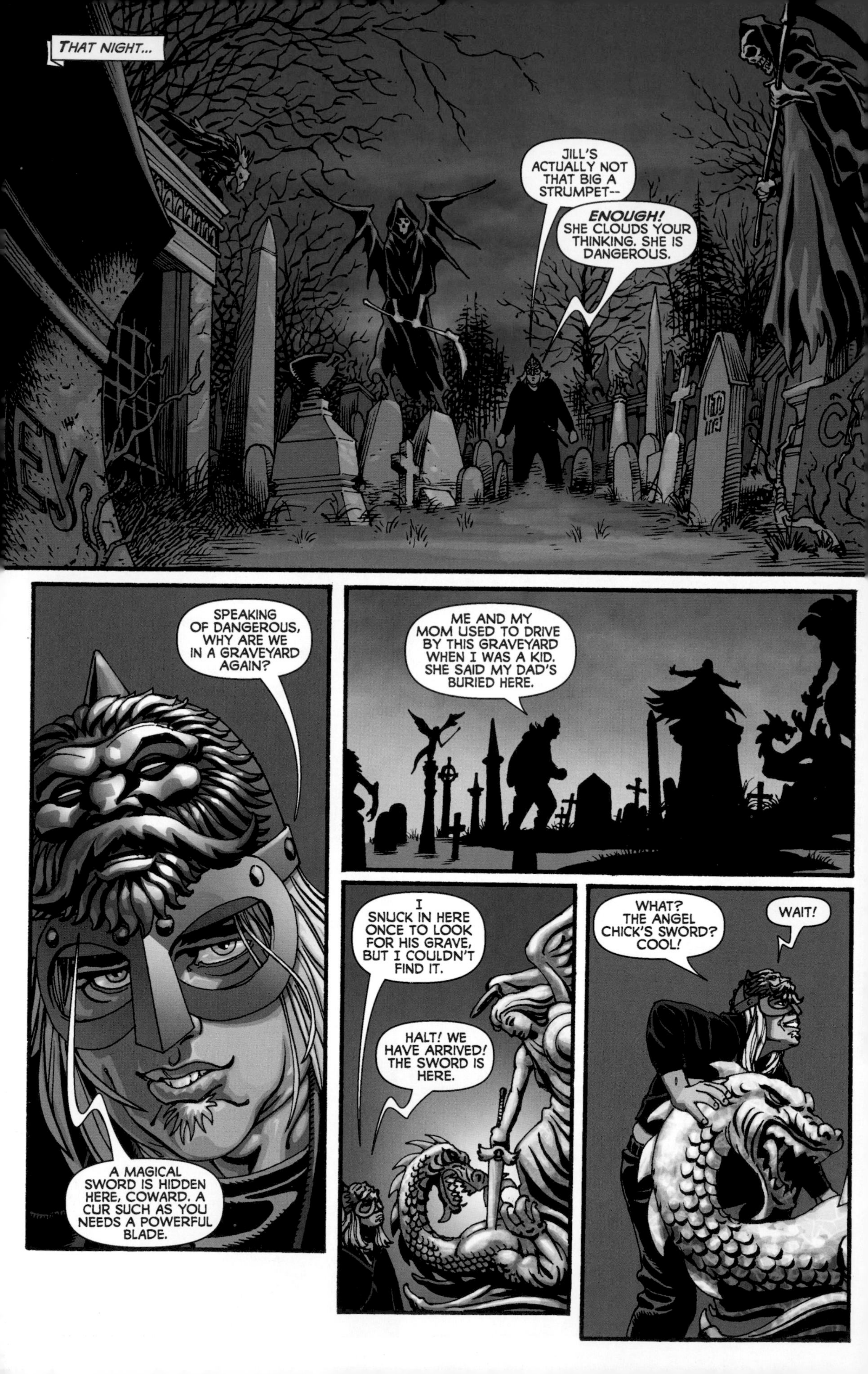
THAT NIGHT...
JILL'S ACTUALLY NOT THAT BIG A STRUMPET--
ENOUGH! SHE CLOUDS YOUR THINKING. SHE IS DANGEROUS.
SPEAKING OF DANGEROUS, WHY ARE WE IN A GRAVEYARD AGAIN?
A MAGICAL SWORD IS HIDDEN HERE, COWARD. A CUR SUCH AS YOU NEEDS A POWERFUL BLADE.
ME AND MY MOM USED TO DRIVE BY THIS GRAVEYARD WHEN I WAS A KID. SHE SAID MY DAD'S BURIED HERE.
I SNUCK IN HERE ONCE TO LOOK FOR HIS GRAVE, BUT I COULDN'T FIND IT.
HALT! WE HAVE ARRIVED! THE SWORD IS HERE.
WHAT? THE ANGEL CHICK'S SWORD? COOL!
WAIT!

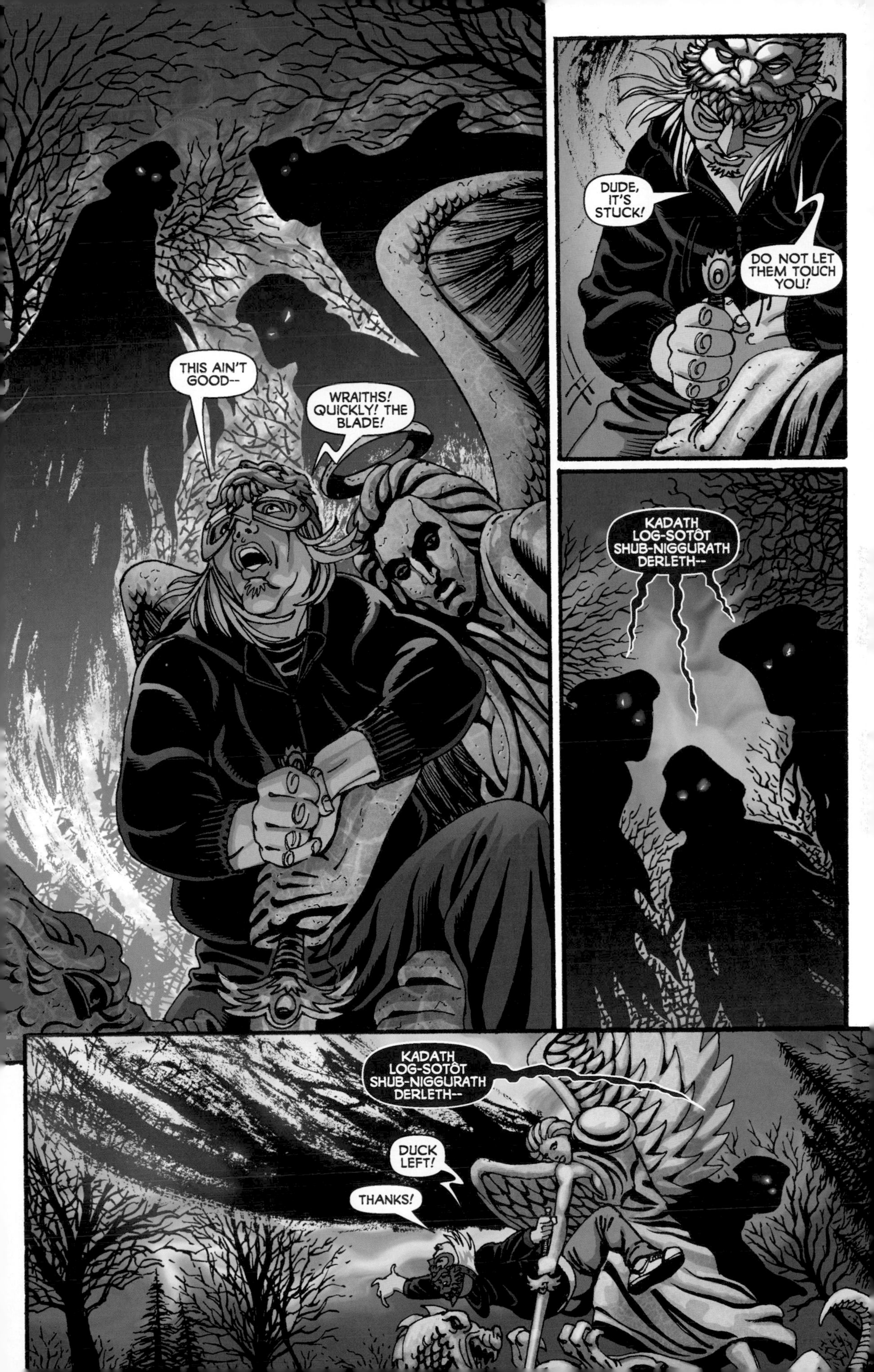
THIS AIN'T GOOD--
WRAITHS! QUICKLY! THE BLADE!
DUDE, IT'S STUCK!
DO NOT LET THEM TOUCH YOU!
KADATH LOG-SOTÔT SHUB-NIGGURATH DERLETH--
KADATH LOG-SOTÔT SHUB-NIGGURATH DERLETH--
DUCK LEFT!
THANKS!

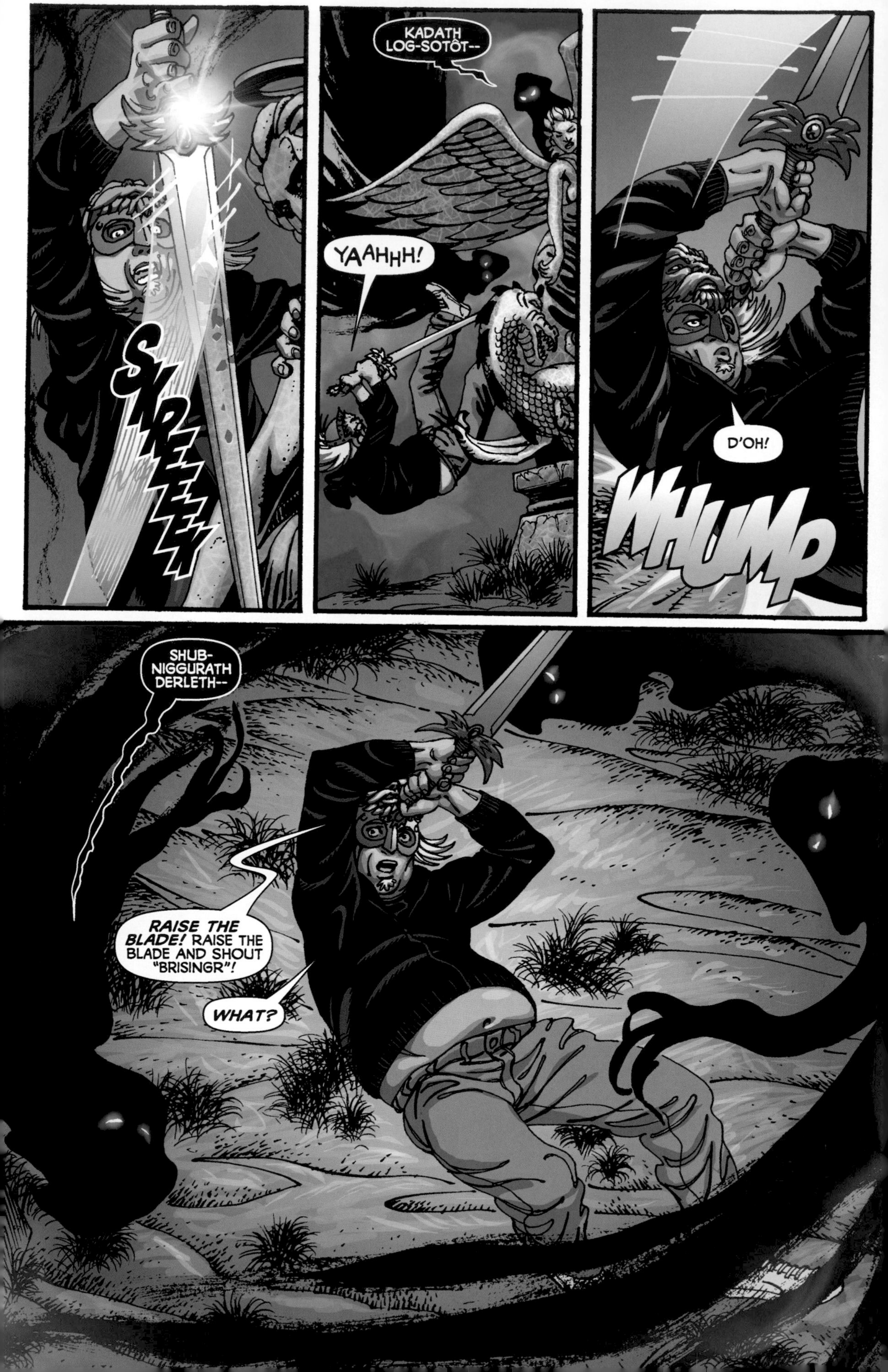
SKREEEEK
KADATH LOG-SOTÔT--
YAAHHH!
D'OH!
WHUMP
SHUB-NIGGURATH DERLETH--
RAISE THE BLADE! RAISE THE BLADE AND SHOUT "BRISINGR"!
WHAT?

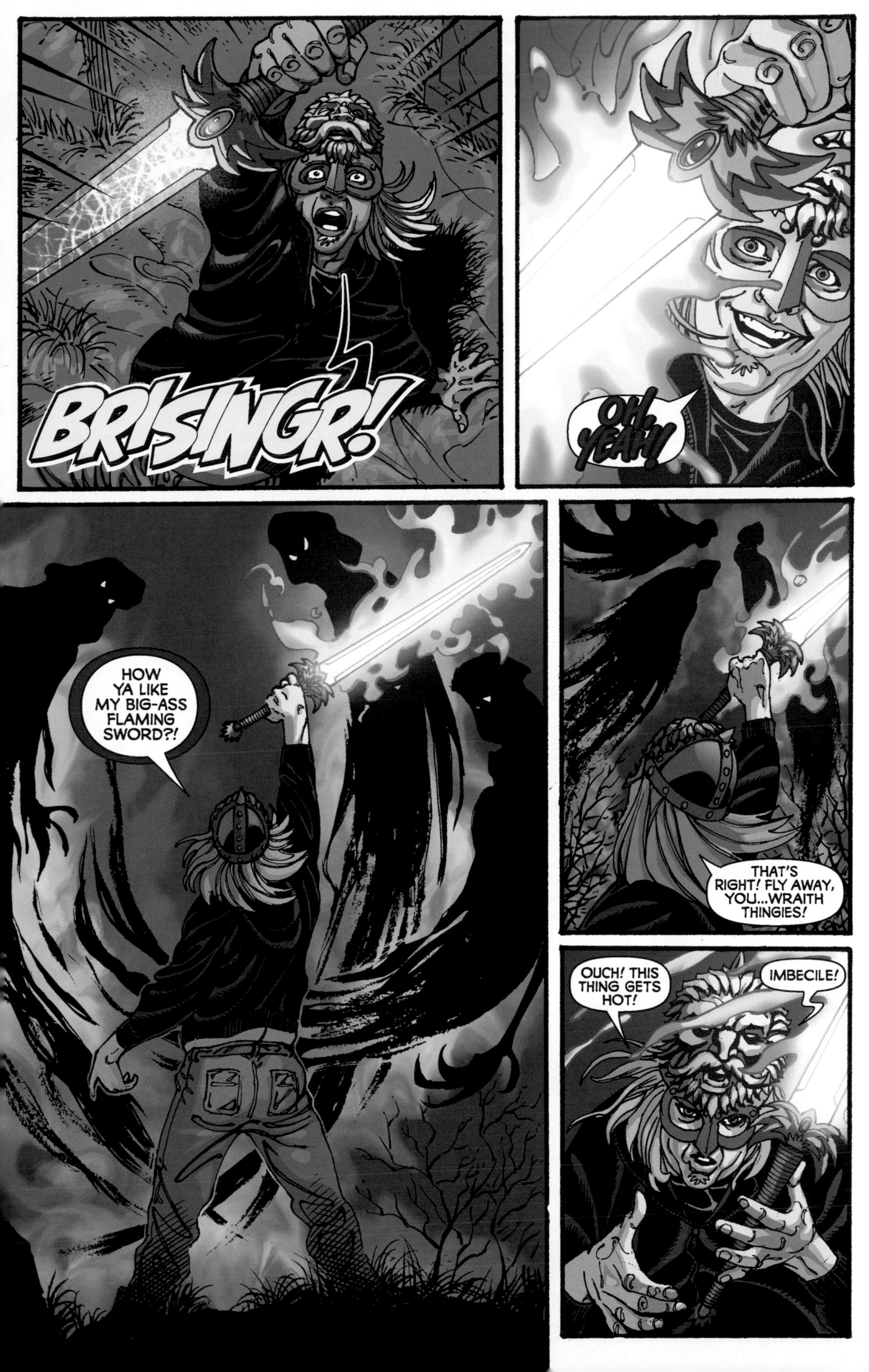
BRISINGR!
OH, YEAH!
HOW YA LIKE MY BIG-ASS FLAMING SWORD?!
THAT'S RIGHT! FLY AWAY, YOU...WRAITH THINGIES!
OUCH! THIS THING GETS HOT!
IMBECILE!

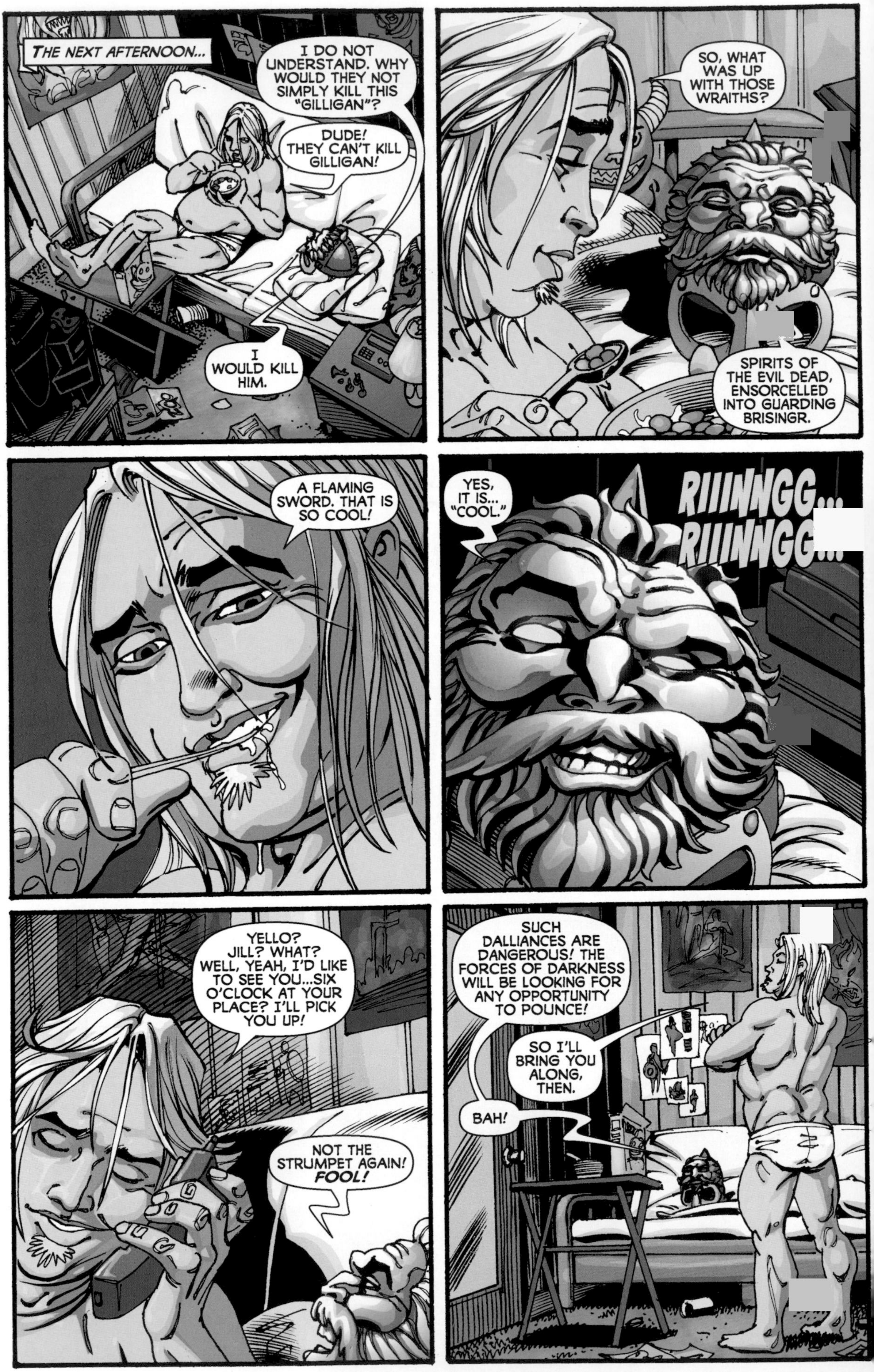
THE NEXT AFTERNOON...
I DO NOT UNDERSTAND. WHY WOULD THEY NOT SIMPLY KILL THIS "GILLIGAN"?
DUDE! THEY CAN'T KILL GILLIGAN!
I WOULD KILL HIM.
SO, WHAT WAS UP WITH THOSE WRAITHS?
SPIRITS OF THE EVIL DEAD, ENSORCELLED INTO GUARDING BRISINGR.
A FLAMING SWORD. THAT IS SO COOL!
YES, IT IS... "COOL."
RIIINNGG... RIIINNGG...
YELLO? JILL? WHAT? WELL, YEAH, I'D LIKE TO SEE YOU...SIX O'CLOCK AT YOUR PLACE? I'LL PICK YOU UP!
NOT THE STRUMPET AGAIN! FOOL!
SUCH DALLIANCES ARE DANGEROUS! THE FORCES OF DARKNESS WILL BE LOOKING FOR ANY OPPORTUNITY TO POUNCE!
SO I'LL BRING YOU ALONG, THEN.
BAH!

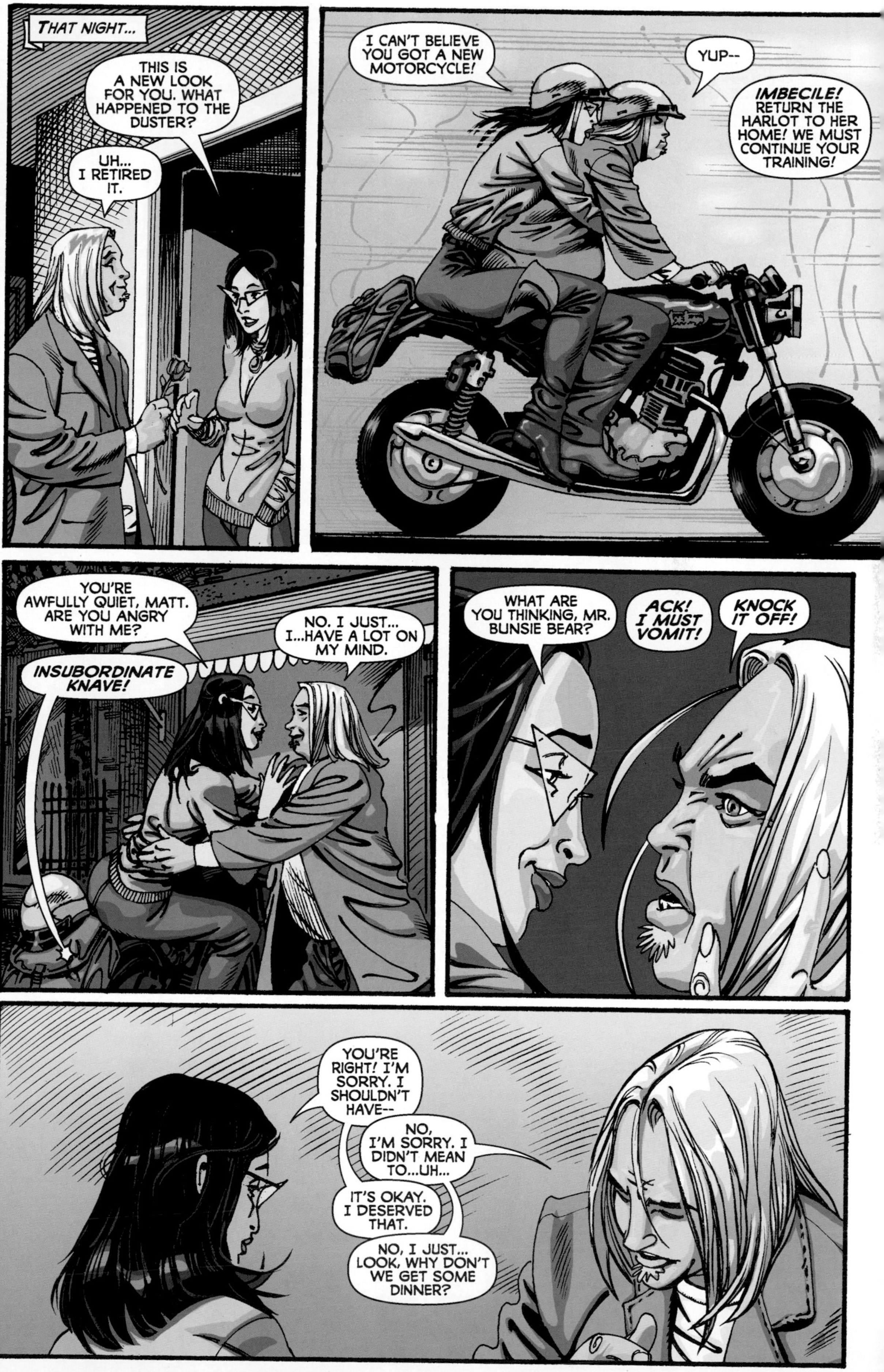
THAT NIGHT...
THIS IS A NEW LOOK FOR YOU. WHAT HAPPENED TO THE DUSTER?
UH... I RETIRED IT.
I CAN'T BELIEVE YOU GOT A NEW MOTORCYCLE!
YUP--
IMBECILE! RETURN THE HARLOT TO HER HOME! WE MUST CONTINUE YOUR TRAINING!
YOU'RE AWFULLY QUIET, MATT. ARE YOU ANGRY WITH ME?
NO. I JUST... I...HAVE A LOT ON MY MIND.
INSUBORDINATE KNAVE!
WHAT ARE YOU THINKING, MR. BUNSIE BEAR?
ACK! I MUST VOMIT!
KNOCK IT OFF!
YOU'RE RIGHT! I'M SORRY. I SHOULDN'T HAVE--
NO, I'M SORRY. I DIDN'T MEAN TO...UH...
IT'S OKAY. I DESERVED THAT.
NO, I JUST... LOOK, WHY DON'T WE GET SOME DINNER?

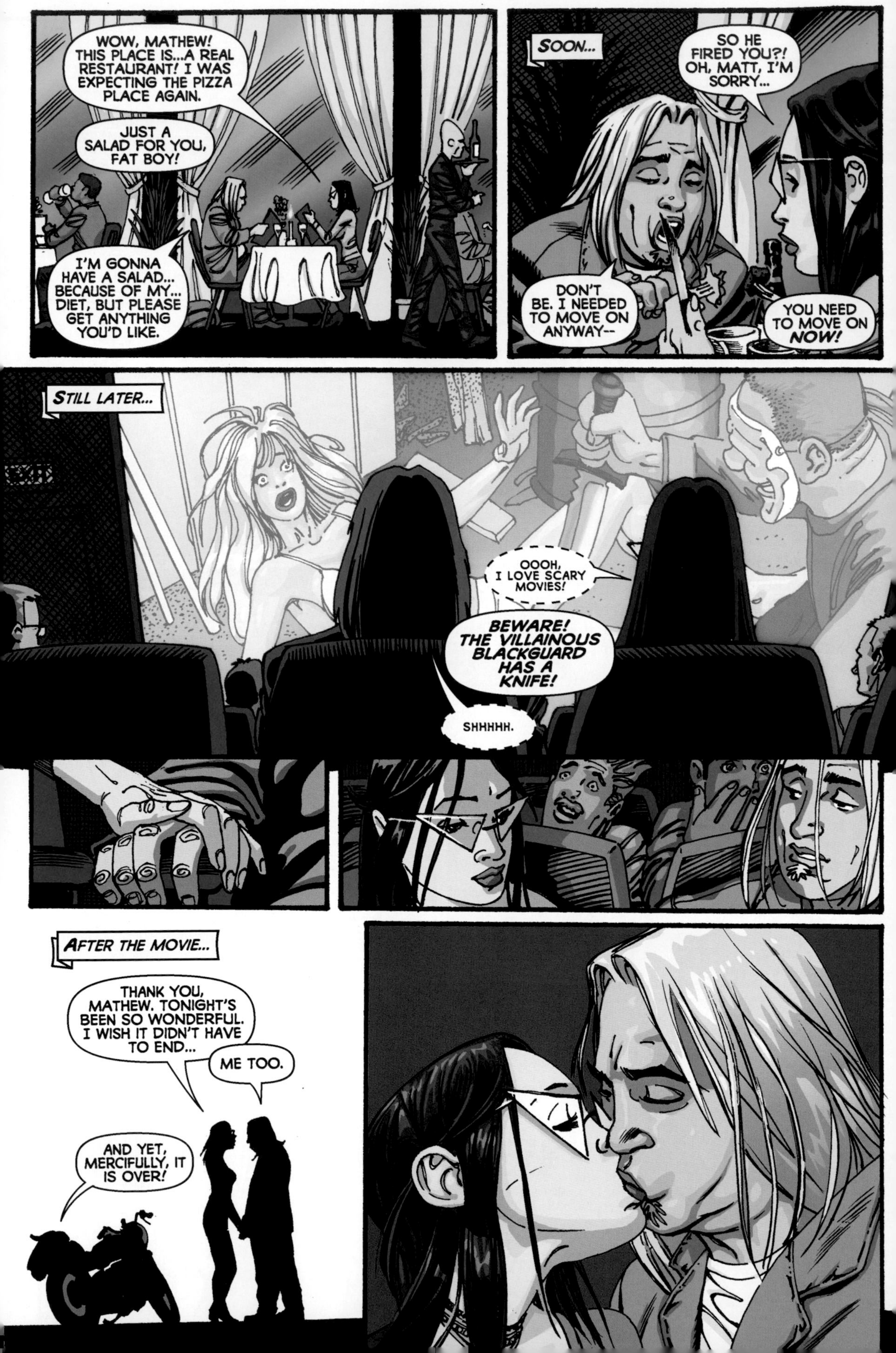
WOW, MATHEW! THIS PLACE IS...A REAL RESTAURANT! I WAS EXPECTING THE PIZZA PLACE AGAIN.
JUST A SALAD FOR YOU, FAT BOY!
I'M GONNA HAVE A SALAD... BECAUSE OF MY... DIET, BUT PLEASE GET ANYTHING YOU'D LIKE.
SOON...
SO HE FIRED YOU?! OH, MATT, I'M SORRY...
DON'T BE. I NEEDED TO MOVE ON ANYWAY--
YOU NEED TO MOVE ON NOW!
STILL LATER...
OOOH, I LOVE SCARY MOVIES!
BEWARE! THE VILLAINOUS BLACKGUARD HAS A KNIFE!
SHHHHH.
AFTER THE MOVIE...
THANK YOU, MATHEW. TONIGHT'S BEEN SO WONDERFUL. I WISH IT DIDN'T HAVE TO END...
ME TOO.
AND YET, MERCIFULLY, IT IS OVER!

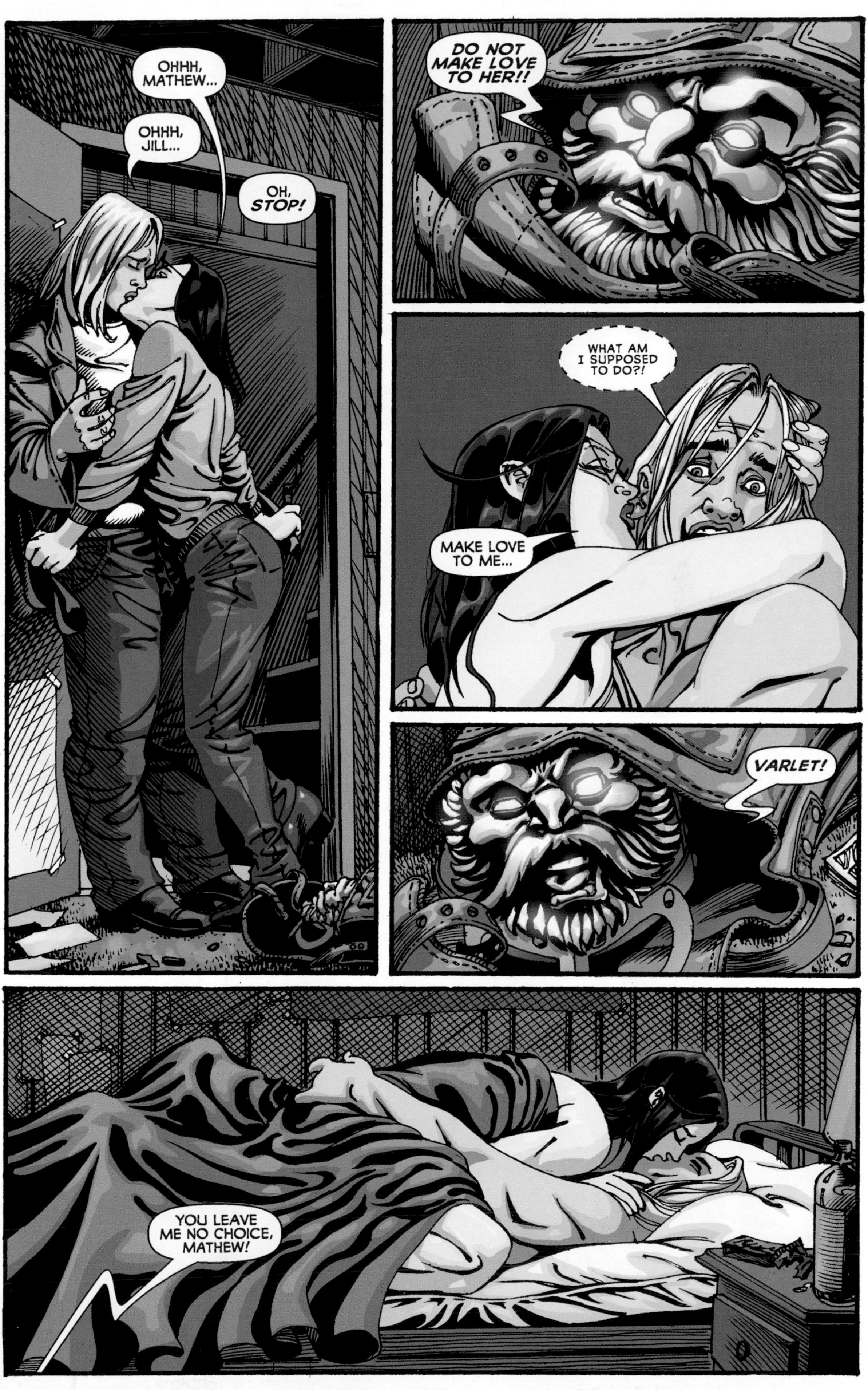
OHHH, MATHEW...
OHHH, JILL...
OH, STOP!
DO NOT MAKE LOVE TO HER!!
WHAT AM I SUPPOSED TO DO?!
MAKE LOVE TO ME...
VARLET!
YOU LEAVE ME NO CHOICE, MATHEW!

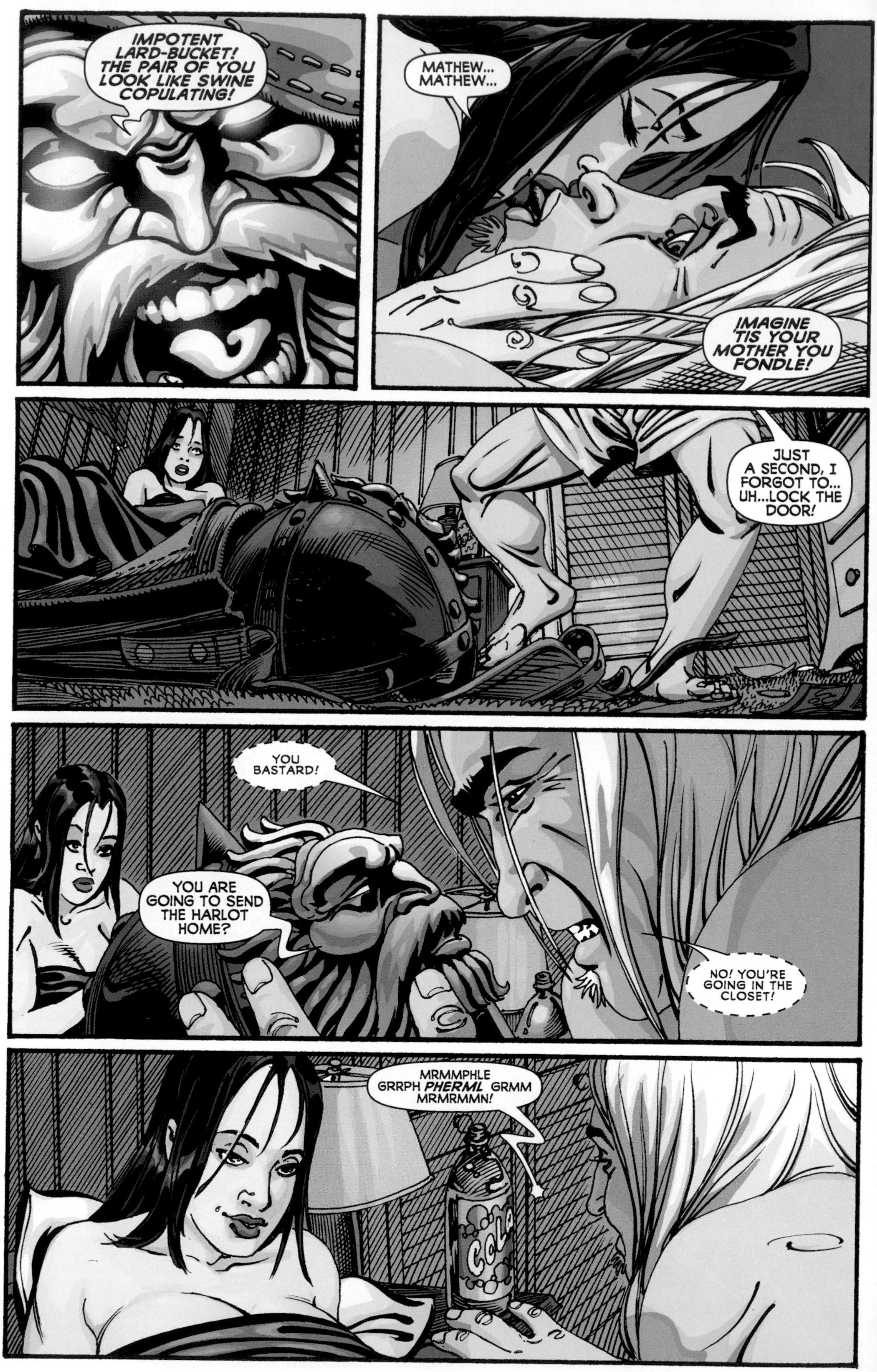
IMPOTENT LARD-BUCKET! THE PAIR OF YOU LOOK LIKE SWINE COPULATING!
MATHEW... MATHEW...
IMAGINE 'TIS YOUR MOTHER YOU FONDLE!
JUST A SECOND, I FORGOT TO... UH...LOCK THE DOOR!
YOU BASTARD!
YOU ARE GOING TO SEND THE HARLOT HOME?
NO! YOU'RE GOING IN THE CLOSET!
MRMMPHLE GRRPH *PHERML* GRMM MRMRMMN!
COLA

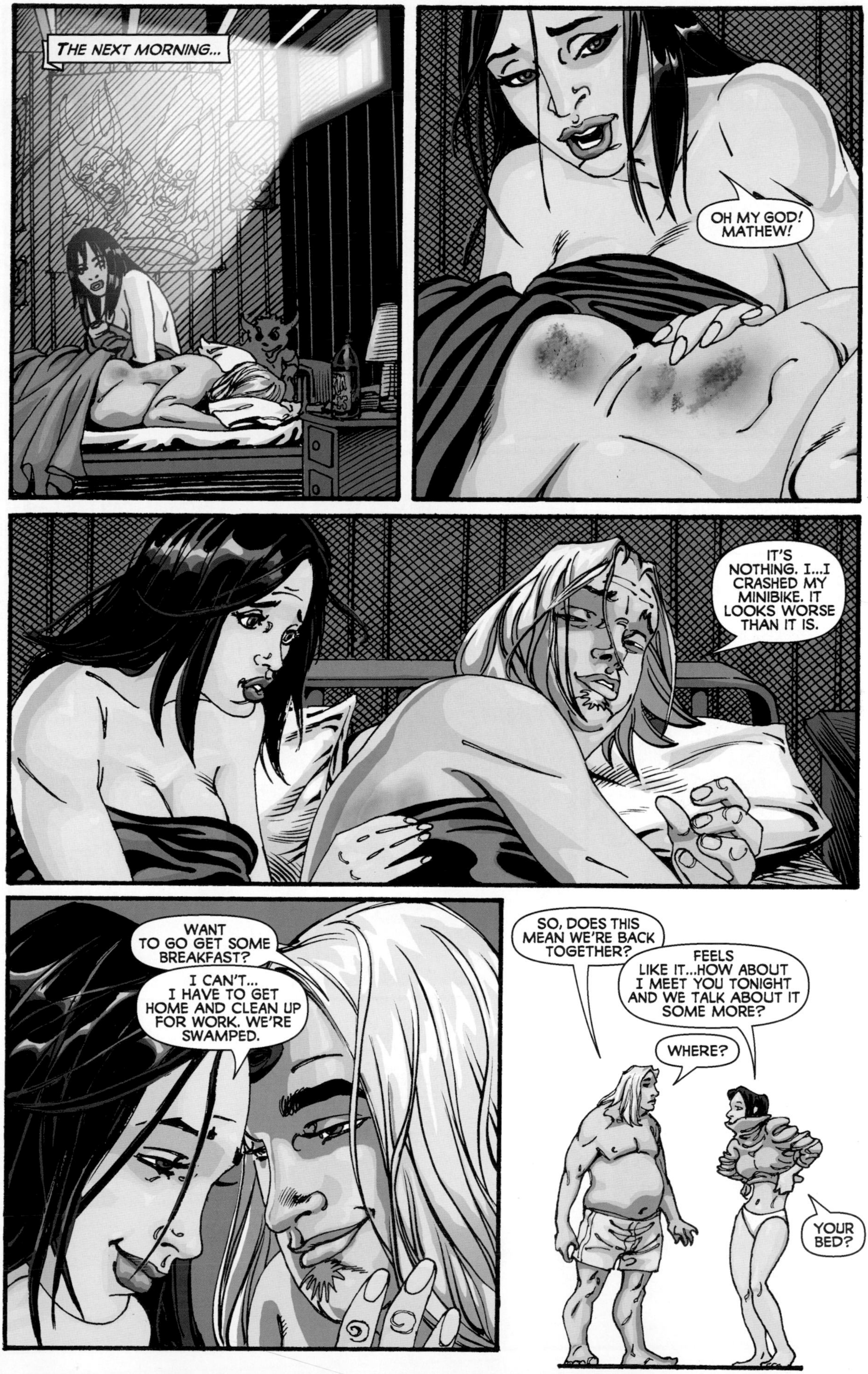
THE NEXT MORNING...
OH MY GOD! MATHEW!
IT'S NOTHING. I...I CRASHED MY MINIBIKE. IT LOOKS WORSE THAN IT IS.
WANT TO GO GET SOME BREAKFAST?
I CAN'T... I HAVE TO GET HOME AND CLEAN UP FOR WORK. WE'RE SWAMPED.
SO, DOES THIS MEAN WE'RE BACK TOGETHER?
FEELS LIKE IT...HOW ABOUT I MEET YOU TONIGHT AND WE TALK ABOUT IT SOME MORE?
WHERE?
YOUR BED?

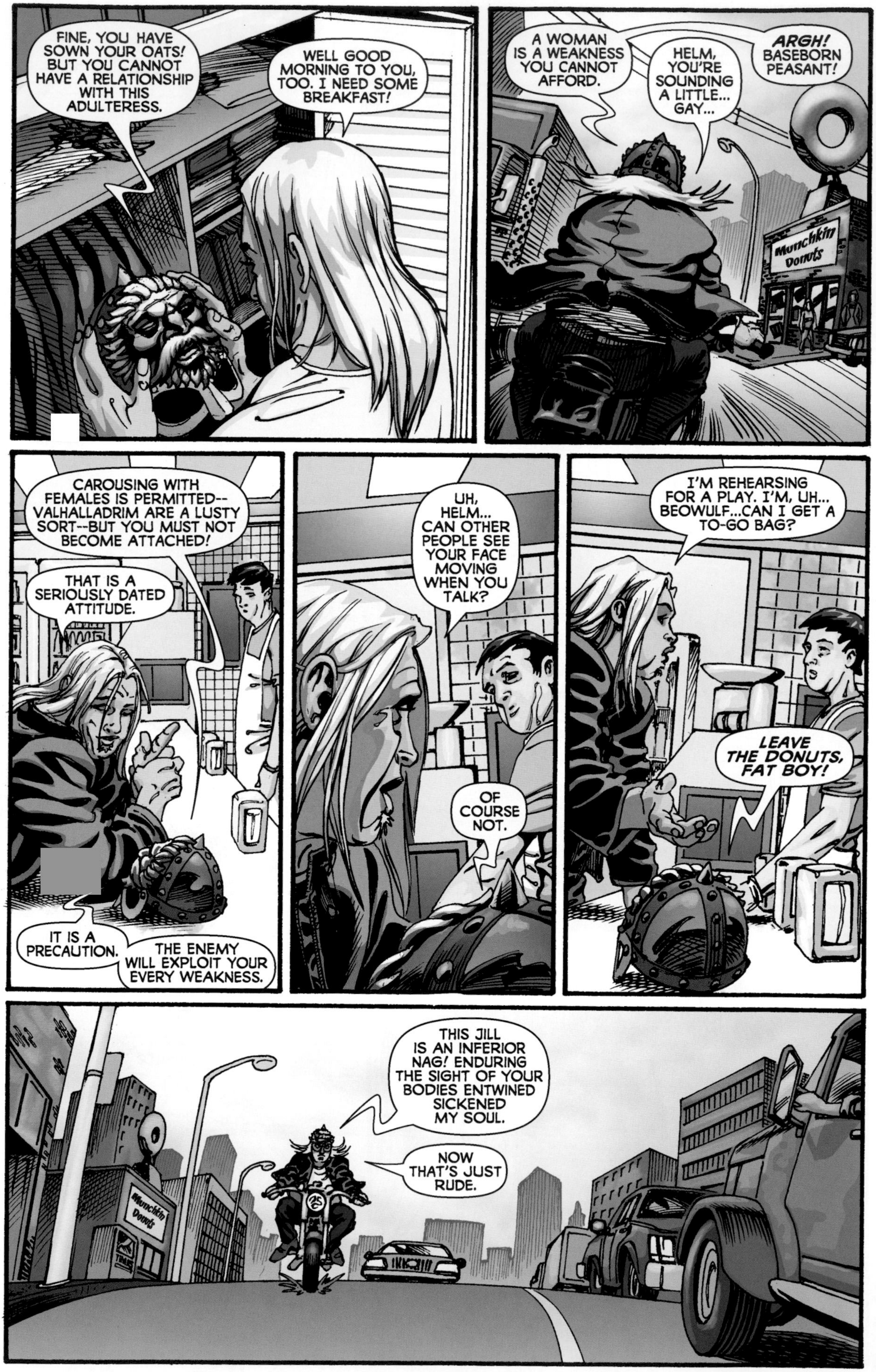
FINE, YOU HAVE SOWN YOUR OATS! BUT YOU CANNOT HAVE A RELATIONSHIP WITH THIS ADULTERESS.
WELL GOOD MORNING TO YOU, TOO. I NEED SOME BREAKFAST!
A WOMAN IS A WEAKNESS YOU CANNOT AFFORD.
HELM, YOU'RE SOUNDING A LITTLE... GAY...
ARGH! BASEBORN PEASANT!
Munchkin Donuts
CAROUSING WITH FEMALES IS PERMITTED-- VALHALLADRIM ARE A LUSTY SORT--BUT YOU MUST NOT BECOME ATTACHED!
THAT IS A SERIOUSLY DATED ATTITUDE.
IT IS A PRECAUTION.
THE ENEMY WILL EXPLOIT YOUR EVERY WEAKNESS.
UH, HELM... CAN OTHER PEOPLE SEE YOUR FACE MOVING WHEN YOU TALK?
OF COURSE NOT.
I'M REHEARSING FOR A PLAY. I'M, UH... BEOWULF...CAN I GET A TO-GO BAG?
LEAVE THE DONUTS, FAT BOY!
THIS JILL IS AN INFERIOR NAG! ENDURING THE SIGHT OF YOUR BODIES ENTWINED SICKENED MY SOUL.
NOW THAT'S JUST RUDE.
Munchkin Donuts

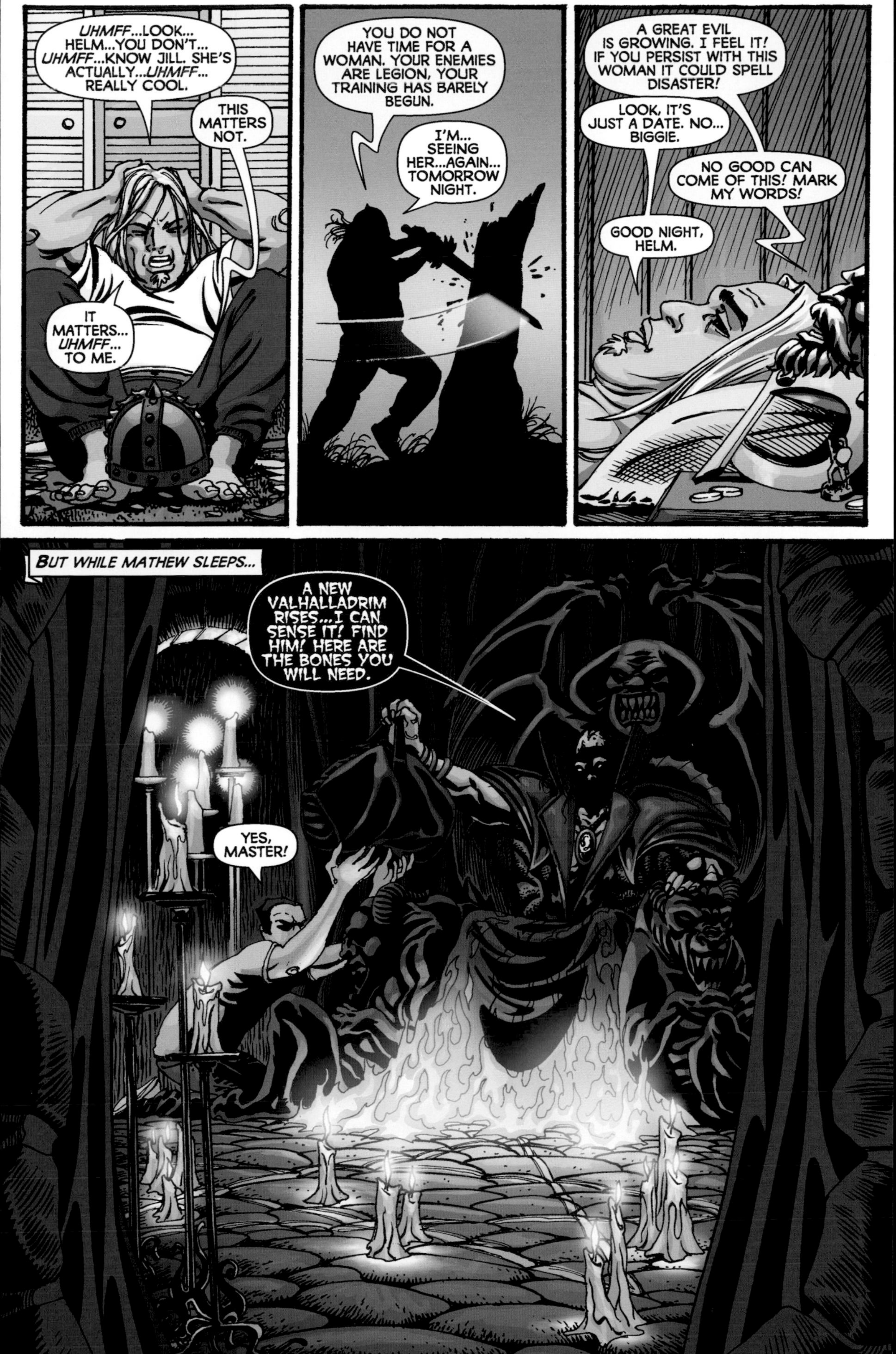
UHMFF...LOOK... HELM...YOU DON'T... UHMFF...KNOW JILL. SHE'S ACTUALLY...UHMFF... REALLY COOL.
THIS MATTERS NOT.
IT MATTERS... UHMFF... TO ME.
YOU DO NOT HAVE TIME FOR A WOMAN. YOUR ENEMIES ARE LEGION, YOUR TRAINING HAS BARELY BEGUN.
I'M... SEEING HER...AGAIN... TOMORROW NIGHT.
A GREAT EVIL IS GROWING. I FEEL IT! IF YOU PERSIST WITH THIS WOMAN IT COULD SPELL DISASTER!
LOOK, IT'S JUST A DATE. NO... BIGGIE.
NO GOOD CAN COME OF THIS! MARK MY WORDS!
GOOD NIGHT, HELM.
BUT WHILE MATHEW SLEEPS...
A NEW VALHALLADRIM RISES...I CAN SENSE IT! FIND HIM! HERE ARE THE BONES YOU WILL NEED.
YES, MASTER!

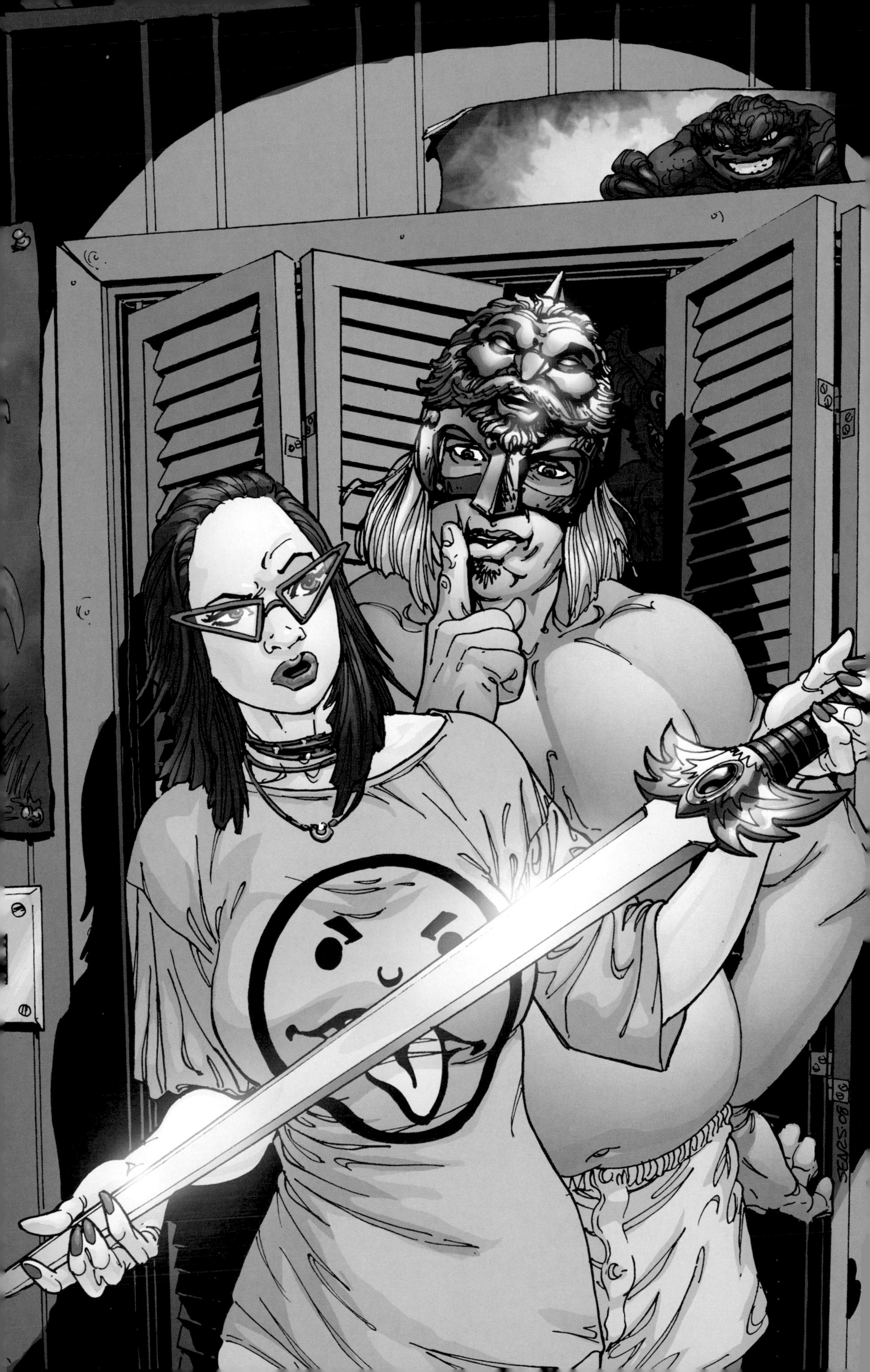

CHAPTER 3
MADNESS

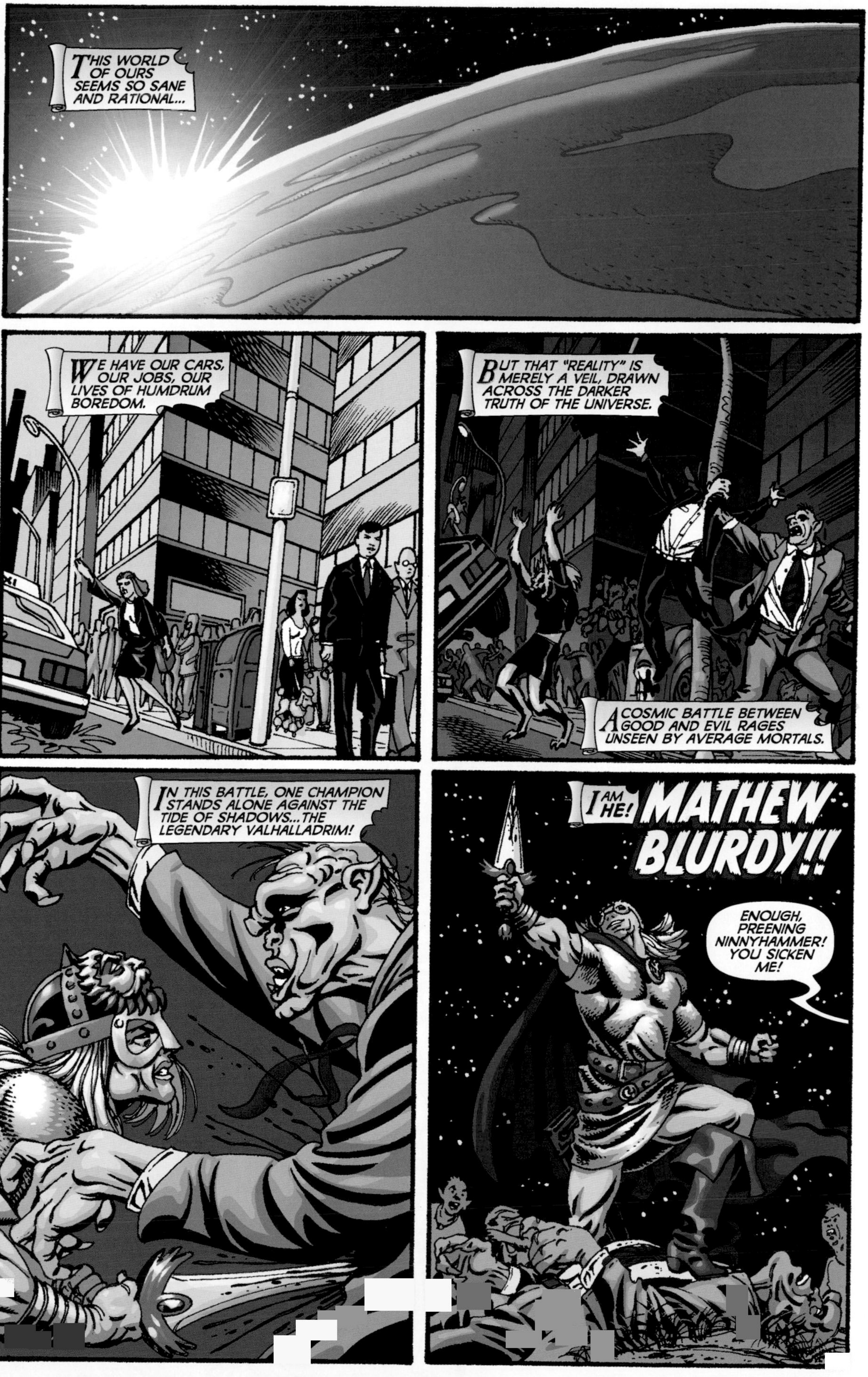
THIS WORLD OF OURS SEEMS SO SANE AND RATIONAL...
WE HAVE OUR CARS, OUR JOBS, OUR LIVES OF HUMDRUM BOREDOM.
BUT THAT "REALITY" IS MERELY A VEIL, DRAWN ACROSS THE DARKER TRUTH OF THE UNIVERSE.
A COSMIC BATTLE BETWEEN GOOD AND EVIL RAGES UNSEEN BY AVERAGE MORTALS.
IN THIS BATTLE, ONE CHAMPION STANDS ALONE AGAINST THE TIDE OF SHADOWS...THE LEGENDARY VALHALLADRIM!
I AM HE! MATHEW BLURDY!!
ENOUGH, PREENING NINNYHAMMER! YOU SICKEN ME!

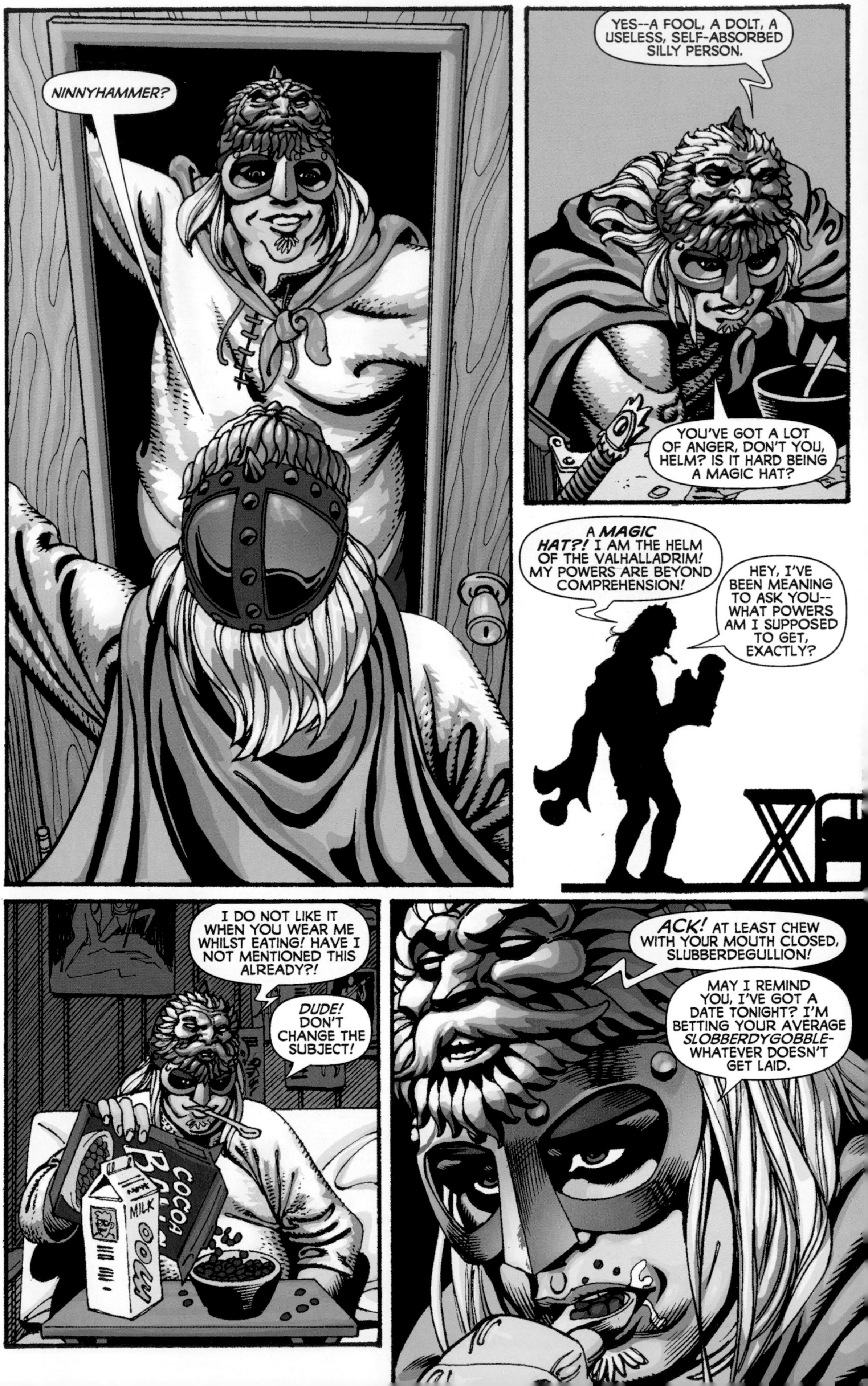
NINNYHAMMER?
YES--A FOOL, A DOLT, A USELESS, SELF-ABSORBED SILLY PERSON.
YOU'VE GOT A LOT OF ANGER, DON'T YOU, HELM? IS IT HARD BEING A MAGIC HAT?
A MAGIC HAT?! I AM THE HELM OF THE VALHALLADRIM! MY POWERS ARE BEYOND COMPREHENSION!
HEY, I'VE BEEN MEANING TO ASK YOU-- WHAT POWERS AM I SUPPOSED TO GET, EXACTLY?
I DO NOT LIKE IT WHEN YOU WEAR ME WHILST EATING! HAVE I NOT MENTIONED THIS ALREADY?!
DUDE! DON'T CHANGE THE SUBJECT!
COCOA
MILK
ACK! AT LEAST CHEW WITH YOUR MOUTH CLOSED, SLUBBERDEGULLION!
MAY I REMIND YOU, I'VE GOT A DATE TONIGHT? I'M BETTING YOUR AVERAGE SLOBBERDYGOBBLE-WHATEVER DOESN'T GET LAID.

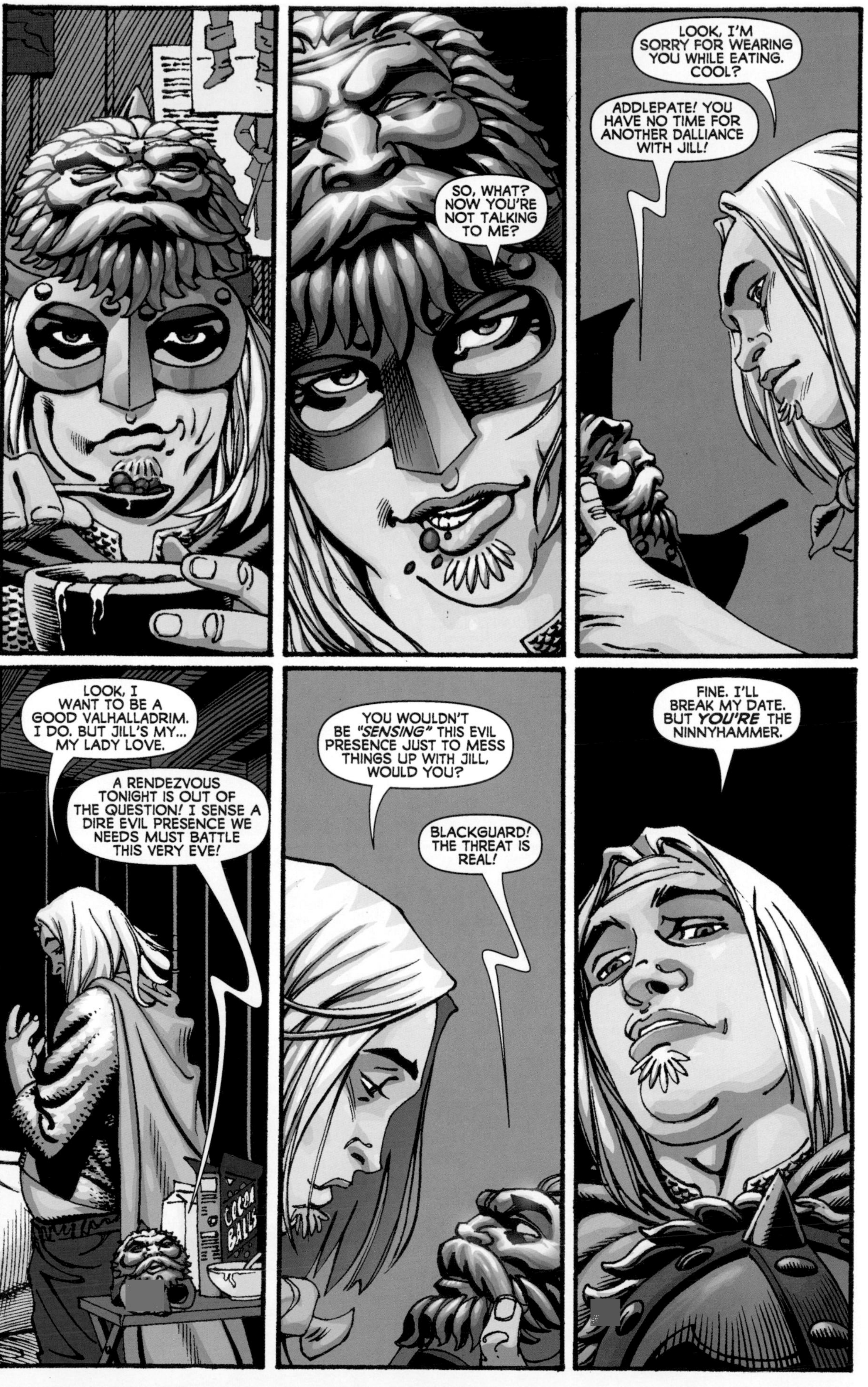
SO, WHAT? NOW YOU'RE NOT TALKING TO ME?
LOOK, I'M SORRY FOR WEARING YOU WHILE EATING. COOL?
ADDLEPATE! YOU HAVE NO TIME FOR ANOTHER DALLIANCE WITH JILL!
LOOK, I WANT TO BE A GOOD VALHALLADRIM. I DO. BUT JILL'S MY... MY LADY LOVE.
A RENDEZVOUS TONIGHT IS OUT OF THE QUESTION! I SENSE A DIRE EVIL PRESENCE WE NEEDS MUST BATTLE THIS VERY EVE!
COCOA BALLS
YOU WOULDN'T BE "SENSING" THIS EVIL PRESENCE JUST TO MESS THINGS UP WITH JILL, WOULD YOU?
BLACKGUARD! THE THREAT IS REAL!
FINE. I'LL BREAK MY DATE. BUT YOU'RE THE NINNYHAMMER.

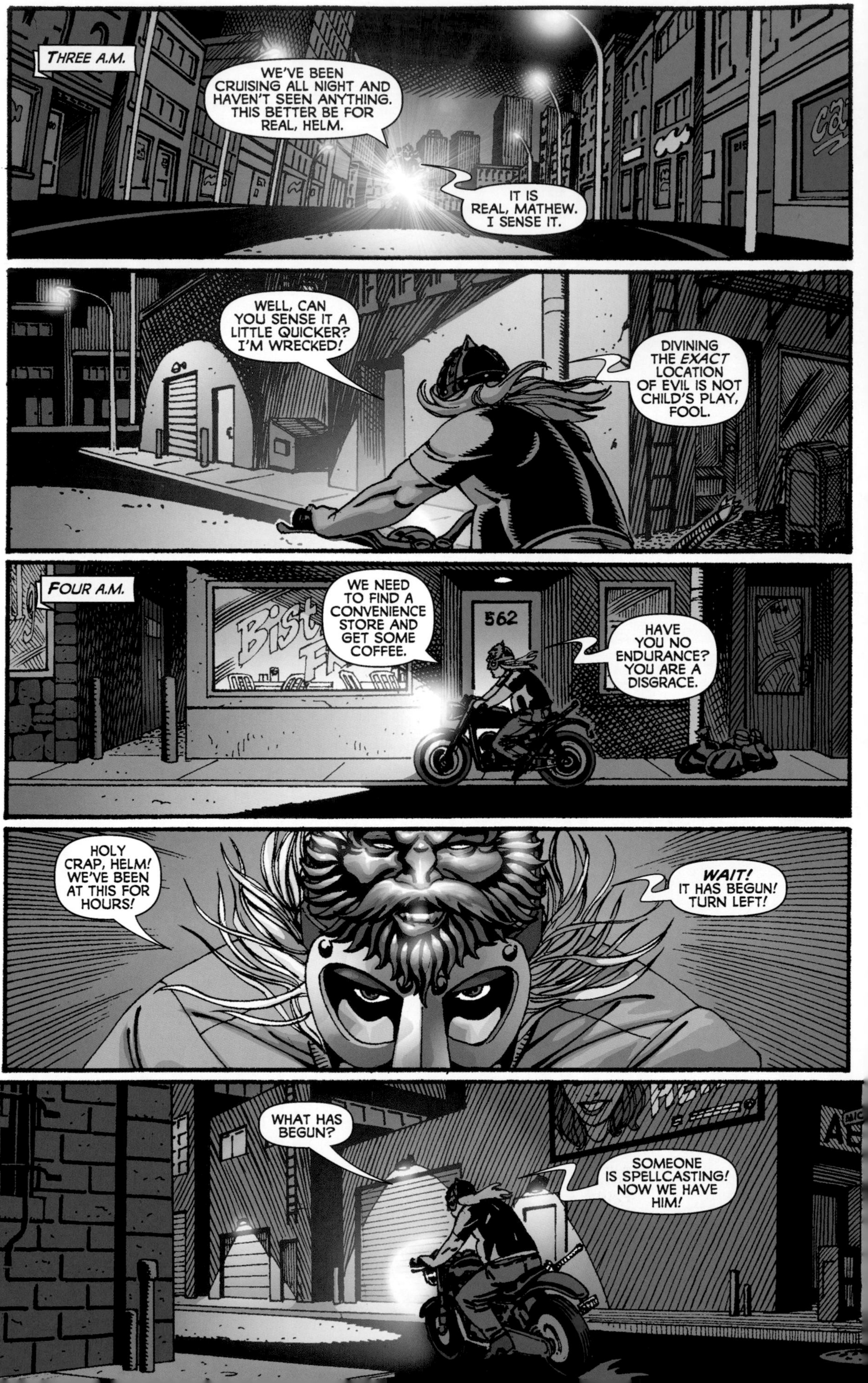
THREE A.M.
WE'VE BEEN CRUISING ALL NIGHT AND HAVEN'T SEEN ANYTHING. THIS BETTER BE FOR REAL, HELM.
IT IS REAL, MATHEW. I SENSE IT.
WELL, CAN YOU SENSE IT A LITTLE QUICKER? I'M WRECKED!
DIVINING THE *EXACT* LOCATION OF EVIL IS NOT CHILD'S PLAY, FOOL.
FOUR A.M.
WE NEED TO FIND A CONVENIENCE STORE AND GET SOME COFFEE.
562
HAVE YOU NO ENDURANCE? YOU ARE A DISGRACE.
HOLY CRAP, HELM! WE'VE BEEN AT THIS FOR HOURS!
WAIT! IT HAS BEGUN! TURN LEFT!
WHAT HAS BEGUN?
SOMEONE IS SPELLCASTING! NOW WE HAVE HIM!

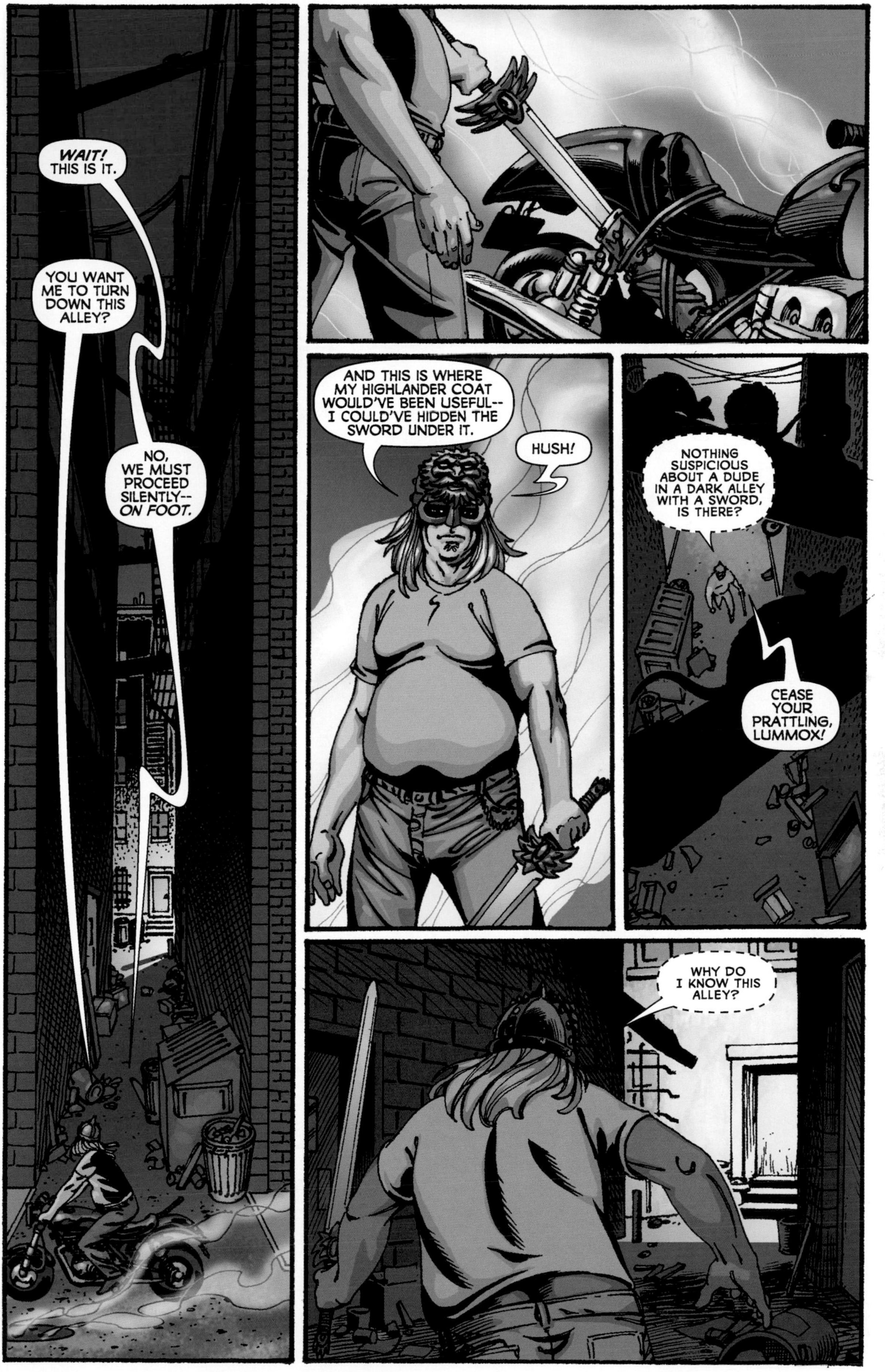
WAIT! THIS IS IT.
YOU WANT ME TO TURN DOWN THIS ALLEY?
NO, WE MUST PROCEED SILENTLY-- ON FOOT.
AND THIS IS WHERE MY HIGHLANDER COAT WOULD'VE BEEN USEFUL-- I COULD'VE HIDDEN THE SWORD UNDER IT.
HUSH!
NOTHING SUSPICIOUS ABOUT A DUDE IN A DARK ALLEY WITH A SWORD, IS THERE?
CEASE YOUR PRATTLING, LUMMOX!
WHY DO I KNOW THIS ALLEY?

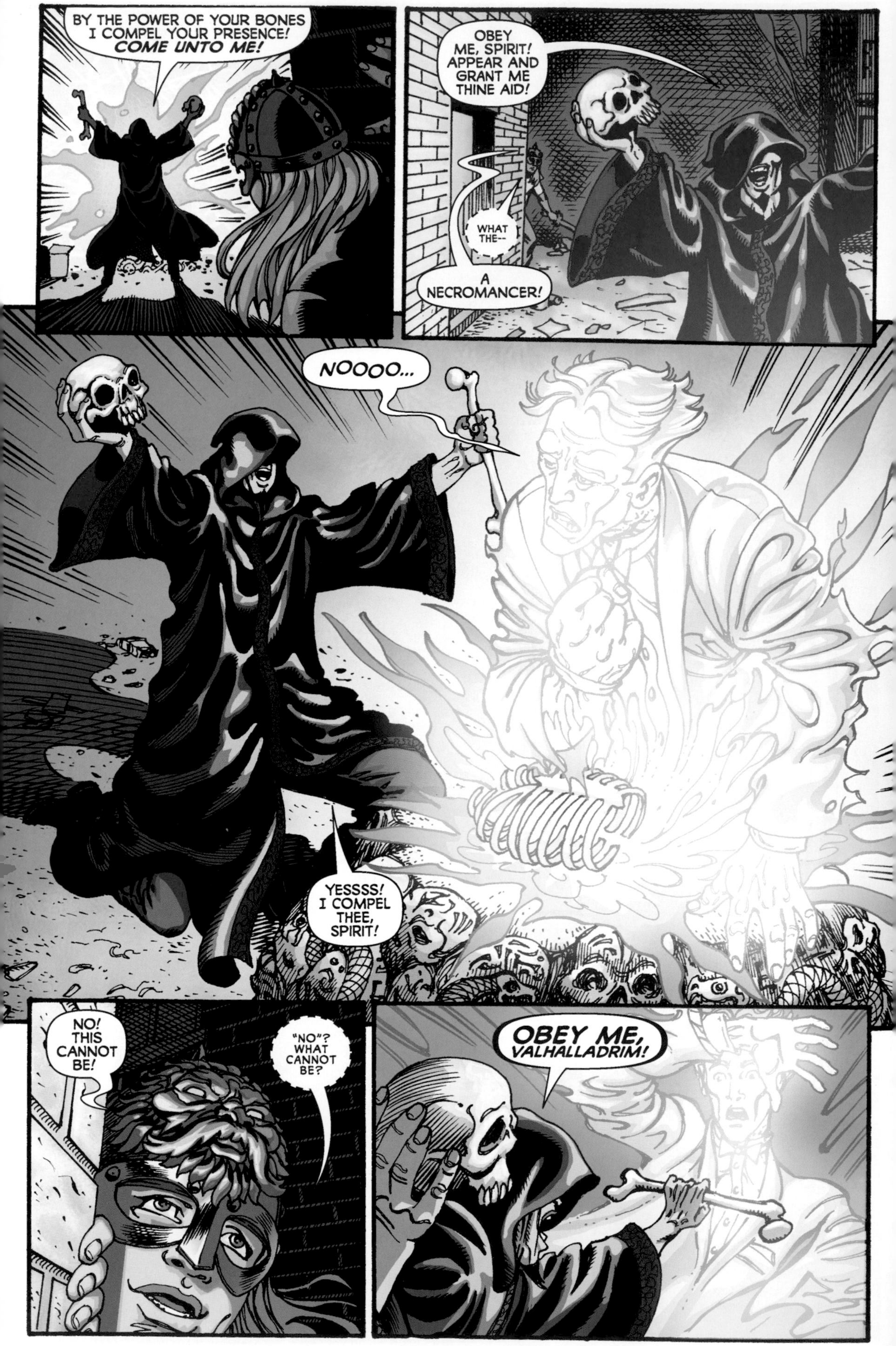
BY THE POWER OF YOUR BONES I COMPEL YOUR PRESENCE! *COME UNTO ME!*
OBEY ME, SPIRIT! APPEAR AND GRANT ME THINE AID!
WHAT THE--
A NECROMANCER!
NOOOO...
YESSSS! I COMPEL THEE, SPIRIT!
NO! THIS CANNOT BE!
"NO"? WHAT CANNOT BE?
OBEY ME, VALHALLADRIM!

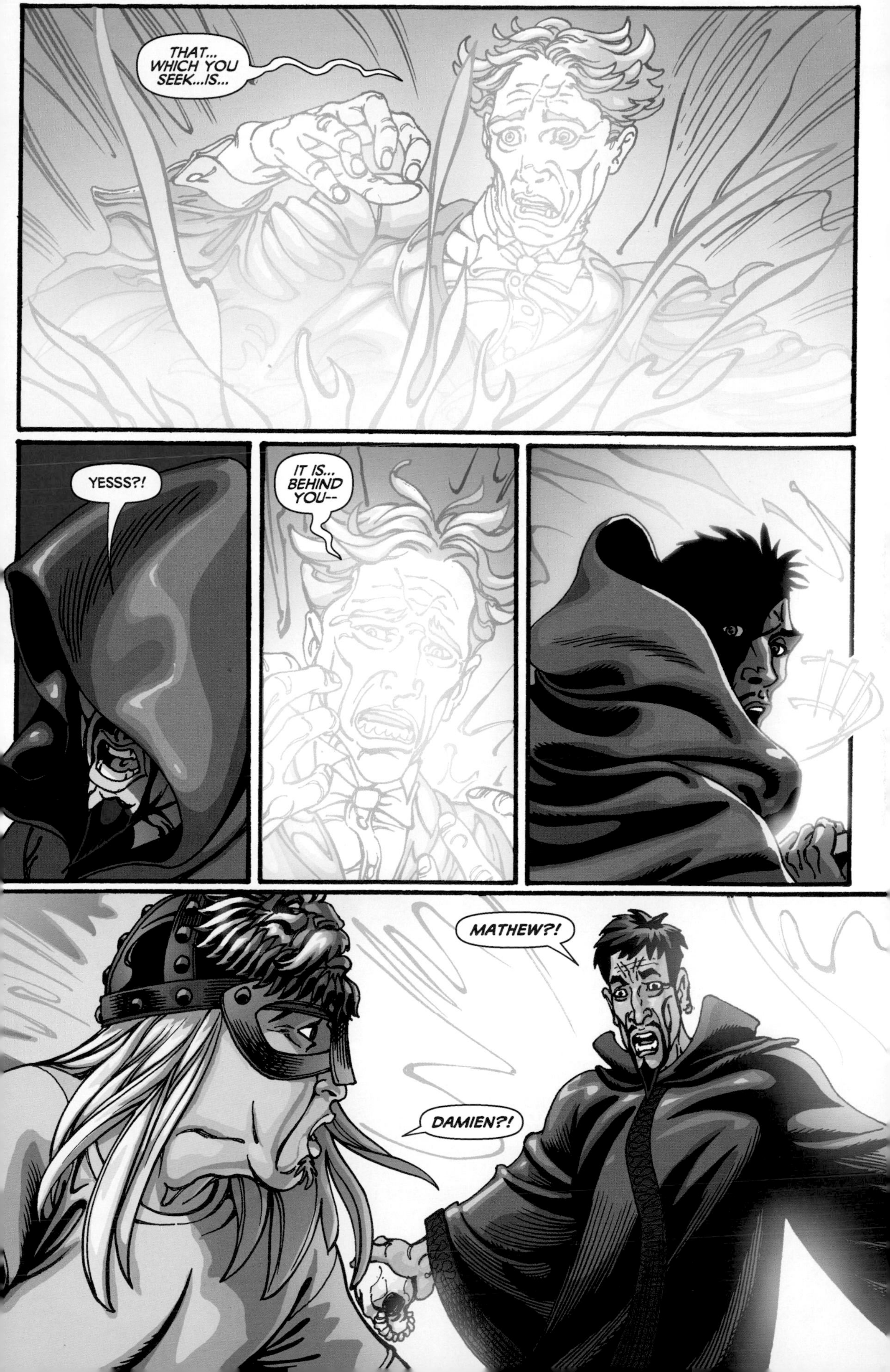
THAT... WHICH YOU SEEK...IS...
YESSS?!
IT IS... BEHIND YOU--
MATHEW?!
DAMIEN?!

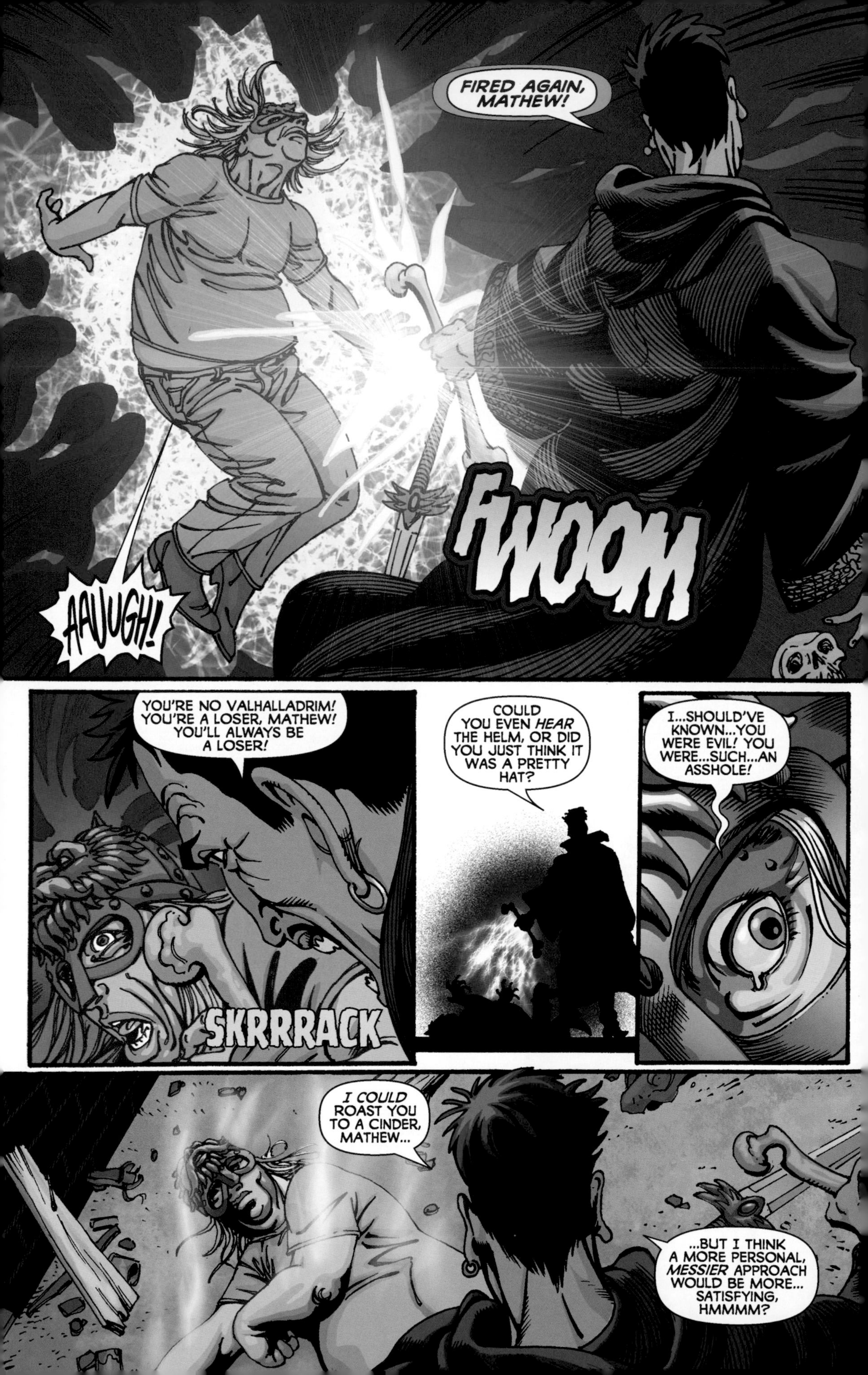
FIRED AGAIN, MATHEW!
FWOOM
AAUUGH!
YOU'RE NO VALHALLADRIM! YOU'RE A LOSER, MATHEW! YOU'LL ALWAYS BE A LOSER!
SKRRRACK
COULD YOU EVEN *HEAR* THE HELM, OR DID YOU JUST THINK IT WAS A PRETTY HAT?
I...SHOULD'VE KNOWN...YOU WERE EVIL! YOU WERE...SUCH...AN ASSHOLE!
I COULD ROAST YOU TO A CINDER, MATHEW...
...BUT I THINK A MORE PERSONAL, *MESSIER* APPROACH WOULD BE MORE... SATISFYING, HMMMM?

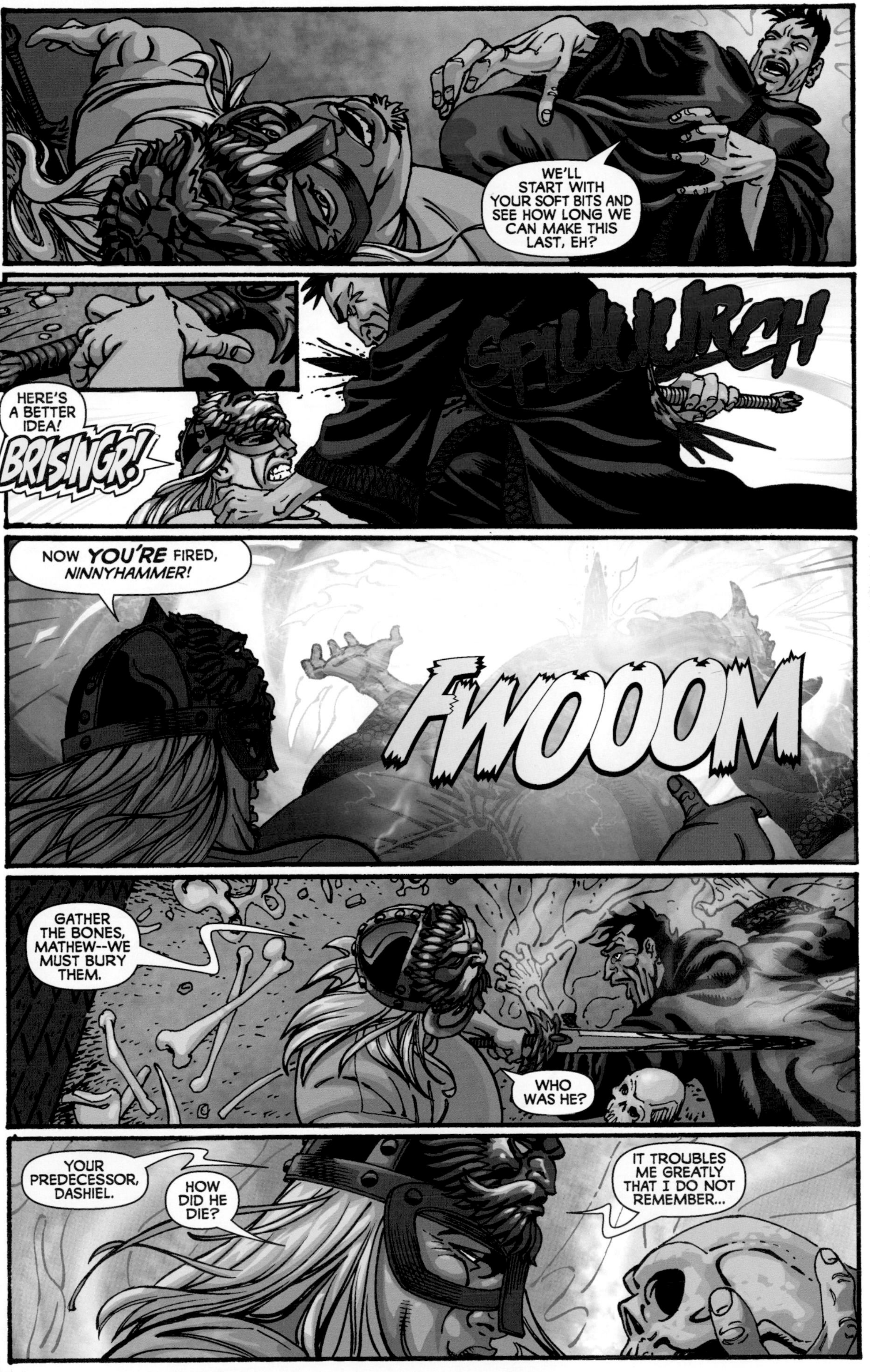
WE'LL START WITH YOUR SOFT BITS AND SEE HOW LONG WE CAN MAKE THIS LAST, EH?
SPLUUURCH
HERE'S A BETTER IDEA!
BRISINGR!
NOW YOU'RE FIRED, NINNYHAMMER!
FWOOOM
GATHER THE BONES, MATHEW--WE MUST BURY THEM.
WHO WAS HE?
YOUR PREDECESSOR, DASHIEL.
HOW DID HE DIE?
IT TROUBLES ME GREATLY THAT I DO NOT REMEMBER...

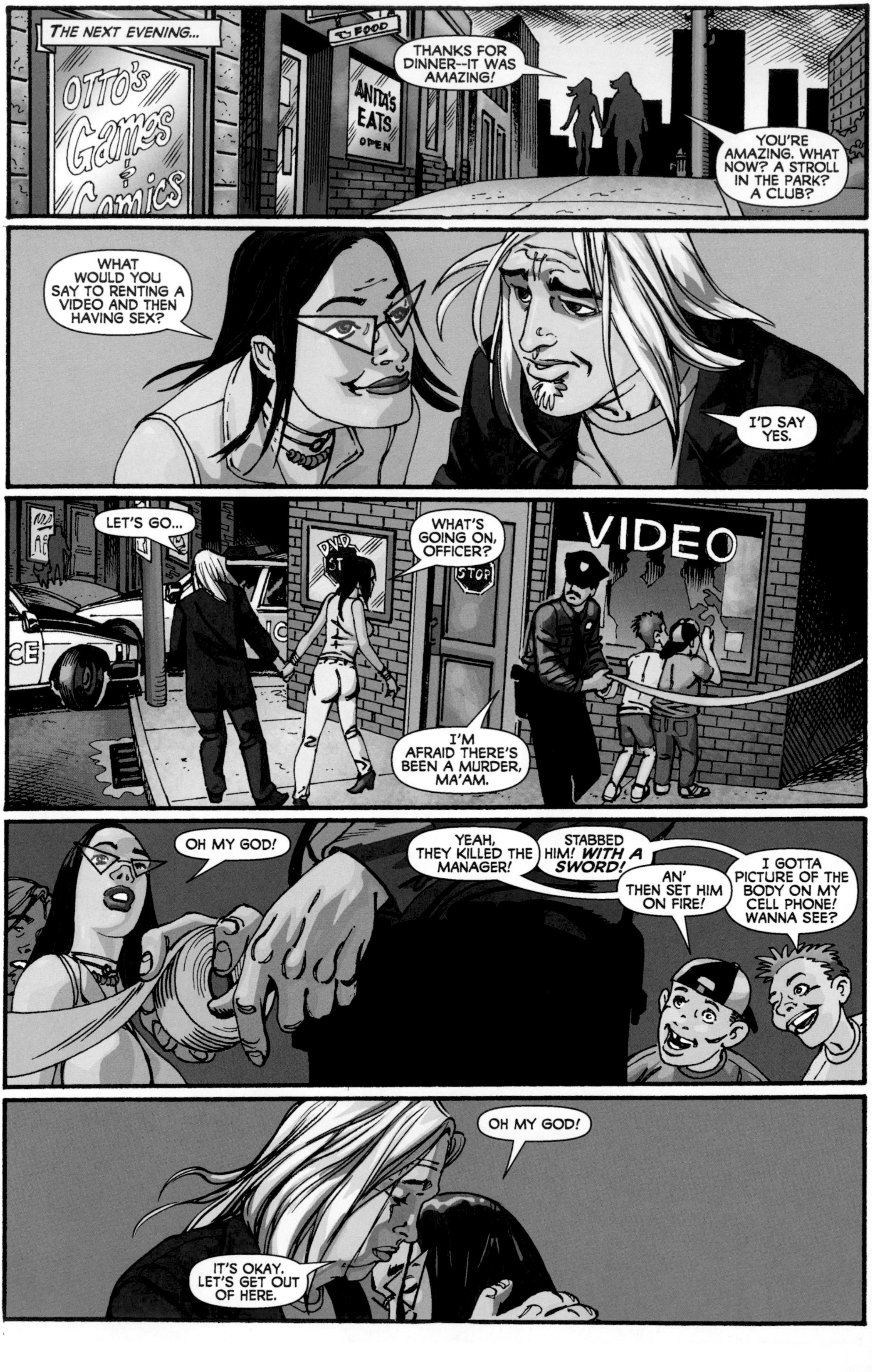
THE NEXT EVENING...
OTTO'S Games & Comics
FOOD
ANITA'S EATS OPEN
THANKS FOR DINNER--IT WAS AMAZING!
YOU'RE AMAZING. WHAT NOW? A STROLL IN THE PARK? A CLUB?
WHAT WOULD YOU SAY TO RENTING A VIDEO AND THEN HAVING SEX?
I'D SAY YES.
LET'S GO...
WHAT'S GOING ON, OFFICER?
VIDEO
STOP
I'M AFRAID THERE'S BEEN A MURDER, MA'AM.
OH MY GOD!
YEAH, THEY KILLED THE MANAGER!
STABBED HIM! ***WITH A SWORD!***
AN' THEN SET HIM ON FIRE!
I GOTTA PICTURE OF THE BODY ON MY CELL PHONE! WANNA SEE?
OH MY GOD!
IT'S OKAY. LET'S GET OUT OF HERE.

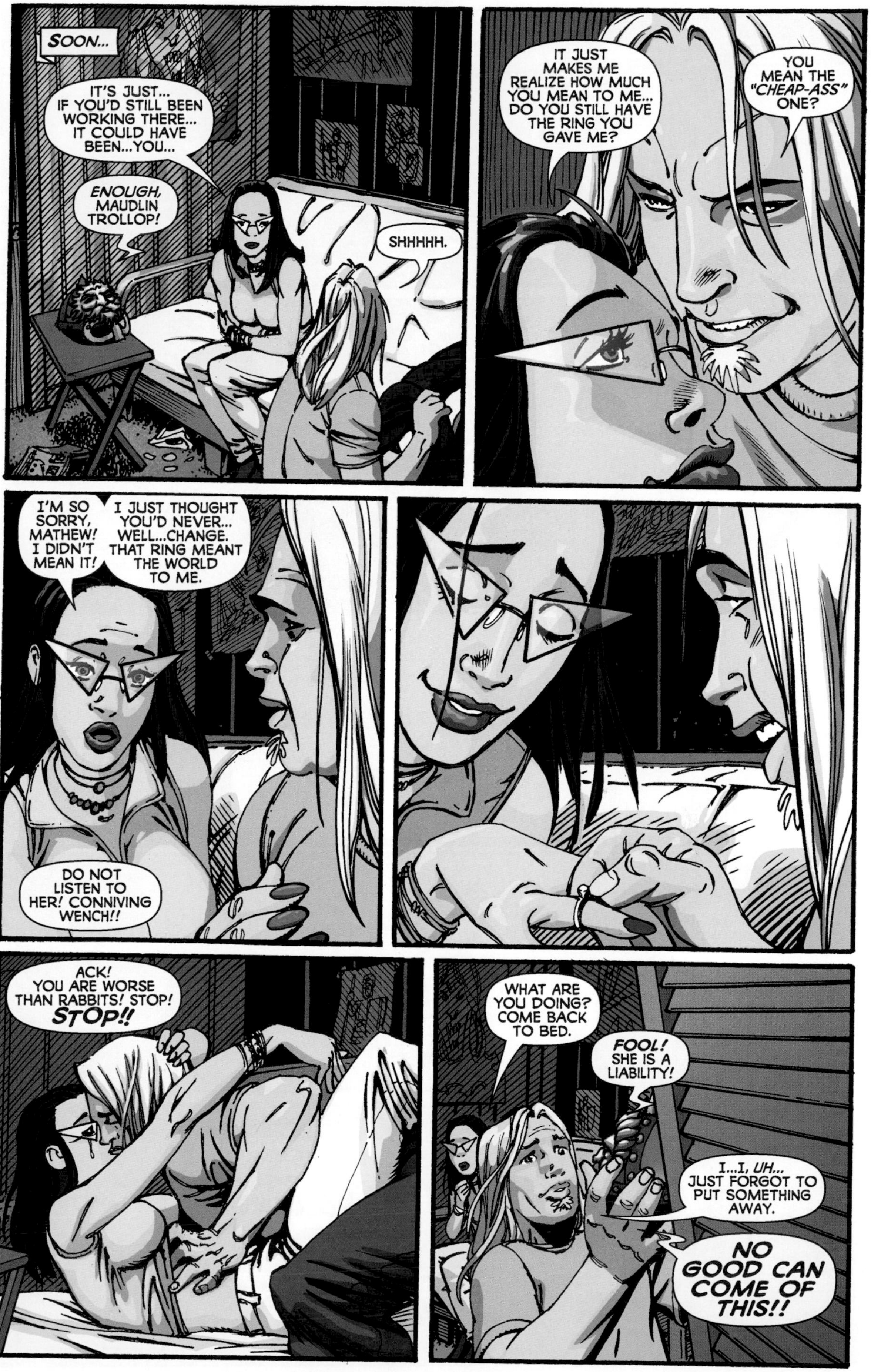
SOON...
IT'S JUST... IF YOU'D STILL BEEN WORKING THERE... IT COULD HAVE BEEN...YOU...
ENOUGH, MAUDLIN TROLLOP!
SHHHHH.
IT JUST MAKES ME REALIZE HOW MUCH YOU MEAN TO ME... DO YOU STILL HAVE THE RING YOU GAVE ME?
YOU MEAN THE "CHEAP-ASS" ONE?
I'M SO SORRY, MATHEW! I DIDN'T MEAN IT!
I JUST THOUGHT YOU'D NEVER... WELL...CHANGE. THAT RING MEANT THE WORLD TO ME.
DO NOT LISTEN TO HER! CONNIVING WENCH!!
ACK! YOU ARE WORSE THAN RABBITS! STOP! STOP!!
WHAT ARE YOU DOING? COME BACK TO BED.
FOOL! SHE IS A LIABILITY!
I...I, UH... JUST FORGOT TO PUT SOMETHING AWAY.
NO GOOD CAN COME OF THIS!!

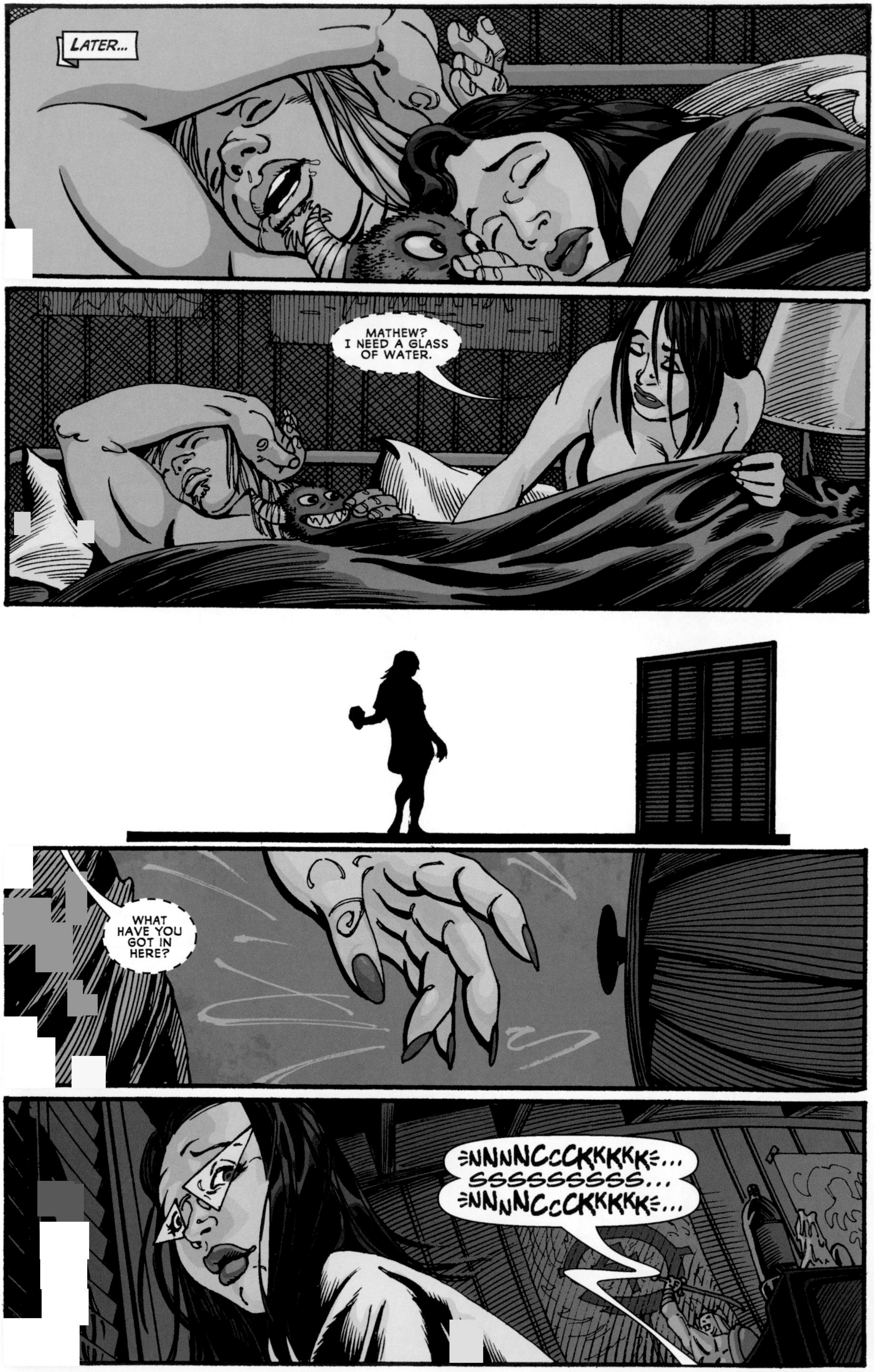
LATER...
MATHEW? I NEED A GLASS OF WATER.
WHAT HAVE YOU GOT IN HERE?
NNNNCcCKKKKK... SSSSSSSSSS... NNNNCcCKKKKK...

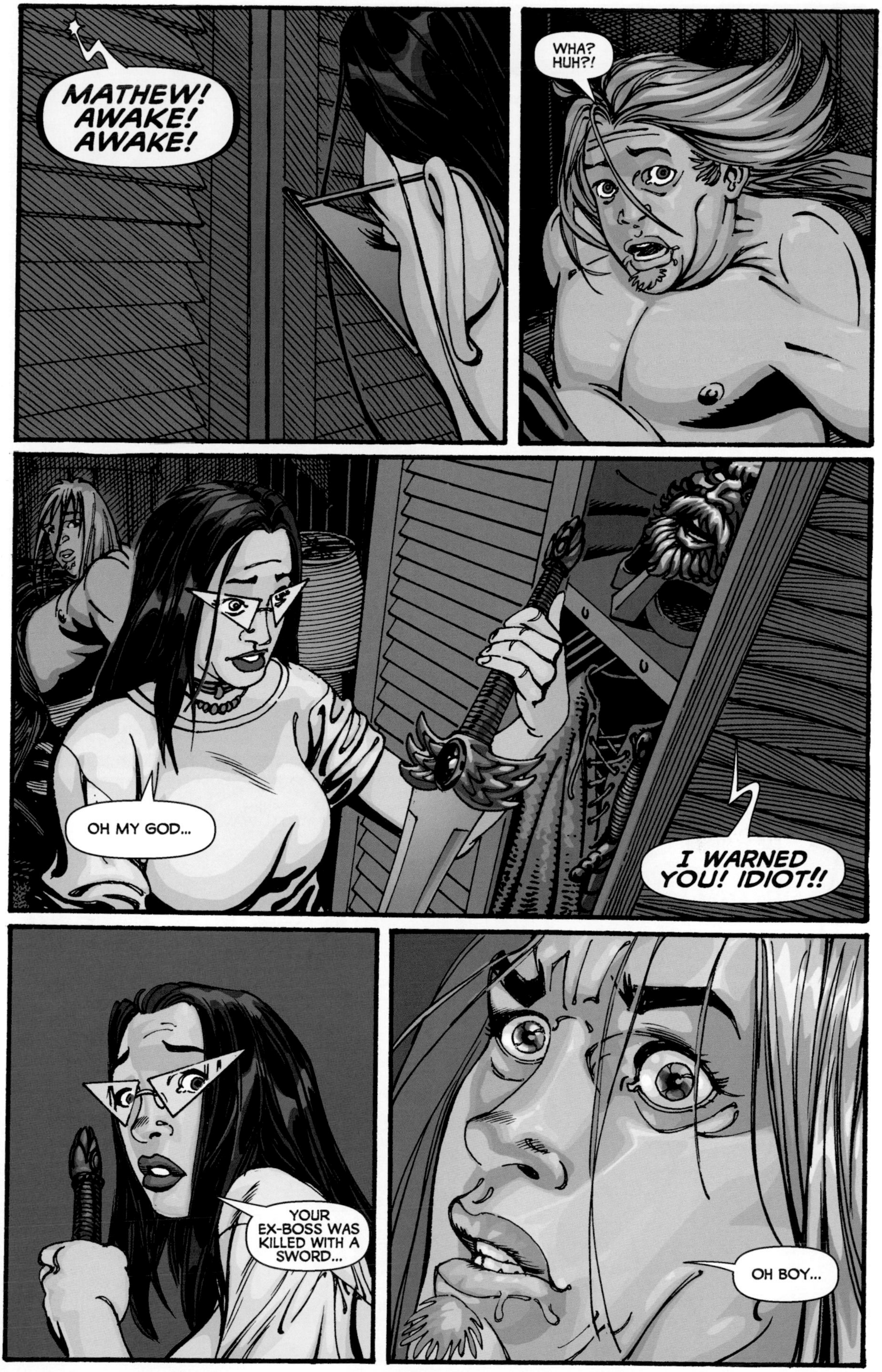
MATHEW! AWAKE! AWAKE!
WHA? HUH?!
OH MY GOD...
I WARNED YOU! IDIOT!!
YOUR EX-BOSS WAS KILLED WITH A SWORD...
OH BOY...

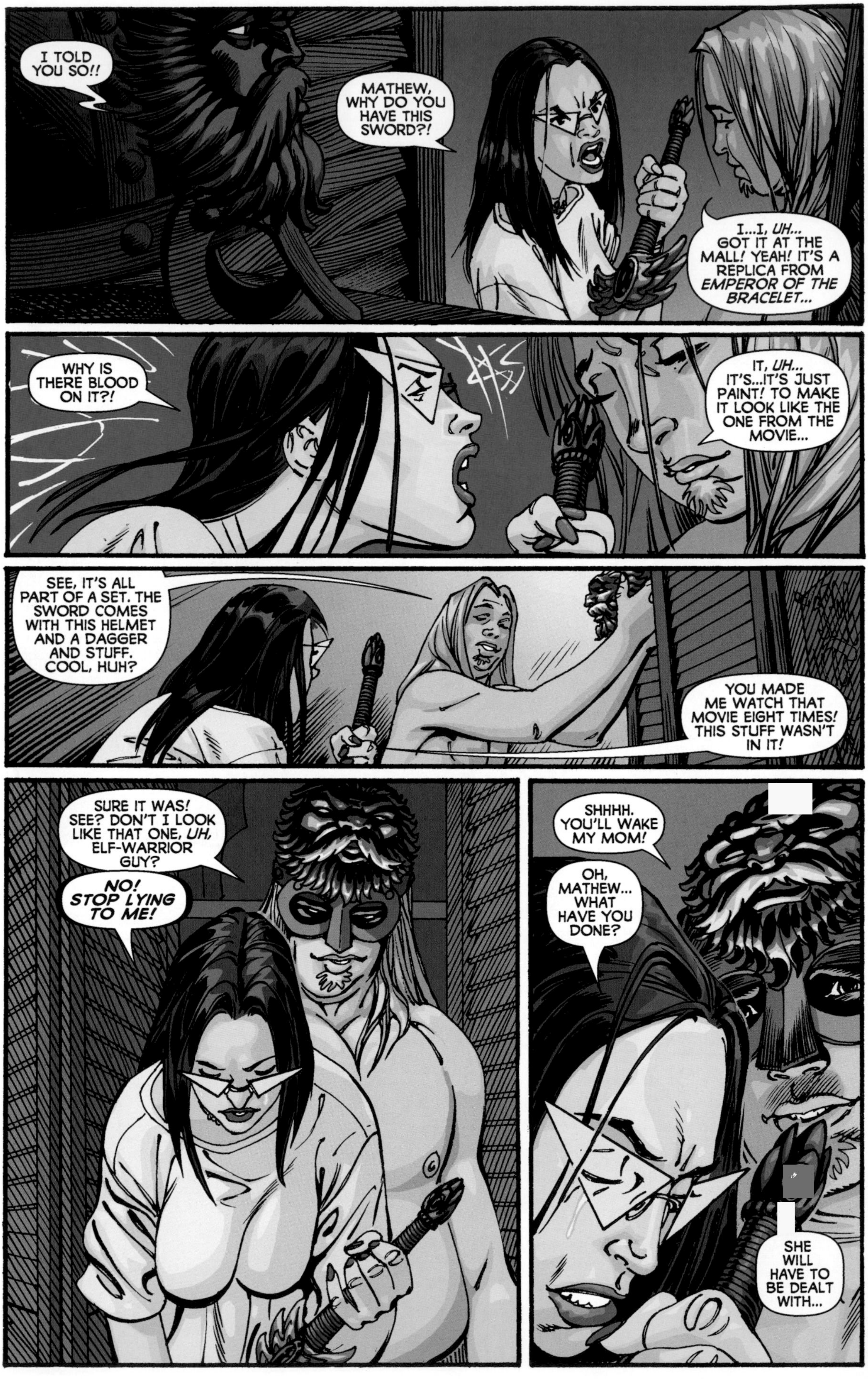
I TOLD YOU SO!!
MATHEW, WHY DO YOU HAVE THIS SWORD?!
I...I, *UH*... GOT IT AT THE MALL! YEAH! IT'S A REPLICA FROM *EMPEROR OF THE BRACELET*...
WHY IS THERE BLOOD ON IT?!
IT, *UH*... IT'S...IT'S JUST PAINT! TO MAKE IT LOOK LIKE THE ONE FROM THE MOVIE...
SEE, IT'S ALL PART OF A SET. THE SWORD COMES WITH THIS HELMET AND A DAGGER AND STUFF. COOL, HUH?
YOU MADE ME WATCH THAT MOVIE EIGHT TIMES! THIS STUFF WASN'T IN IT!
SURE IT WAS! SEE? DON'T I LOOK LIKE THAT ONE, *UH*, ELF-WARRIOR GUY?
NO! STOP LYING TO ME!
SHHHH. YOU'LL WAKE MY MOM!
OH, MATHEW... WHAT HAVE YOU DONE?
SHE WILL HAVE TO BE DEALT WITH...

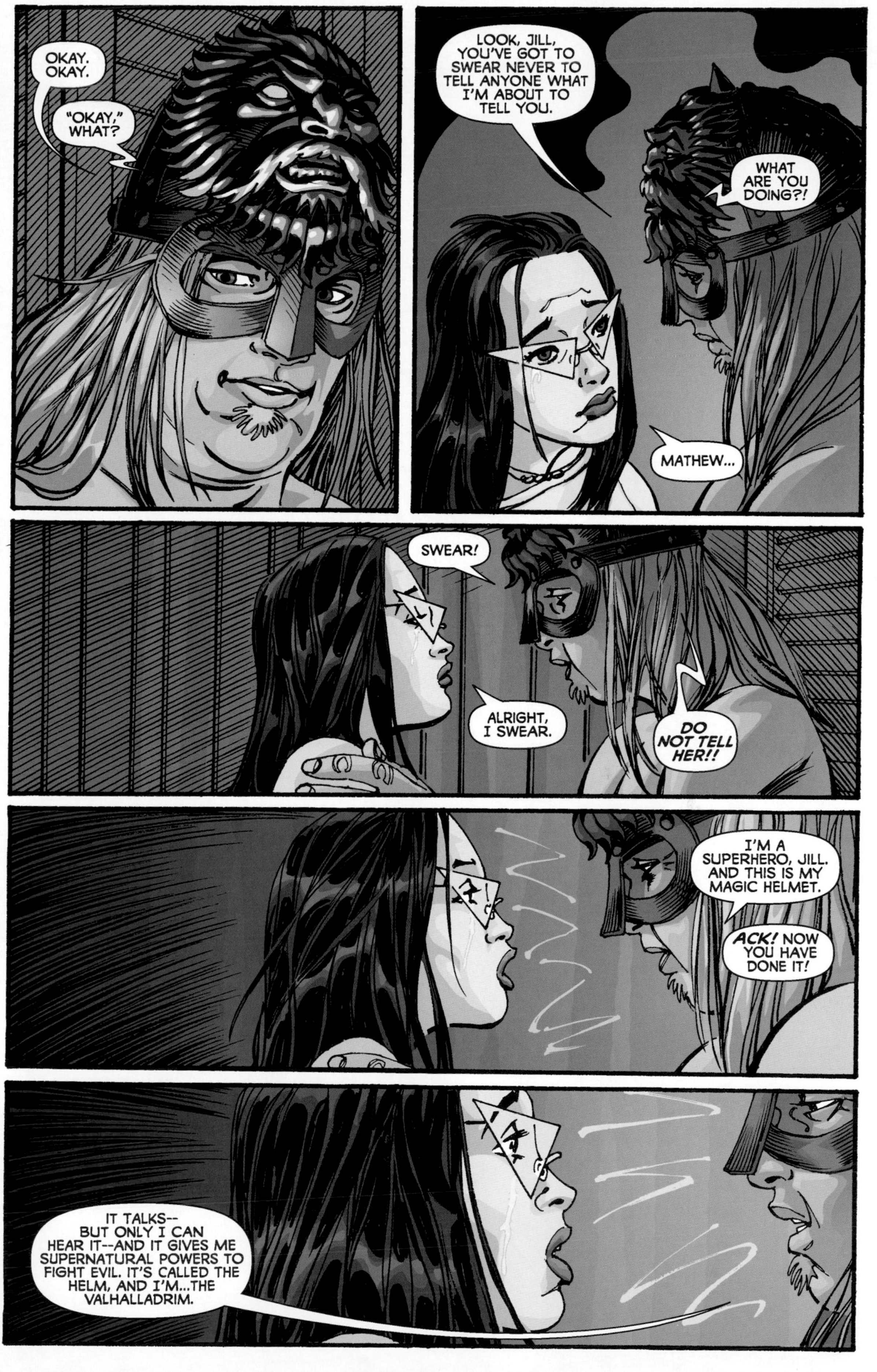
OKAY. OKAY.
"OKAY," WHAT?
LOOK, JILL, YOU'VE GOT TO SWEAR NEVER TO TELL ANYONE WHAT I'M ABOUT TO TELL YOU.
WHAT ARE YOU DOING?!
MATHEW...
SWEAR!
ALRIGHT, I SWEAR.
DO NOT TELL HER!!
I'M A SUPERHERO, JILL. AND THIS IS MY MAGIC HELMET.
ACK! NOW YOU HAVE DONE IT!
IT TALKS-- BUT ONLY I CAN HEAR IT--AND IT GIVES ME SUPERNATURAL POWERS TO FIGHT EVIL. IT'S CALLED THE HELM, AND I'M...THE VALHALLADRIM.

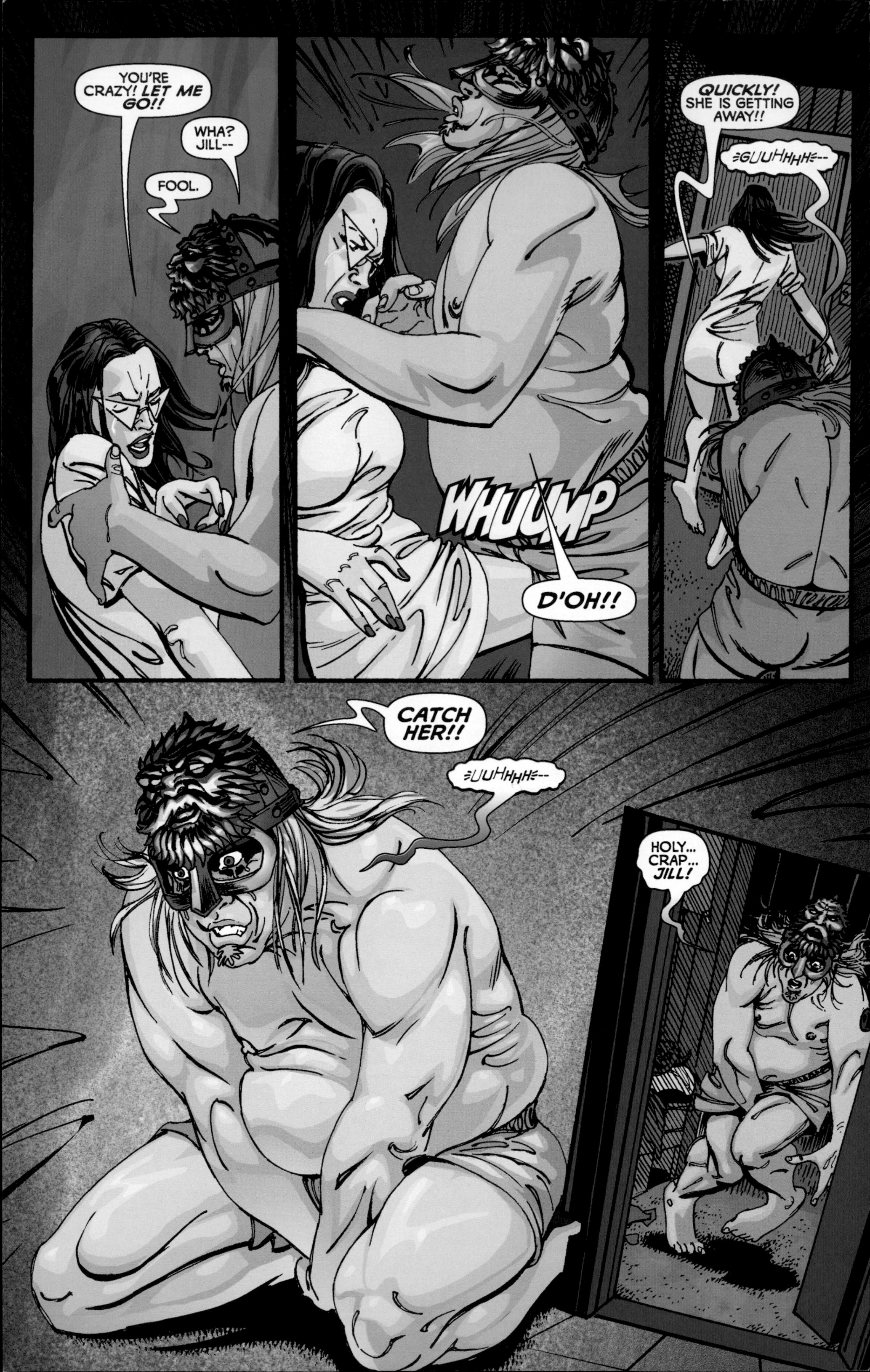
YOU'RE CRAZY!! LET ME GO!!
WHA? JILL--
FOOL.
WHUUMP
D'OH!!
QUICKLY! SHE IS GETTING AWAY!!
GUUHHHH--
CATCH HER!!
UUHHHH--
HOLY... CRAP... JILL!

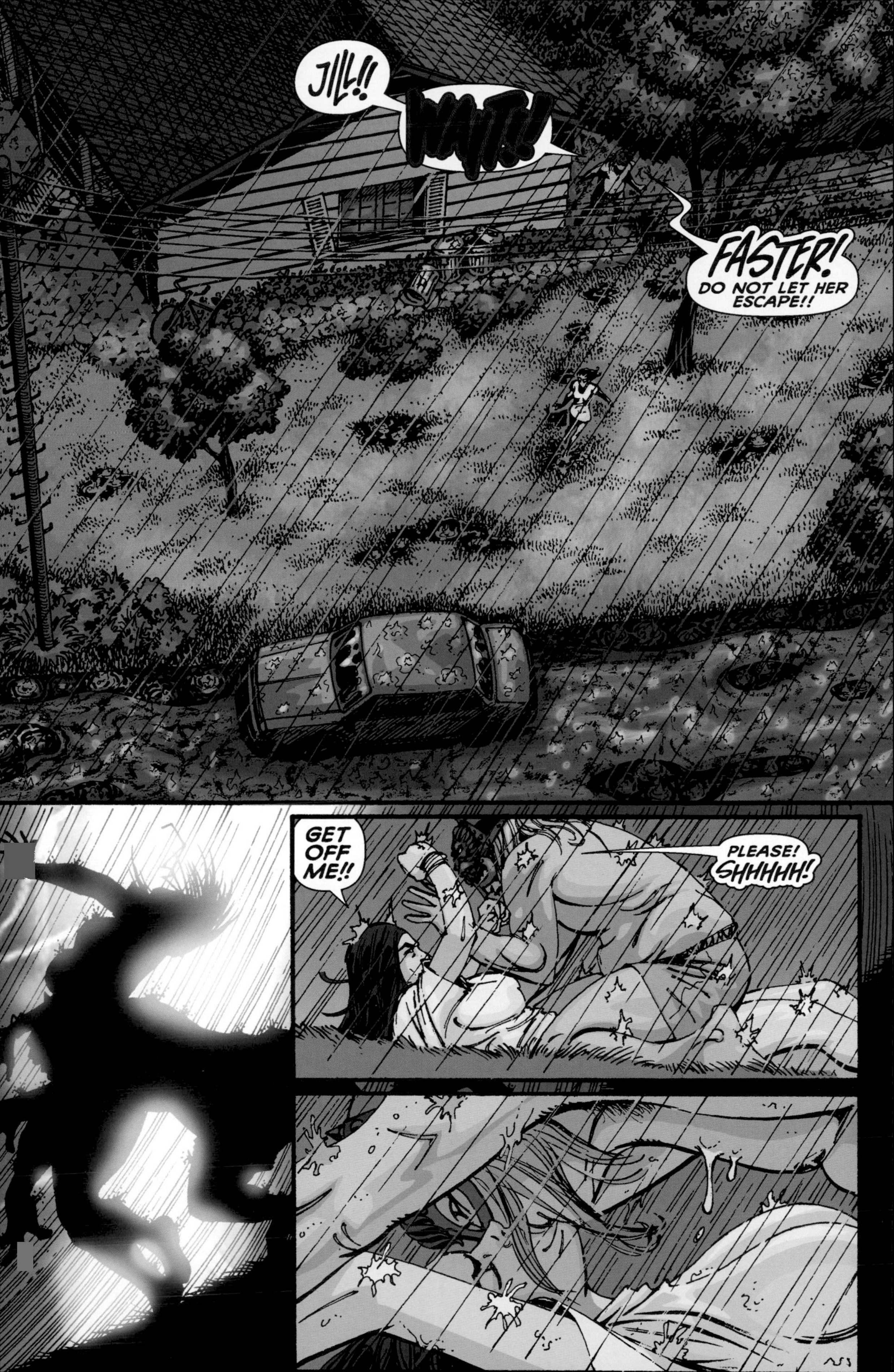
JILL!!
WAIT!!
FASTER! DO NOT LET HER ESCAPE!!
GET OFF ME!!
PLEASE! SHHHHH!

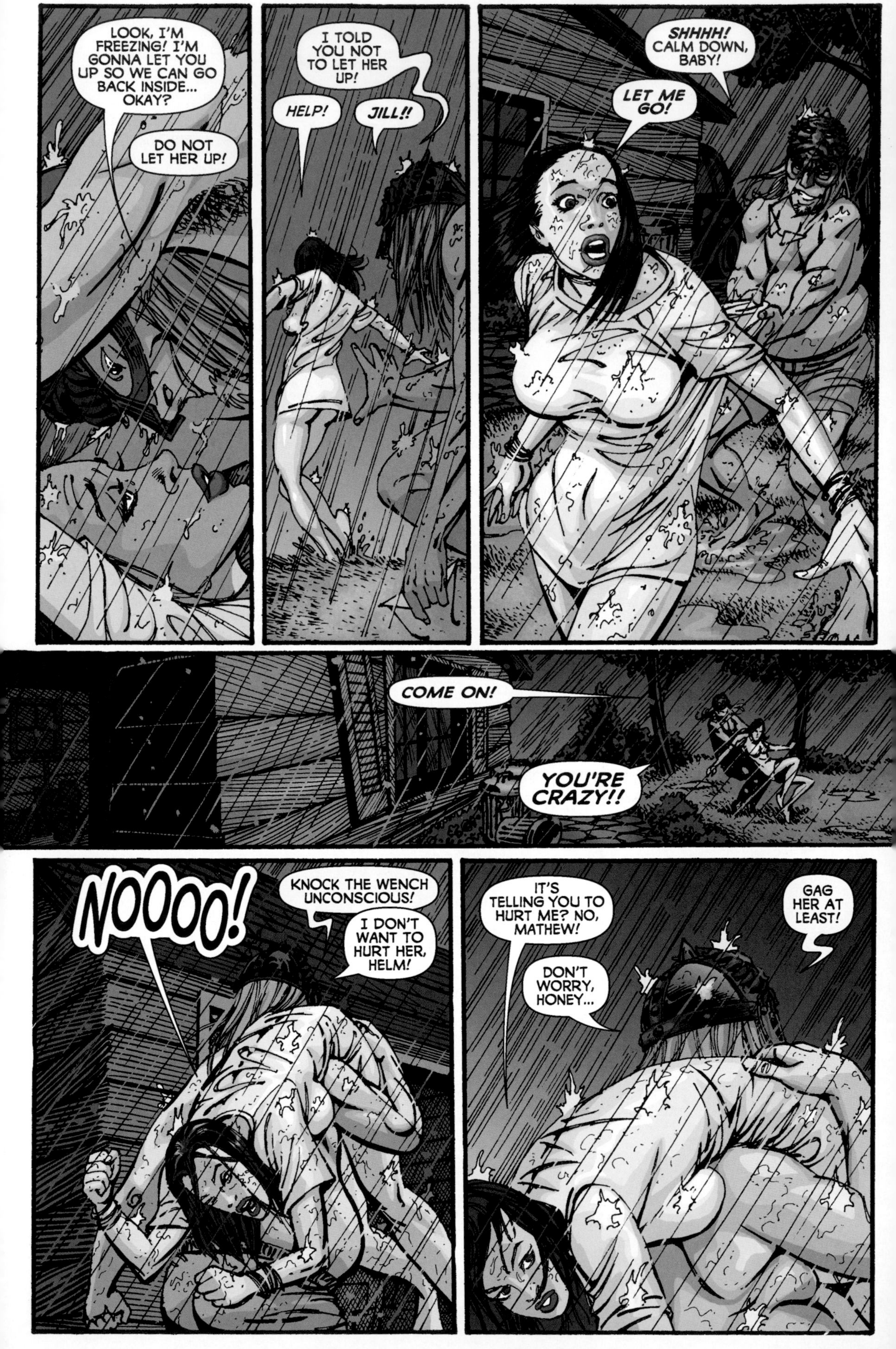
LOOK, I'M FREEZING! I'M GONNA LET YOU UP SO WE CAN GO BACK INSIDE... OKAY?
DO NOT LET HER UP!
I TOLD YOU NOT TO LET HER UP!
HELP!
JILL!!
SHHHH! CALM DOWN, BABY!
LET ME GO!
COME ON!
YOU'RE CRAZY!!
NOOOO!
KNOCK THE WENCH UNCONSCIOUS!
I DON'T WANT TO HURT HER, HELM!
IT'S TELLING YOU TO HURT ME? NO, MATHEW!
GAG HER AT LEAST!
DON'T WORRY, HONEY...

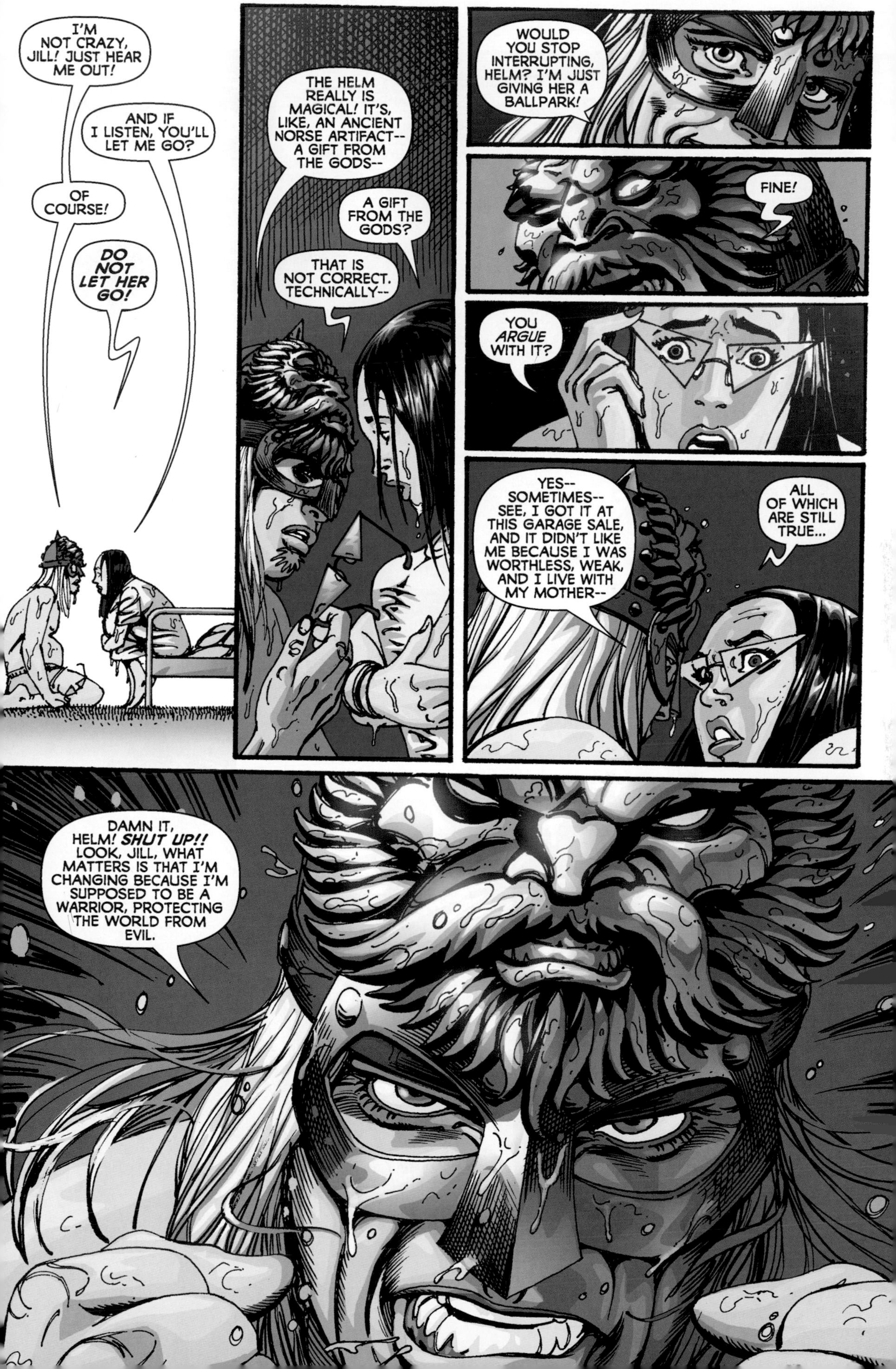
I'M NOT CRAZY, JILL! JUST HEAR ME OUT!
AND IF I LISTEN, YOU'LL LET ME GO?
OF COURSE!
DO NOT LET HER GO!
THE HELM REALLY IS MAGICAL! IT'S, LIKE, AN ANCIENT NORSE ARTIFACT-- A GIFT FROM THE GODS--
A GIFT FROM THE GODS?
THAT IS NOT CORRECT. TECHNICALLY--
WOULD YOU STOP INTERRUPTING, HELM? I'M JUST GIVING HER A BALLPARK!
FINE!
YOU ARGUE WITH IT?
YES-- SOMETIMES-- SEE, I GOT IT AT THIS GARAGE SALE, AND IT DIDN'T LIKE ME BECAUSE I WAS WORTHLESS, WEAK, AND I LIVE WITH MY MOTHER--
ALL OF WHICH ARE STILL TRUE...
DAMN IT, HELM! SHUT UP!! LOOK, JILL, WHAT MATTERS IS THAT I'M CHANGING BECAUSE I'M SUPPOSED TO BE A WARRIOR, PROTECTING THE WORLD FROM EVIL.

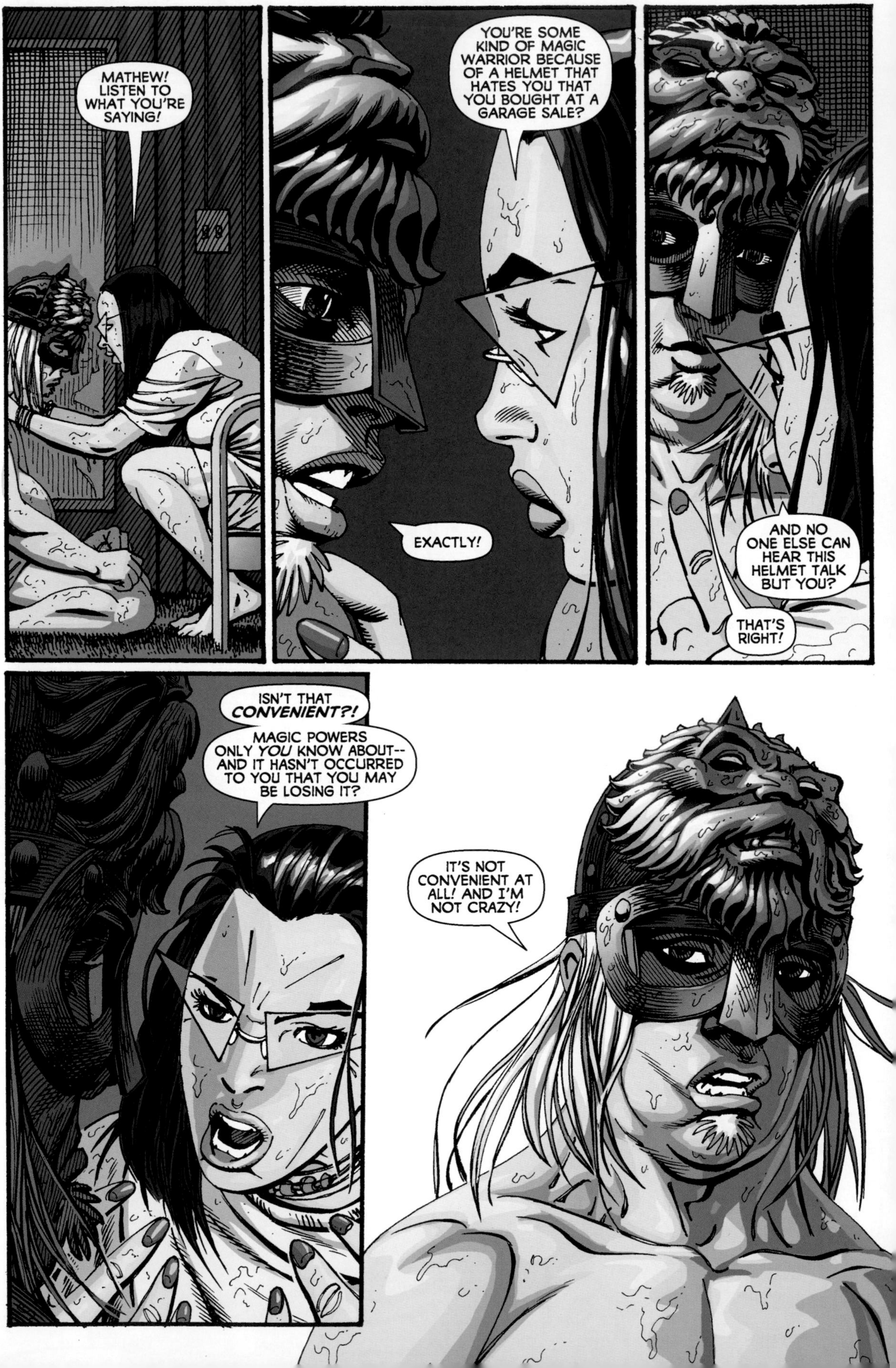
MATHEW! LISTEN TO WHAT YOU'RE SAYING!
YOU'RE SOME KIND OF MAGIC WARRIOR BECAUSE OF A HELMET THAT HATES YOU THAT YOU BOUGHT AT A GARAGE SALE?
EXACTLY!
AND NO ONE ELSE CAN HEAR THIS HELMET TALK BUT YOU?
THAT'S RIGHT!
ISN'T THAT *CONVENIENT?!*
MAGIC POWERS ONLY *YOU* KNOW ABOUT-- AND IT HASN'T OCCURRED TO YOU THAT YOU MAY BE LOSING IT?
IT'S NOT CONVENIENT AT ALL! AND I'M NOT CRAZY!

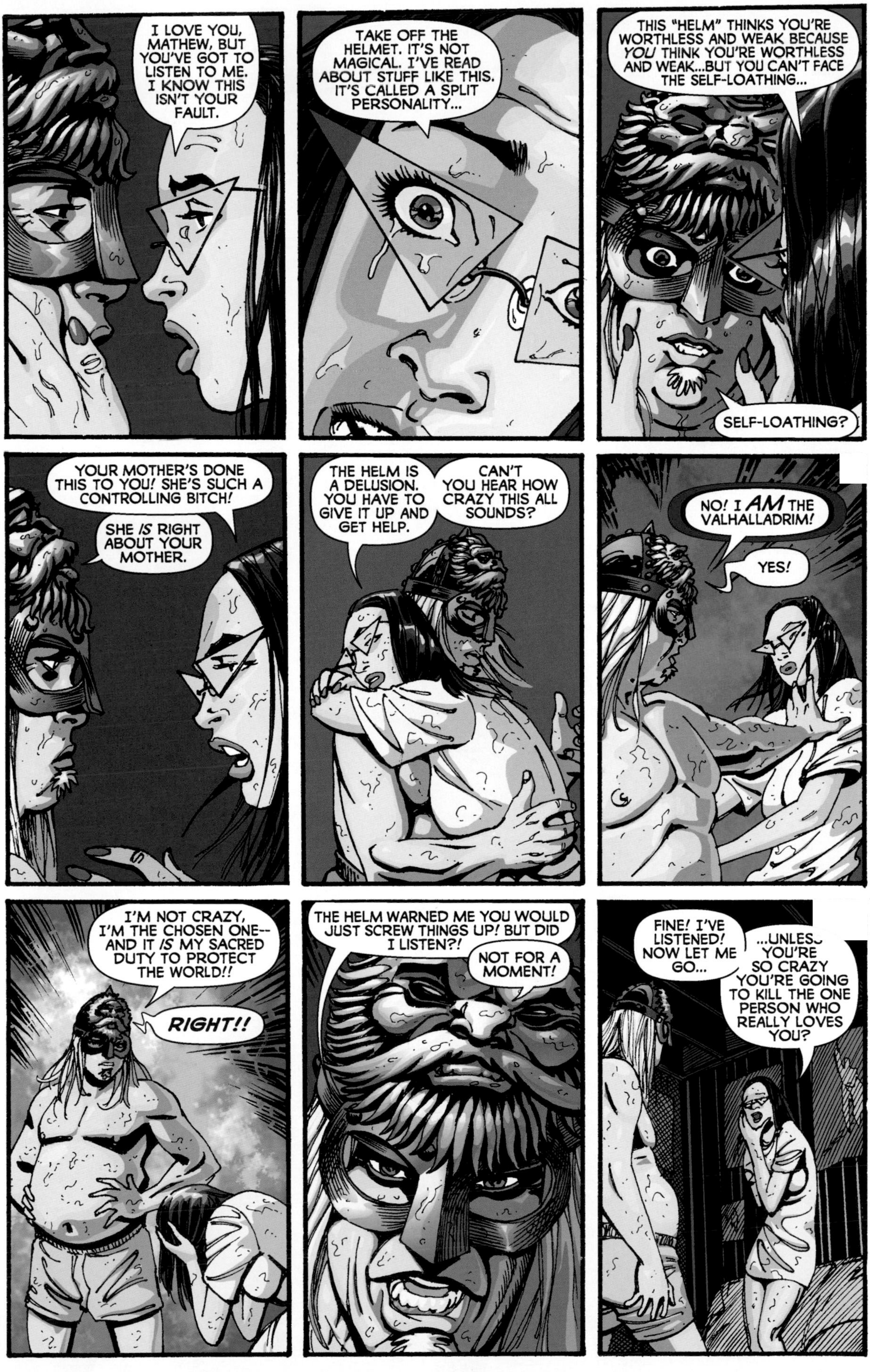
I LOVE YOU, MATHEW, BUT YOU'VE GOT TO LISTEN TO ME. I KNOW THIS ISN'T YOUR FAULT.
TAKE OFF THE HELMET. IT'S NOT MAGICAL. I'VE READ ABOUT STUFF LIKE THIS. IT'S CALLED A SPLIT PERSONALITY...
THIS "HELM" THINKS YOU'RE WORTHLESS AND WEAK BECAUSE *YOU* THINK YOU'RE WORTHLESS AND WEAK...BUT YOU CAN'T FACE THE SELF-LOATHING...
SELF-LOATHING?
YOUR MOTHER'S DONE THIS TO YOU! SHE'S SUCH A CONTROLLING BITCH!
SHE *IS* RIGHT ABOUT YOUR MOTHER.
THE HELM IS A DELUSION. YOU HAVE TO GIVE IT UP AND GET HELP.
CAN'T YOU HEAR HOW CRAZY THIS ALL SOUNDS?
NO! I *AM* THE VALHALLADRIM!
YES!
I'M NOT CRAZY, I'M THE CHOSEN ONE-- AND IT *IS* MY SACRED DUTY TO PROTECT THE WORLD!!
RIGHT!!
THE HELM WARNED ME YOU WOULD JUST SCREW THINGS UP! BUT DID I LISTEN?!
NOT FOR A MOMENT!
FINE! I'VE LISTENED! NOW LET ME GO...
...UNLESS YOU'RE SO CRAZY YOU'RE GOING TO KILL THE ONE PERSON WHO REALLY LOVES YOU?

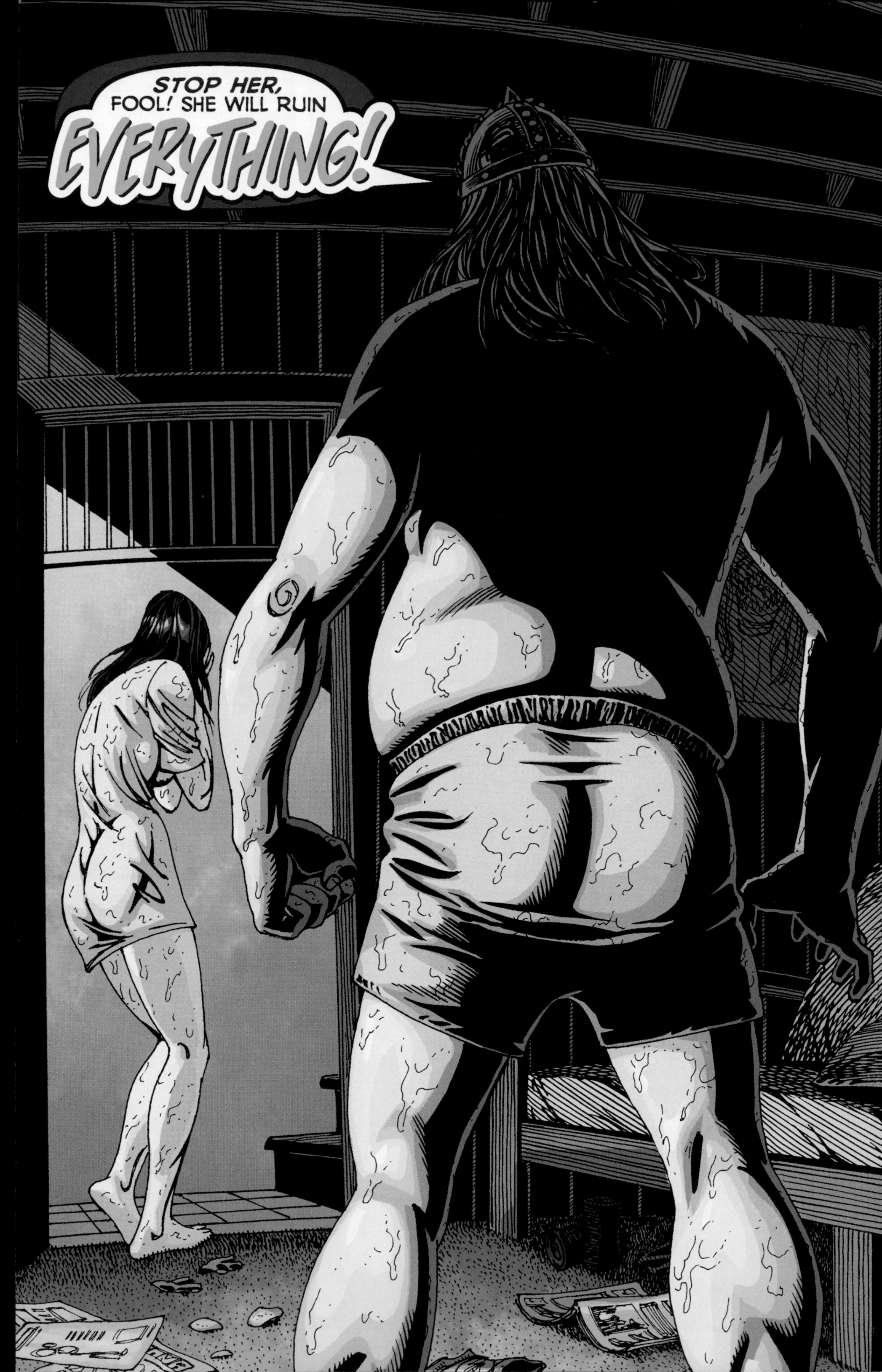
STOP HER, FOOL! SHE WILL RUIN EVERYTHING!

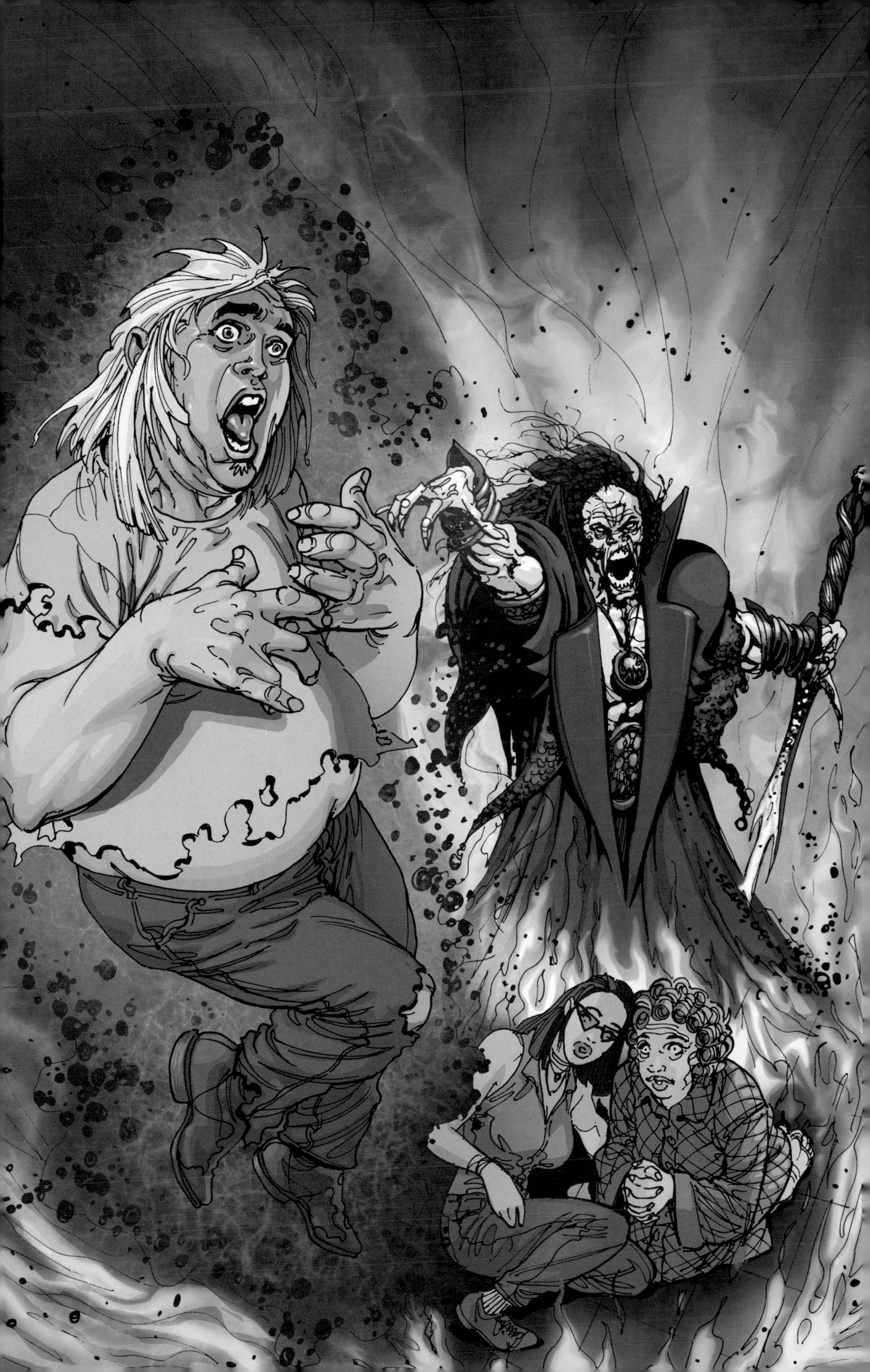

CHAPTER **4**
LITTLE RAGNARÖK

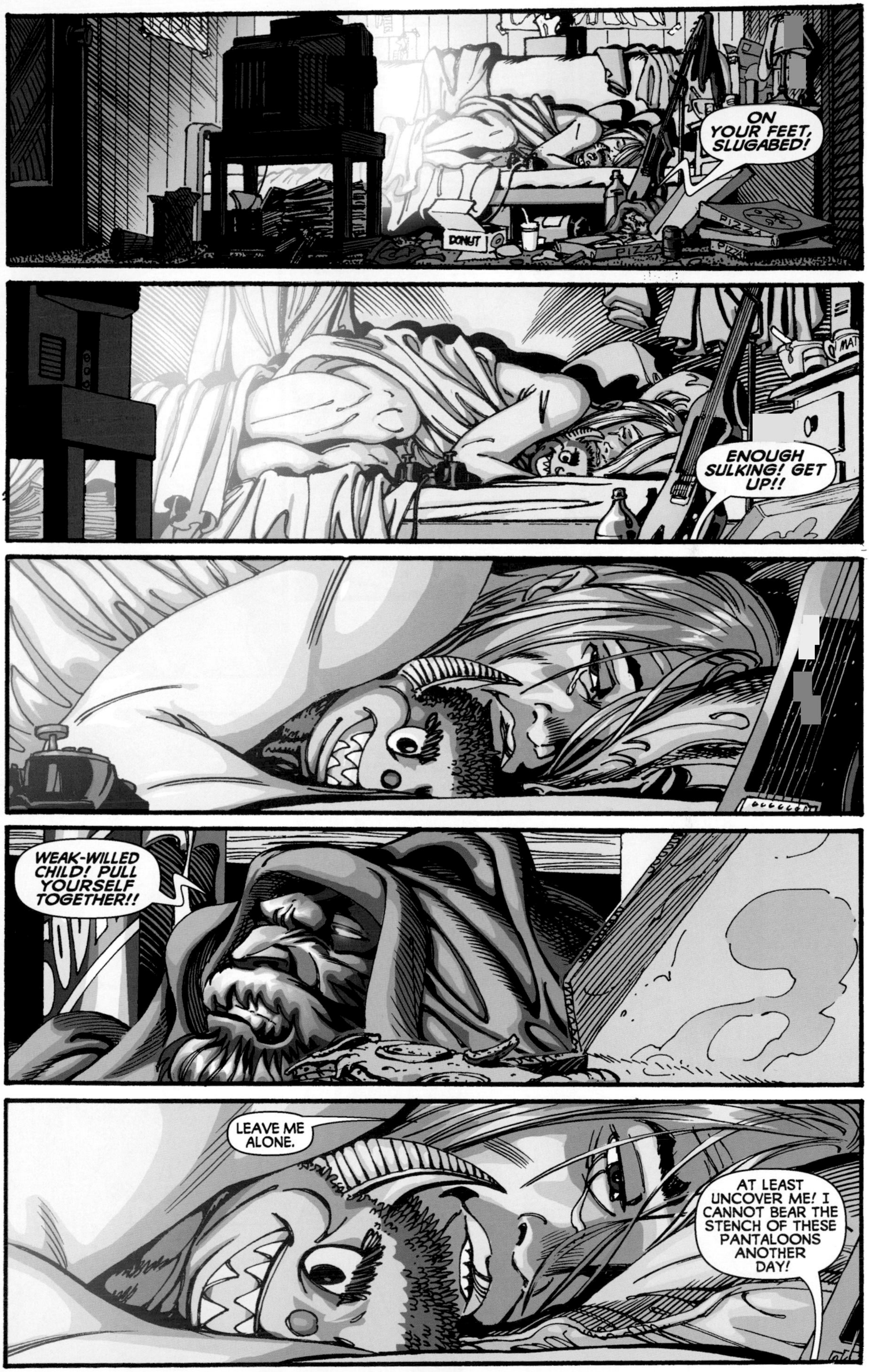
ON YOUR FEET, SLUGABED!
ENOUGH SULKING! GET UP!!
WEAK-WILLED CHILD! PULL YOURSELF TOGETHER!!
LEAVE ME ALONE.
AT LEAST UNCOVER ME! I CANNOT BEAR THE STENCH OF THESE PANTALOONS ANOTHER DAY!

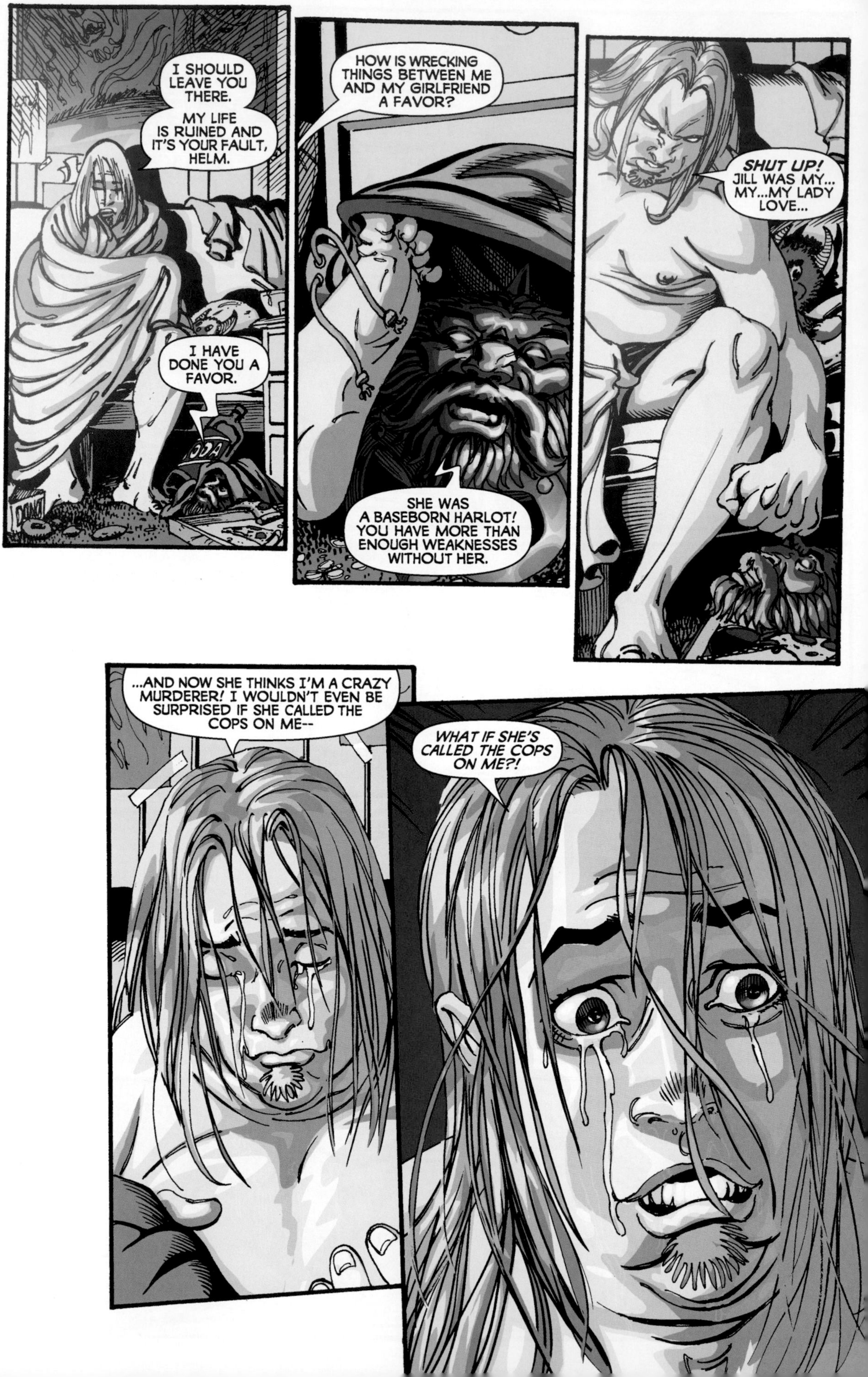
I SHOULD LEAVE YOU THERE.
MY LIFE IS RUINED AND IT'S YOUR FAULT, HELM.
I HAVE DONE YOU A FAVOR.
HOW IS WRECKING THINGS BETWEEN ME AND MY GIRLFRIEND A FAVOR?
SHE WAS A BASEBORN HARLOT! YOU HAVE MORE THAN ENOUGH WEAKNESSES WITHOUT HER.
SHUT UP! JILL WAS MY... MY...MY LADY LOVE...
...AND NOW SHE THINKS I'M A CRAZY MURDERER! I WOULDN'T EVEN BE SURPRISED IF SHE CALLED THE COPS ON ME--
WHAT IF SHE'S CALLED THE COPS ON ME?!

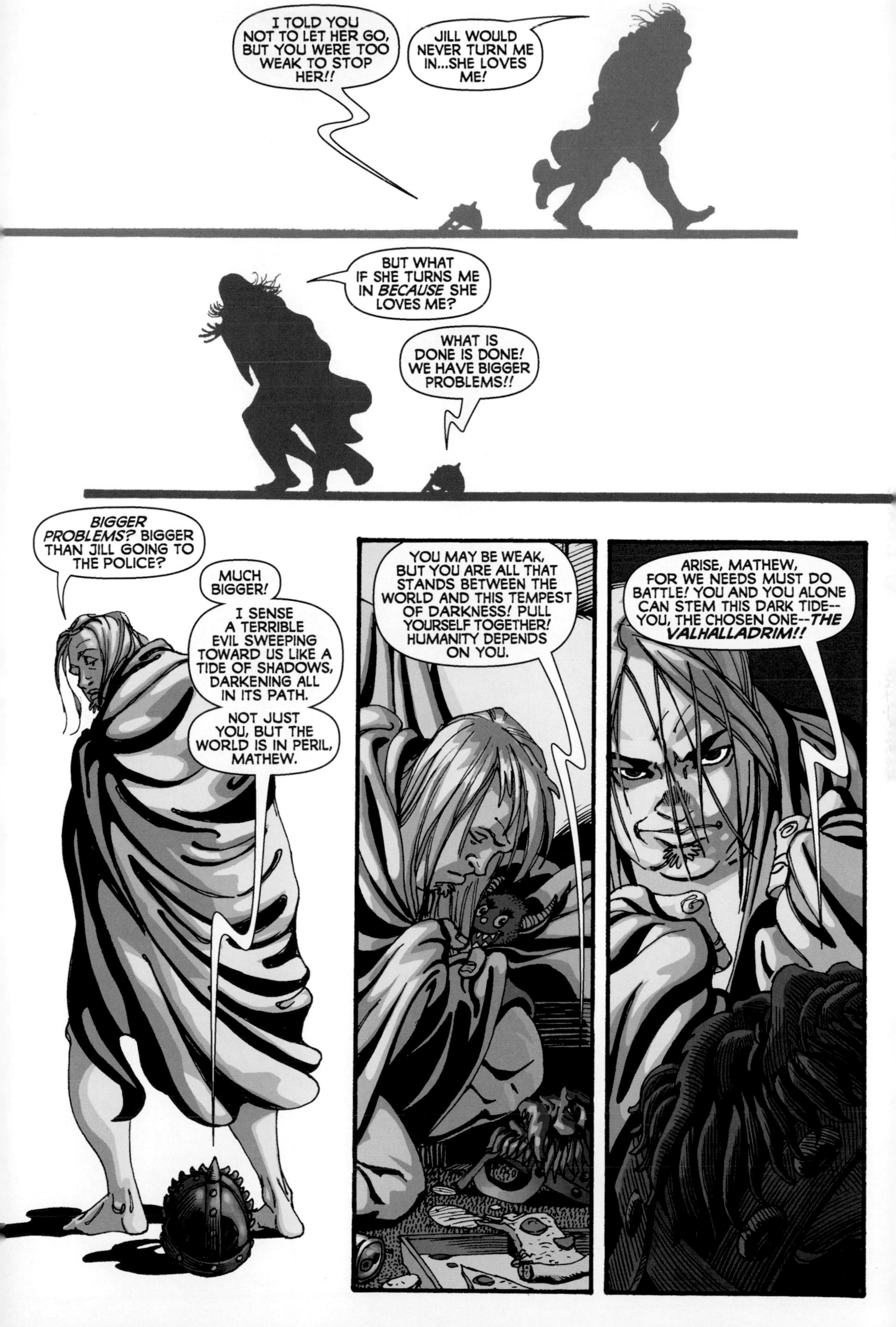
I TOLD YOU NOT TO LET HER GO, BUT YOU WERE TOO WEAK TO STOP HER!!
JILL WOULD NEVER TURN ME IN...SHE LOVES ME!
BUT WHAT IF SHE TURNS ME IN BECAUSE SHE LOVES ME?
WHAT IS DONE IS DONE! WE HAVE BIGGER PROBLEMS!!
BIGGER PROBLEMS? BIGGER THAN JILL GOING TO THE POLICE?
MUCH BIGGER!
I SENSE A TERRIBLE EVIL SWEEPING TOWARD US LIKE A TIDE OF SHADOWS, DARKENING ALL IN ITS PATH.
NOT JUST YOU, BUT THE WORLD IS IN PERIL, MATHEW.
YOU MAY BE WEAK, BUT YOU ARE ALL THAT STANDS BETWEEN THE WORLD AND THIS TEMPEST OF DARKNESS! PULL YOURSELF TOGETHER! HUMANITY DEPENDS ON YOU.
ARISE, MATHEW, FOR WE NEEDS MUST DO BATTLE! YOU AND YOU ALONE CAN STEM THIS DARK TIDE-- YOU, THE CHOSEN ONE--THE VALHALLADRIM!!

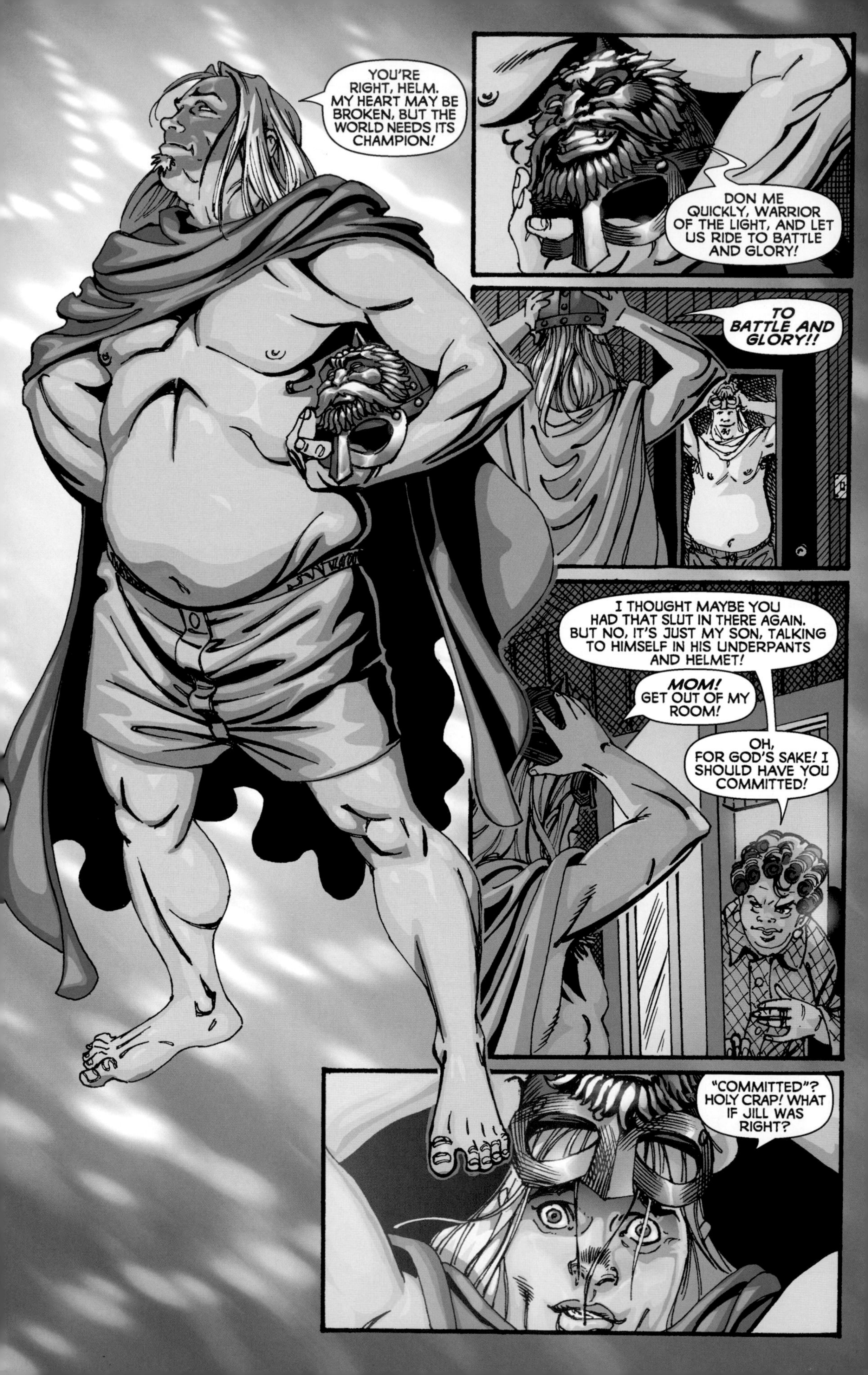
YOU'RE RIGHT, HELM. MY HEART MAY BE BROKEN, BUT THE WORLD NEEDS ITS CHAMPION!
DON ME QUICKLY, WARRIOR OF THE LIGHT, AND LET US RIDE TO BATTLE AND GLORY!
TO BATTLE AND GLORY!!
I THOUGHT MAYBE YOU HAD THAT SLUT IN THERE AGAIN. BUT NO, IT'S JUST MY SON, TALKING TO HIMSELF IN HIS UNDERPANTS AND HELMET!
MOM! GET OUT OF MY ROOM!
OH, FOR GOD'S SAKE! I SHOULD HAVE YOU COMMITTED!
"COMMITTED"? HOLY CRAP! WHAT IF JILL WAS RIGHT?

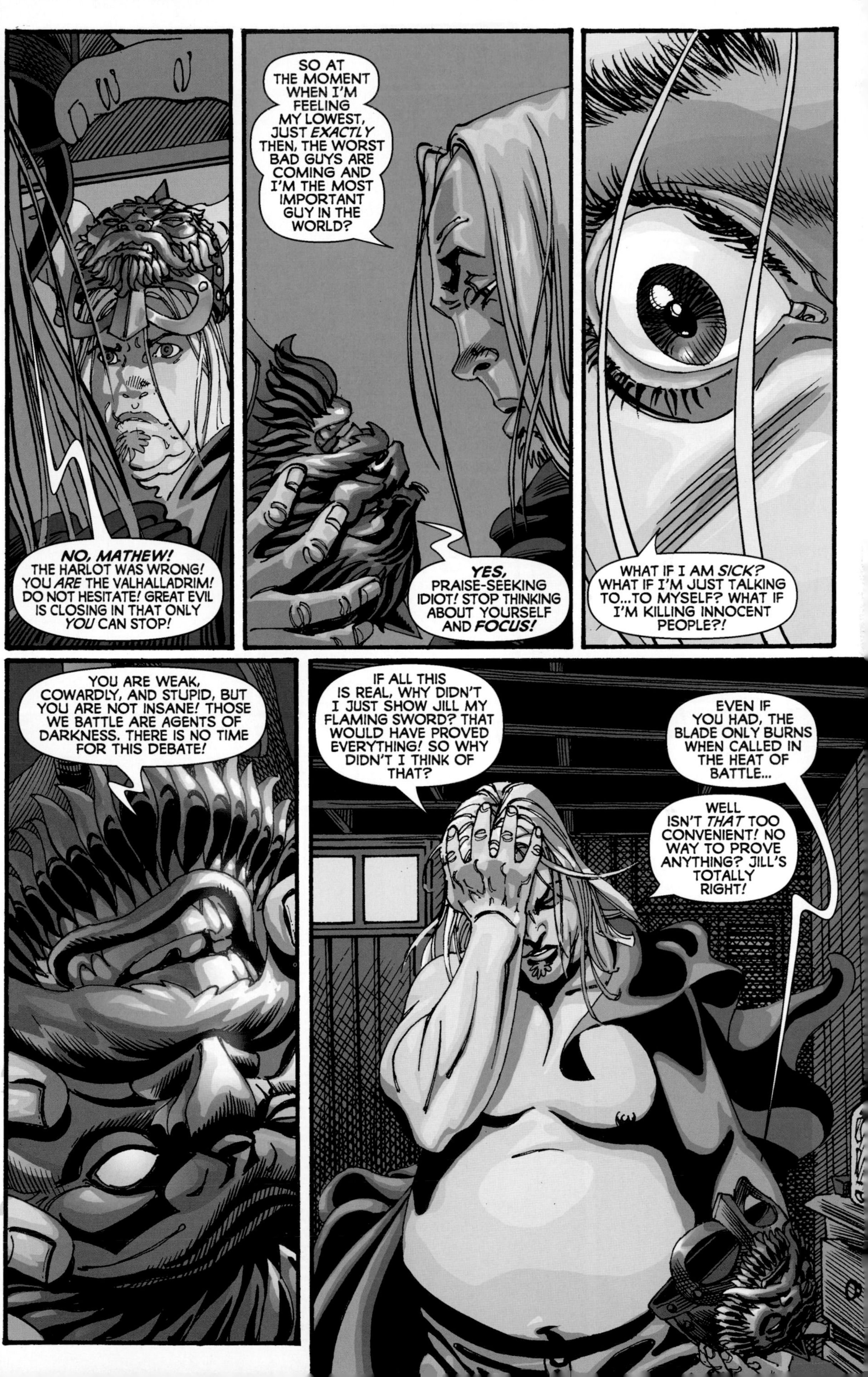
SO AT THE MOMENT WHEN I'M FEELING MY LOWEST, JUST EXACTLY THEN, THE WORST BAD GUYS ARE COMING AND I'M THE MOST IMPORTANT GUY IN THE WORLD?
NO, MATHEW! THE HARLOT WAS WRONG! YOU ARE THE VALHALLADRIM! DO NOT HESITATE! GREAT EVIL IS CLOSING IN THAT ONLY YOU CAN STOP!
YES, PRAISE-SEEKING IDIOT! STOP THINKING ABOUT YOURSELF AND FOCUS!
WHAT IF I AM SICK? WHAT IF I'M JUST TALKING TO...TO MYSELF? WHAT IF I'M KILLING INNOCENT PEOPLE?!
YOU ARE WEAK, COWARDLY, AND STUPID, BUT YOU ARE NOT INSANE! THOSE WE BATTLE ARE AGENTS OF DARKNESS. THERE IS NO TIME FOR THIS DEBATE!
IF ALL THIS IS REAL, WHY DIDN'T I JUST SHOW JILL MY FLAMING SWORD? THAT WOULD HAVE PROVED EVERYTHING! SO WHY DIDN'T I THINK OF THAT?
EVEN IF YOU HAD, THE BLADE ONLY BURNS WHEN CALLED IN THE HEAT OF BATTLE...
WELL ISN'T THAT TOO CONVENIENT! NO WAY TO PROVE ANYTHING? JILL'S TOTALLY RIGHT!

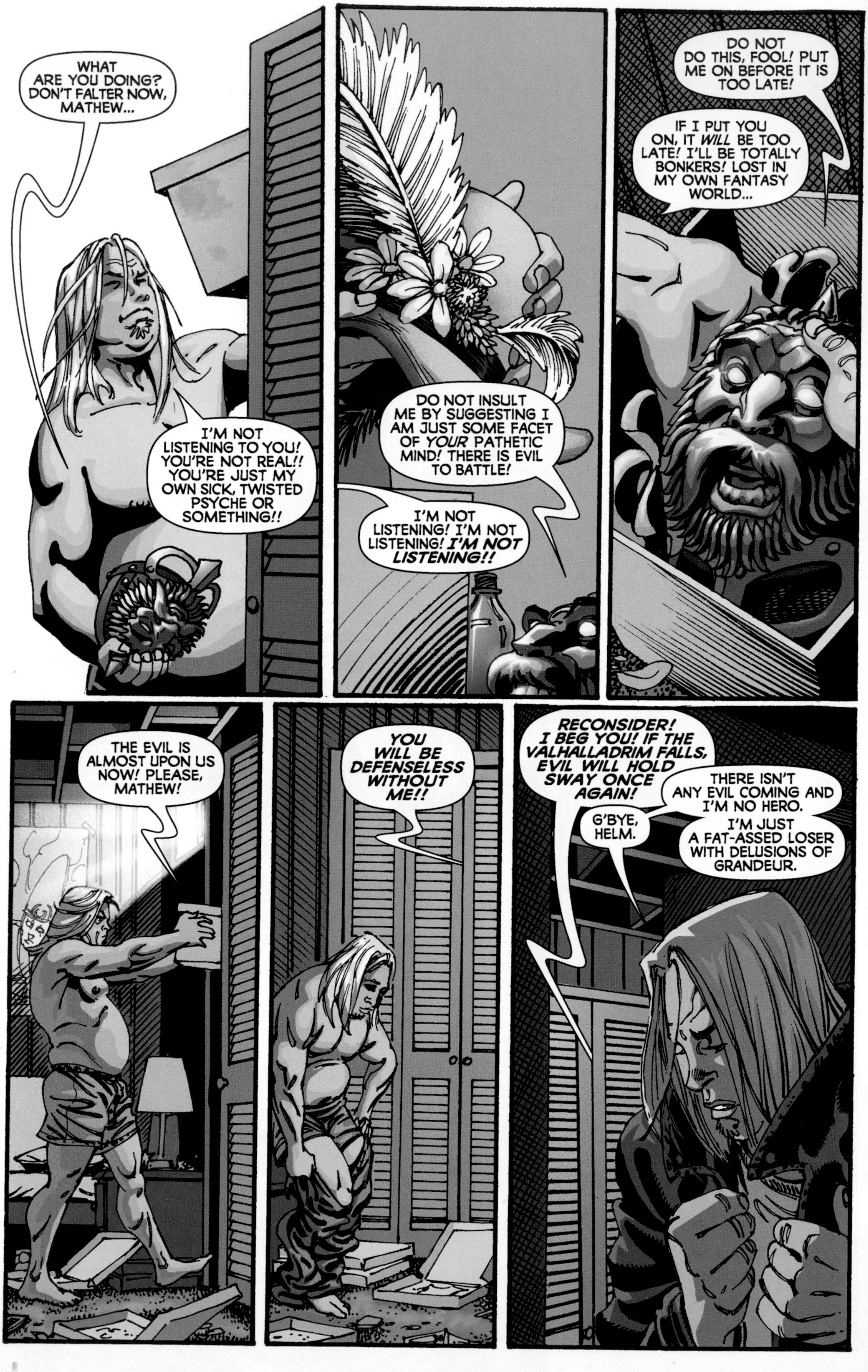
WHAT ARE YOU DOING? DON'T FALTER NOW, MATHEW...
I'M NOT LISTENING TO YOU! YOU'RE NOT REAL!! YOU'RE JUST MY OWN SICK, TWISTED PSYCHE OR SOMETHING!!
DO NOT INSULT ME BY SUGGESTING I AM JUST SOME FACET OF *YOUR* PATHETIC MIND! THERE IS EVIL TO BATTLE!
I'M NOT LISTENING! I'M NOT LISTENING! ***I'M NOT LISTENING!!***
DO NOT DO THIS, FOOL! PUT ME ON BEFORE IT IS TOO LATE!
IF I PUT YOU ON, IT *WILL* BE TOO LATE! I'LL BE TOTALLY BONKERS! LOST IN MY OWN FANTASY WORLD...
THE EVIL IS ALMOST UPON US NOW! PLEASE, MATHEW!
YOU WILL BE DEFENSELESS WITHOUT ME!!
RECONSIDER! I BEG YOU! IF THE VALHALLADRIM FALLS, EVIL WILL HOLD SWAY ONCE AGAIN!
THERE ISN'T ANY EVIL COMING AND I'M NO HERO.
I'M JUST A FAT-ASSED LOSER WITH DELUSIONS OF GRANDEUR.
G'BYE, HELM.

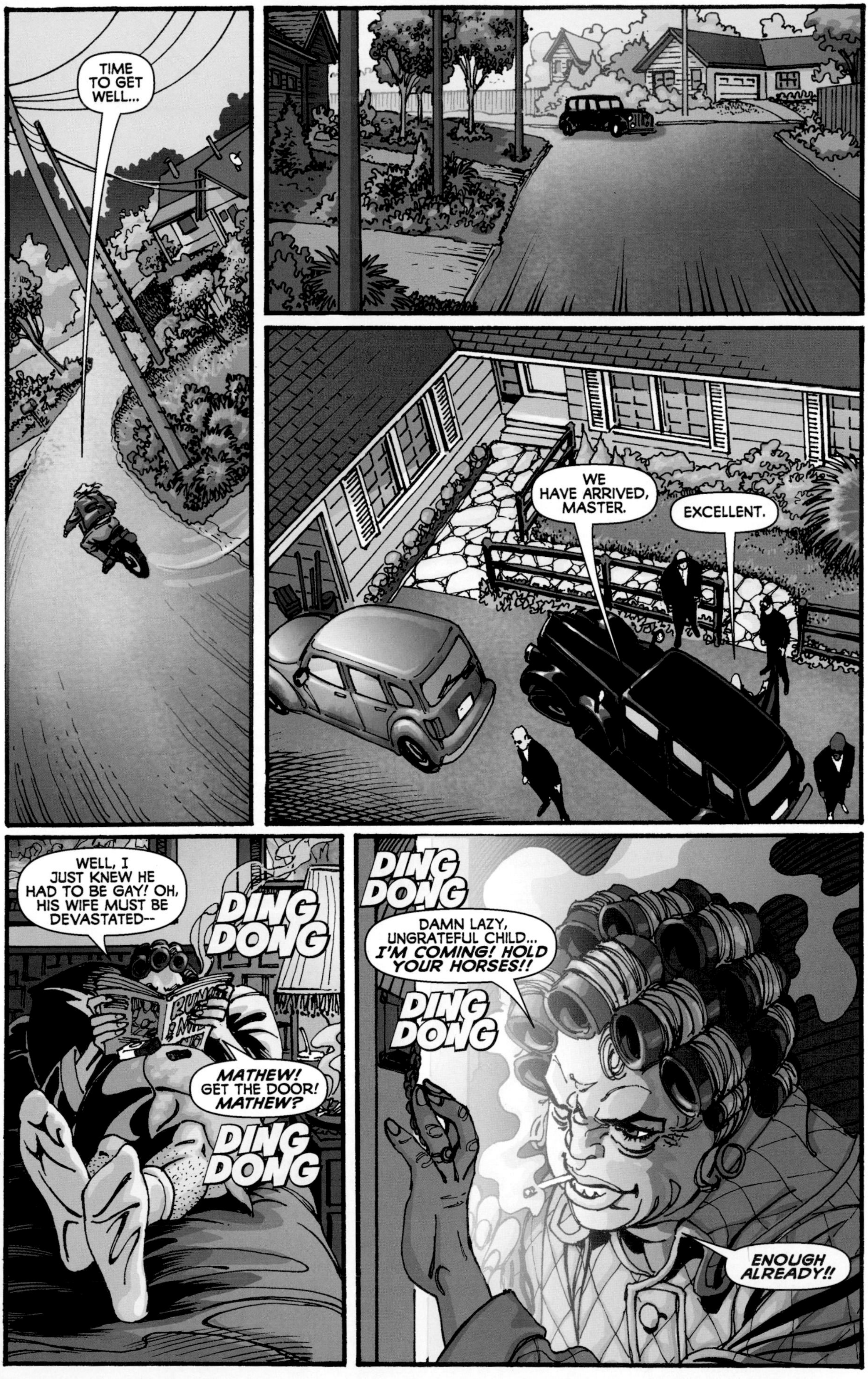
TIME TO GET WELL...
WE HAVE ARRIVED, MASTER.
EXCELLENT.
WELL, I JUST KNEW HE HAD TO BE GAY! OH, HIS WIFE MUST BE DEVASTATED--
DING DONG
MATHEW! GET THE DOOR! MATHEW?
DING DONG
DING DONG
DAMN LAZY, UNGRATEFUL CHILD... I'M COMING! HOLD YOUR HORSES!!
DING DONG
ENOUGH ALREADY!!

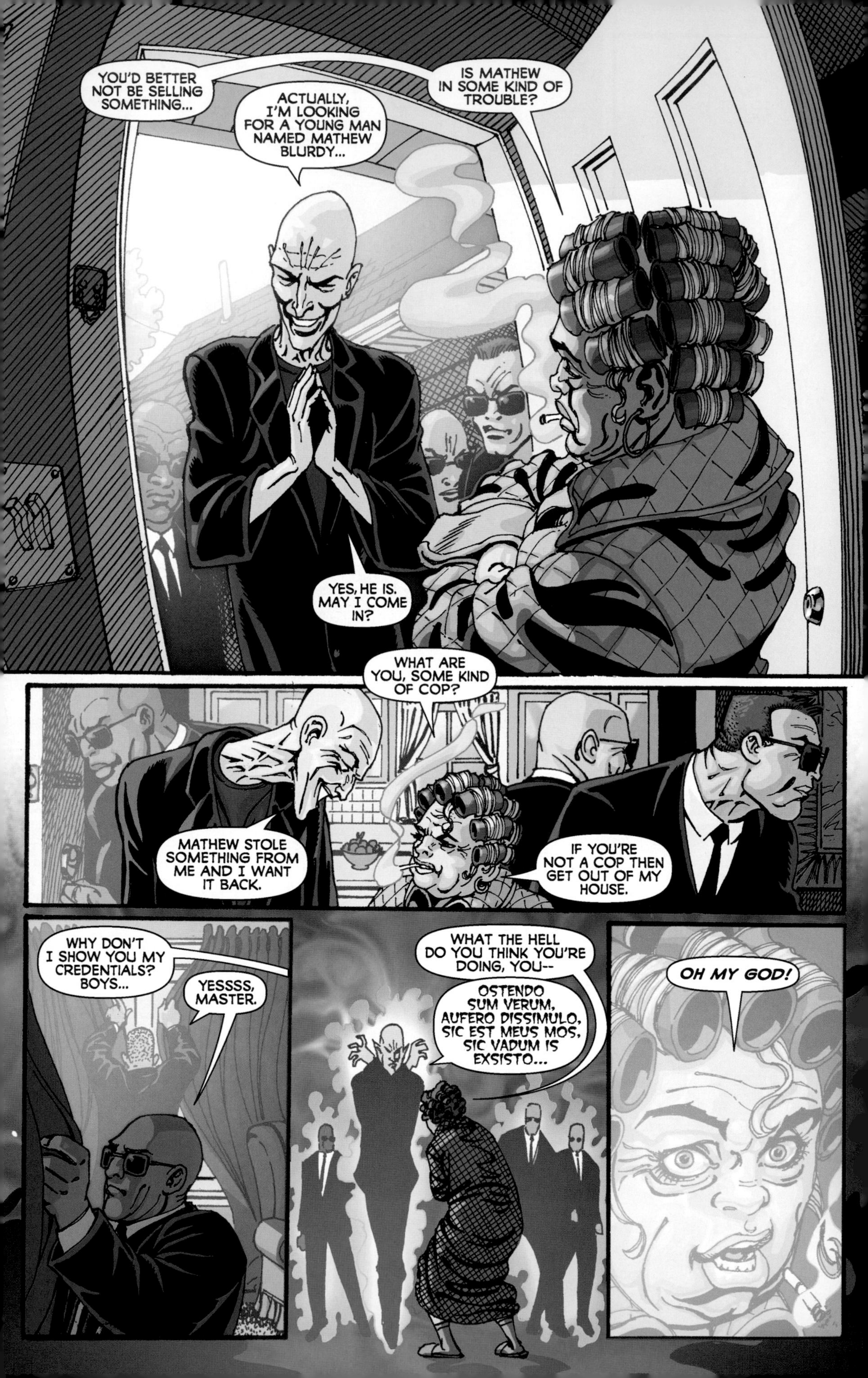
YOU'D BETTER NOT BE SELLING SOMETHING...
ACTUALLY, I'M LOOKING FOR A YOUNG MAN NAMED MATHEW BLURDY...
IS MATHEW IN SOME KIND OF TROUBLE?
YES, HE IS. MAY I COME IN?
WHAT ARE YOU, SOME KIND OF COP?
MATHEW STOLE SOMETHING FROM ME AND I WANT IT BACK.
IF YOU'RE NOT A COP THEN GET OUT OF MY HOUSE.
WHY DON'T I SHOW YOU MY CREDENTIALS? BOYS...
YESSSS, MASTER.
WHAT THE HELL DO YOU THINK YOU'RE DOING, YOU--
OSTENDO SUM VERUM, AUFERO DISSIMULO, SIC EST MEUS MOS, SIC VADUM IS EXSISTO...
OH MY GOD!

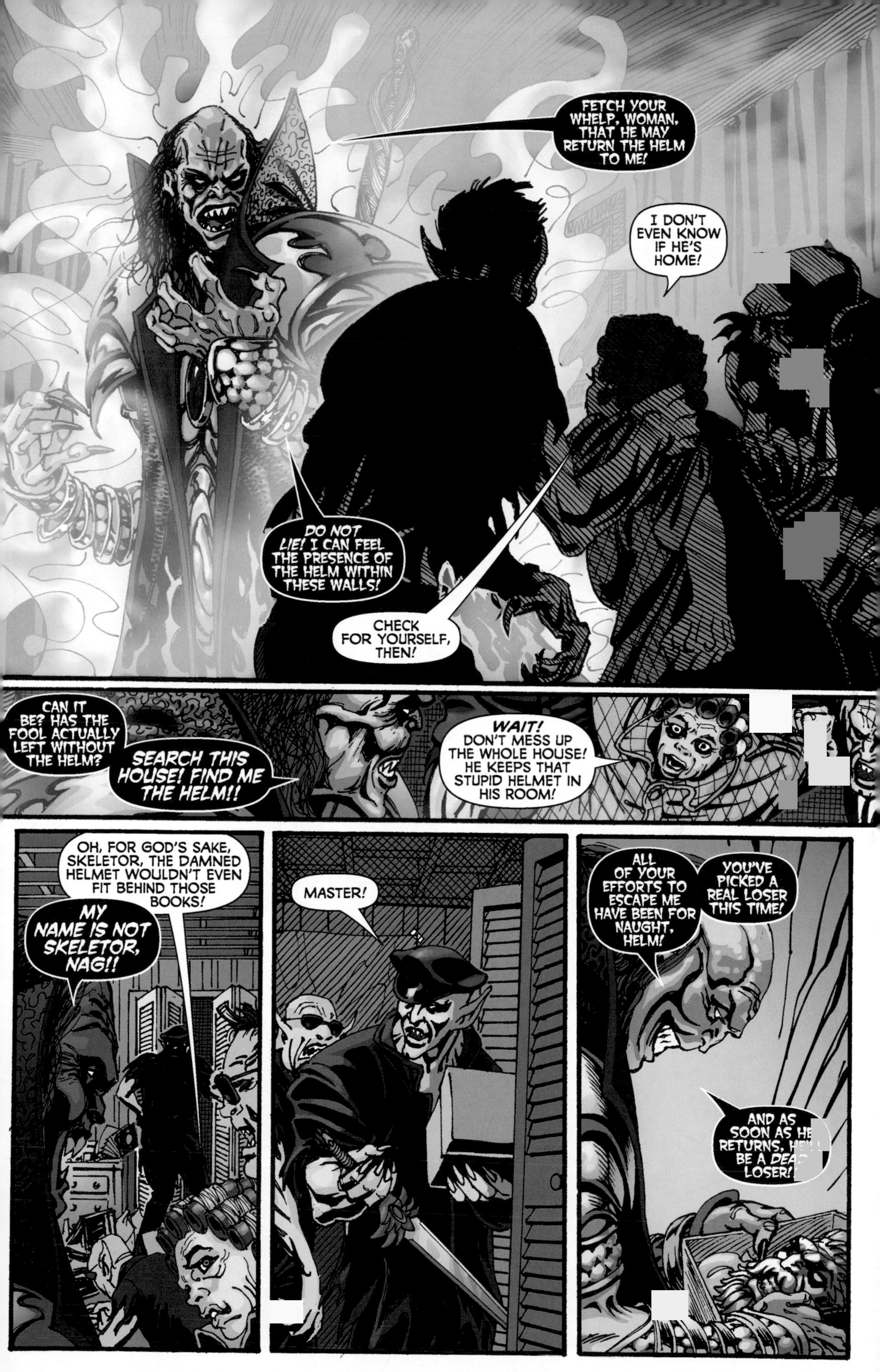
FETCH YOUR WHELP, WOMAN, THAT HE MAY RETURN THE HELM TO ME!
I DON'T EVEN KNOW IF HE'S HOME!
DO NOT LIE! I CAN FEEL THE PRESENCE OF THE HELM WITHIN THESE WALLS!
CHECK FOR YOURSELF, THEN!
CAN IT BE? HAS THE FOOL ACTUALLY LEFT WITHOUT THE HELM?
SEARCH THIS HOUSE! FIND ME THE HELM!!
WAIT! DON'T MESS UP THE WHOLE HOUSE! HE KEEPS THAT STUPID HELMET IN HIS ROOM!
OH, FOR GOD'S SAKE, SKELETOR, THE DAMNED HELMET WOULDN'T EVEN FIT BEHIND THOSE BOOKS!
MY NAME IS NOT SKELETOR, NAG!!
MASTER!
ALL OF YOUR EFFORTS TO ESCAPE ME HAVE BEEN FOR NAUGHT, HELM!
YOU'VE PICKED A REAL LOSER THIS TIME!
AND AS SOON AS HE RETURNS, HE'LL BE A DEAD LOSER!

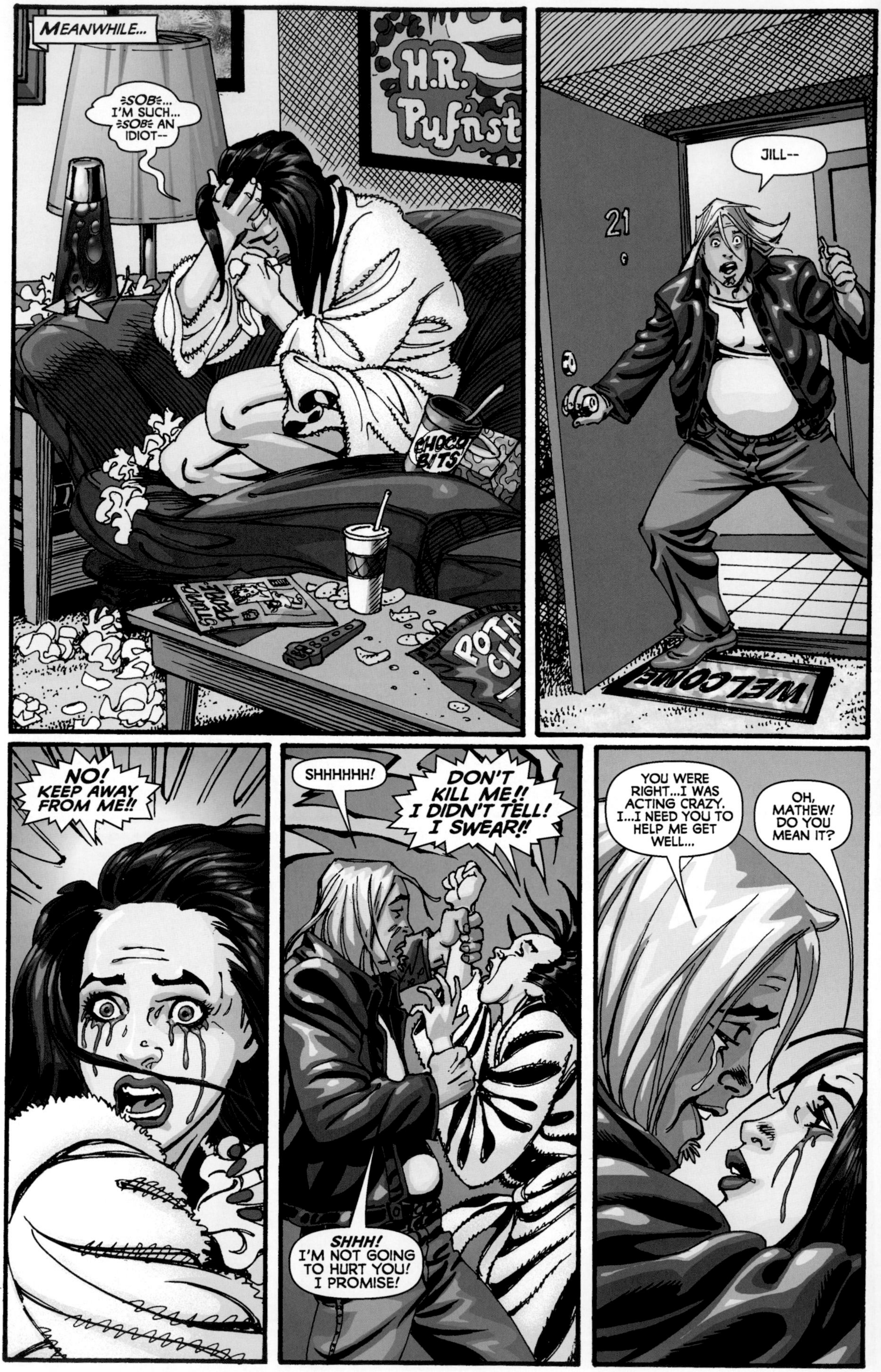
MEANWHILE...
H.R. Pufnst
≈SOB≈... I'M SUCH... ≈SOB≈ AN IDIOT--
CHOCO BITS
POTA CHI
JILL--
21
WELCOME
NO! KEEP AWAY FROM ME!!
SHHHHHH!
DON'T KILL ME!! I DIDN'T TELL! I SWEAR!!
SHHH! I'M NOT GOING TO HURT YOU! I PROMISE!
YOU WERE RIGHT...I WAS ACTING CRAZY. I...I NEED YOU TO HELP ME GET WELL...
OH, MATHEW! DO YOU MEAN IT?

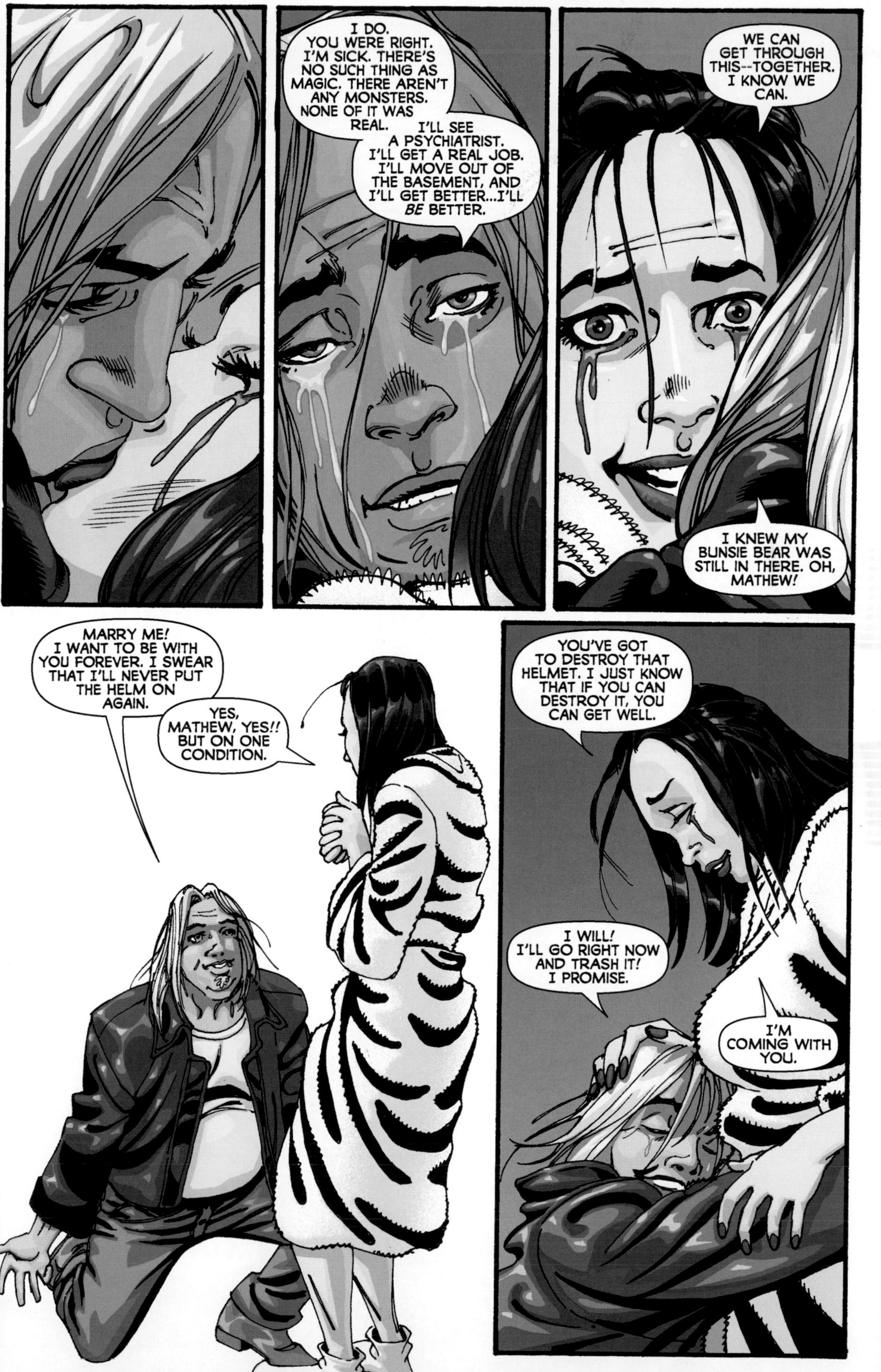
I DO. YOU WERE RIGHT. I'M SICK. THERE'S NO SUCH THING AS MAGIC. THERE AREN'T ANY MONSTERS. NONE OF IT WAS REAL.
I'LL SEE A PSYCHIATRIST. I'LL GET A REAL JOB. I'LL MOVE OUT OF THE BASEMENT, AND I'LL GET BETTER...I'LL *BE* BETTER.
WE CAN GET THROUGH THIS--TOGETHER. I KNOW WE CAN.
I KNEW MY BUNSIE BEAR WAS STILL IN THERE. OH, MATHEW!
MARRY ME! I WANT TO BE WITH YOU FOREVER. I SWEAR THAT I'LL NEVER PUT THE HELM ON AGAIN.
YES, MATHEW, YES!! BUT ON ONE CONDITION.
YOU'VE GOT TO DESTROY THAT HELMET. I JUST KNOW THAT IF YOU CAN DESTROY IT, YOU CAN GET WELL.
I WILL! I'LL GO RIGHT NOW AND TRASH IT! I PROMISE.
I'M COMING WITH YOU.

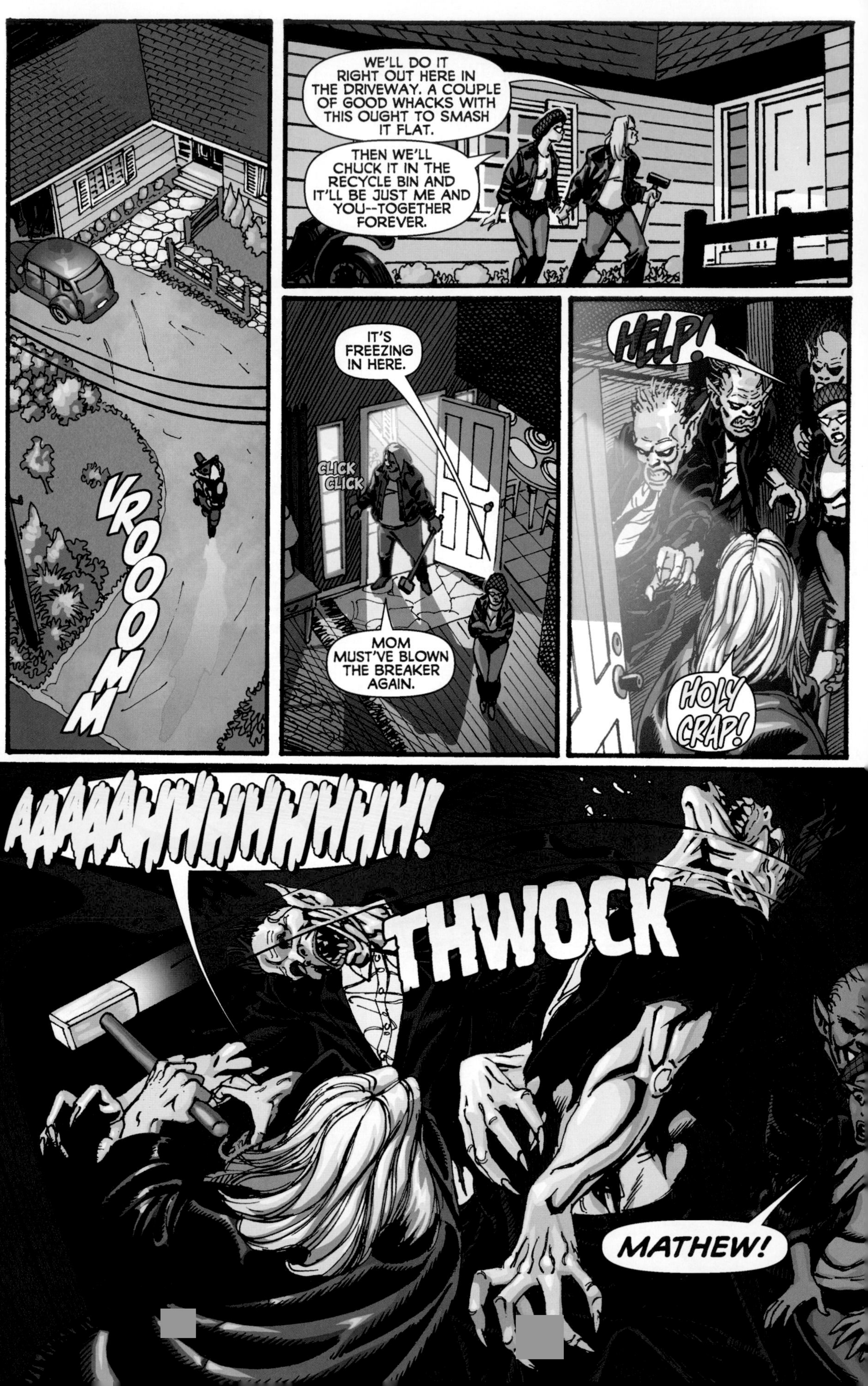
VROOOOMMM
WE'LL DO IT RIGHT OUT HERE IN THE DRIVEWAY. A COUPLE OF GOOD WHACKS WITH THIS OUGHT TO SMASH IT FLAT.
THEN WE'LL CHUCK IT IN THE RECYCLE BIN AND IT'LL BE JUST ME AND YOU--TOGETHER FOREVER.
IT'S FREEZING IN HERE.
CLICK CLICK
MOM MUST'VE BLOWN THE BREAKER AGAIN.
HELP!
HOLY CRAP!
AAAAAHHHHHHHHH!
THWOCK
MATHEW!

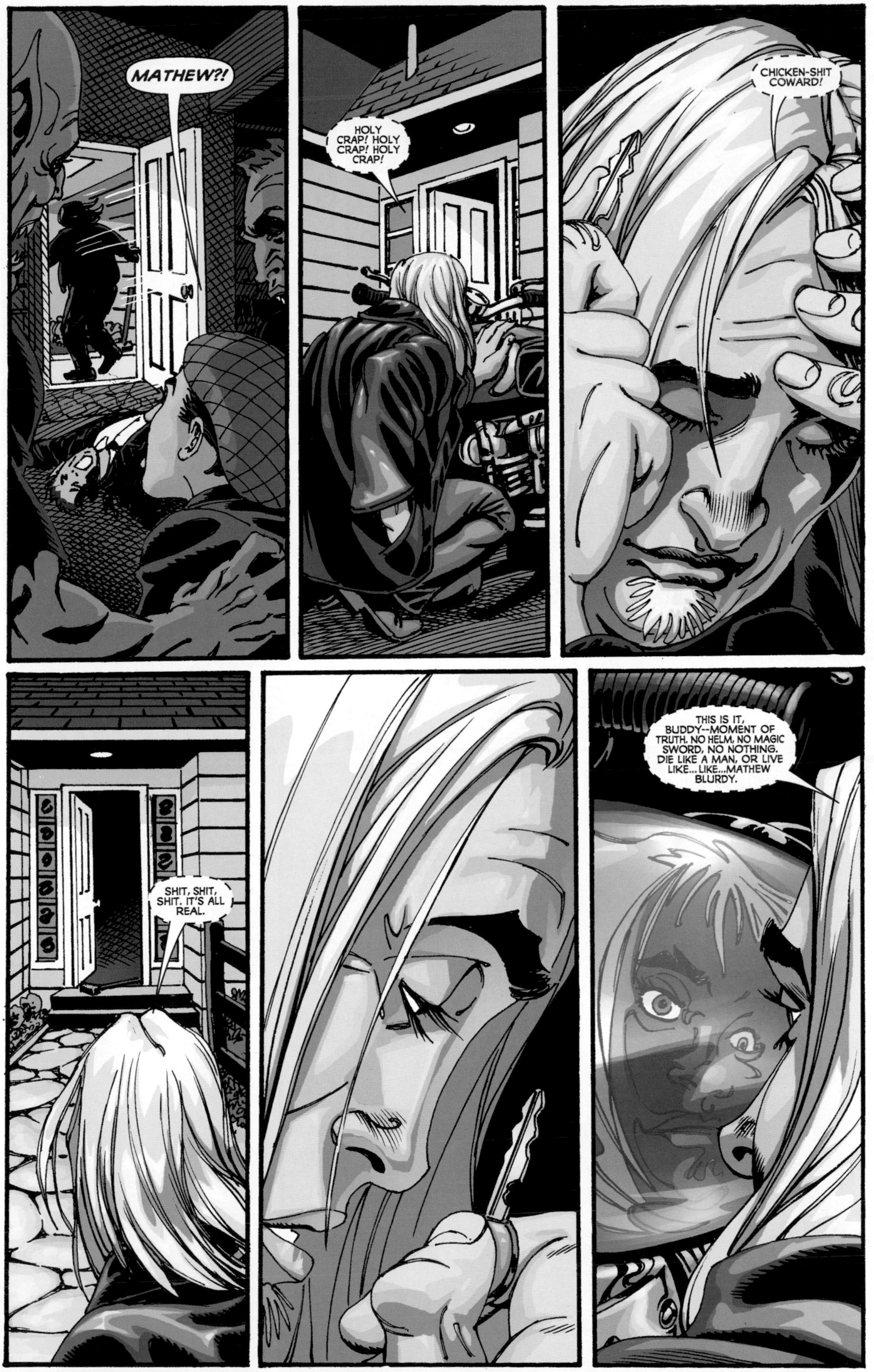
MATHEW?!
HOLY CRAP! HOLY CRAP! HOLY CRAP!
CHICKEN-SHIT COWARD!
SHIT, SHIT, SHIT. IT'S ALL REAL.
THIS IS IT, BUDDY--MOMENT OF TRUTH. NO HELM, NO MAGIC SWORD, NO NOTHING. DIE LIKE A MAN, OR LIVE LIKE... LIKE...MATHEW BLURDY.

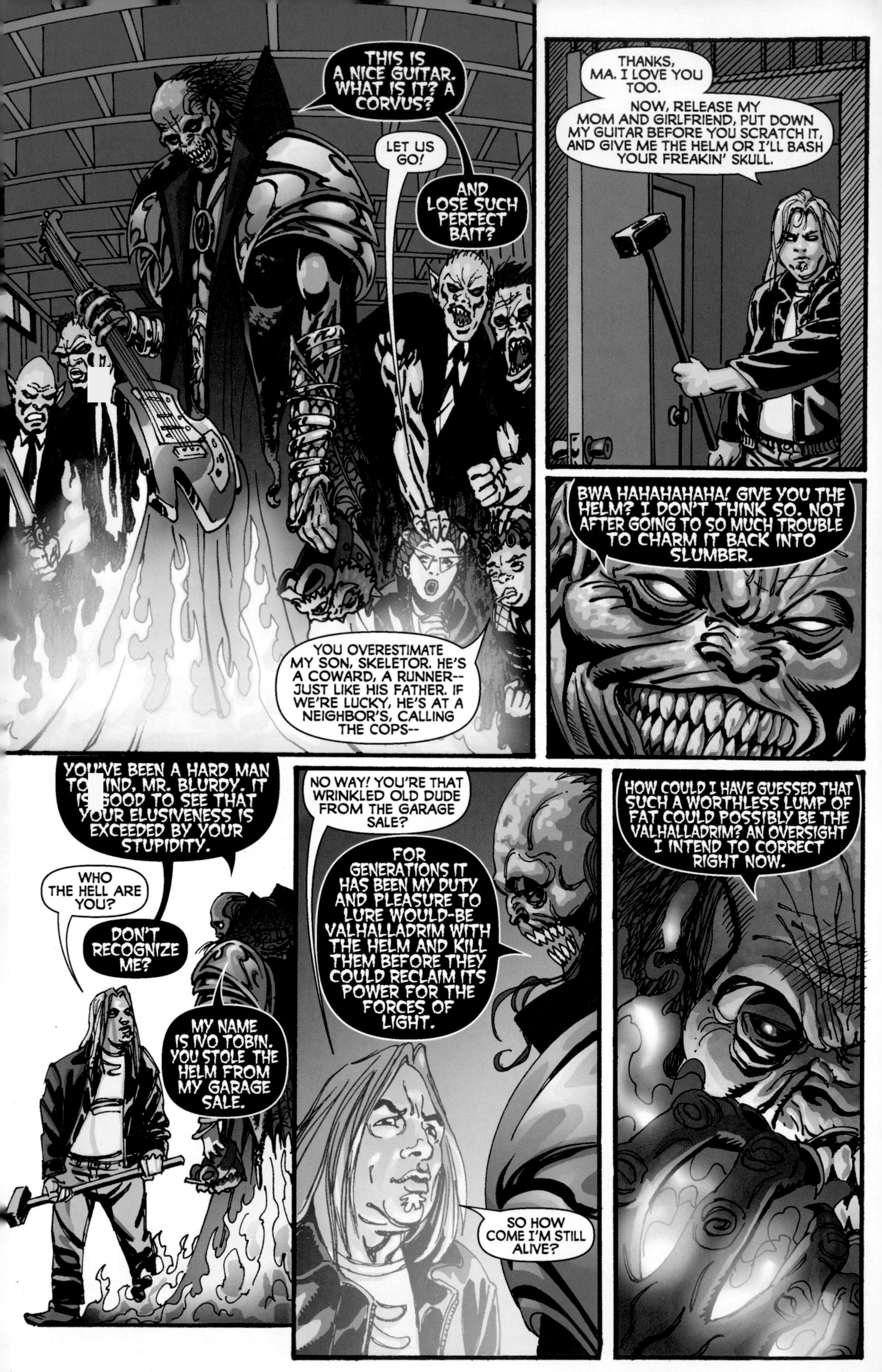
THIS IS A NICE GUITAR. WHAT IS IT? A CORVUS?
LET US GO!
AND LOSE SUCH PERFECT BAIT?
YOU OVERESTIMATE MY SON, SKELETOR. HE'S A COWARD, A RUNNER-- JUST LIKE HIS FATHER. IF WE'RE LUCKY, HE'S AT A NEIGHBOR'S, CALLING THE COPS--
THANKS, MA. I LOVE YOU TOO.
NOW, RELEASE MY MOM AND GIRLFRIEND, PUT DOWN MY GUITAR BEFORE YOU SCRATCH IT, AND GIVE ME THE HELM OR I'LL BASH YOUR FREAKIN' SKULL.
BWA HAHAHAHAHA! GIVE YOU THE HELM? I DON'T THINK SO. NOT AFTER GOING TO SO MUCH TROUBLE TO CHARM IT BACK INTO SLUMBER.
YOU'VE BEEN A HARD MAN TO FIND, MR. BLURDY. IT IS GOOD TO SEE THAT YOUR ELUSIVENESS IS EXCEEDED BY YOUR STUPIDITY.
WHO THE HELL ARE YOU?
DON'T RECOGNIZE ME?
MY NAME IS IVO TOBIN. YOU STOLE THE HELM FROM MY GARAGE SALE.
NO WAY! YOU'RE THAT WRINKLED OLD DUDE FROM THE GARAGE SALE?
FOR GENERATIONS IT HAS BEEN MY DUTY AND PLEASURE TO LURE WOULD-BE VALHALLADRIM WITH THE HELM AND KILL THEM BEFORE THEY COULD RECLAIM ITS POWER FOR THE FORCES OF LIGHT.
SO HOW COME I'M STILL ALIVE?
HOW COULD I HAVE GUESSED THAT SUCH A WORTHLESS LUMP OF FAT COULD POSSIBLY BE THE VALHALLADRIM? AN OVERSIGHT I INTEND TO CORRECT RIGHT NOW.

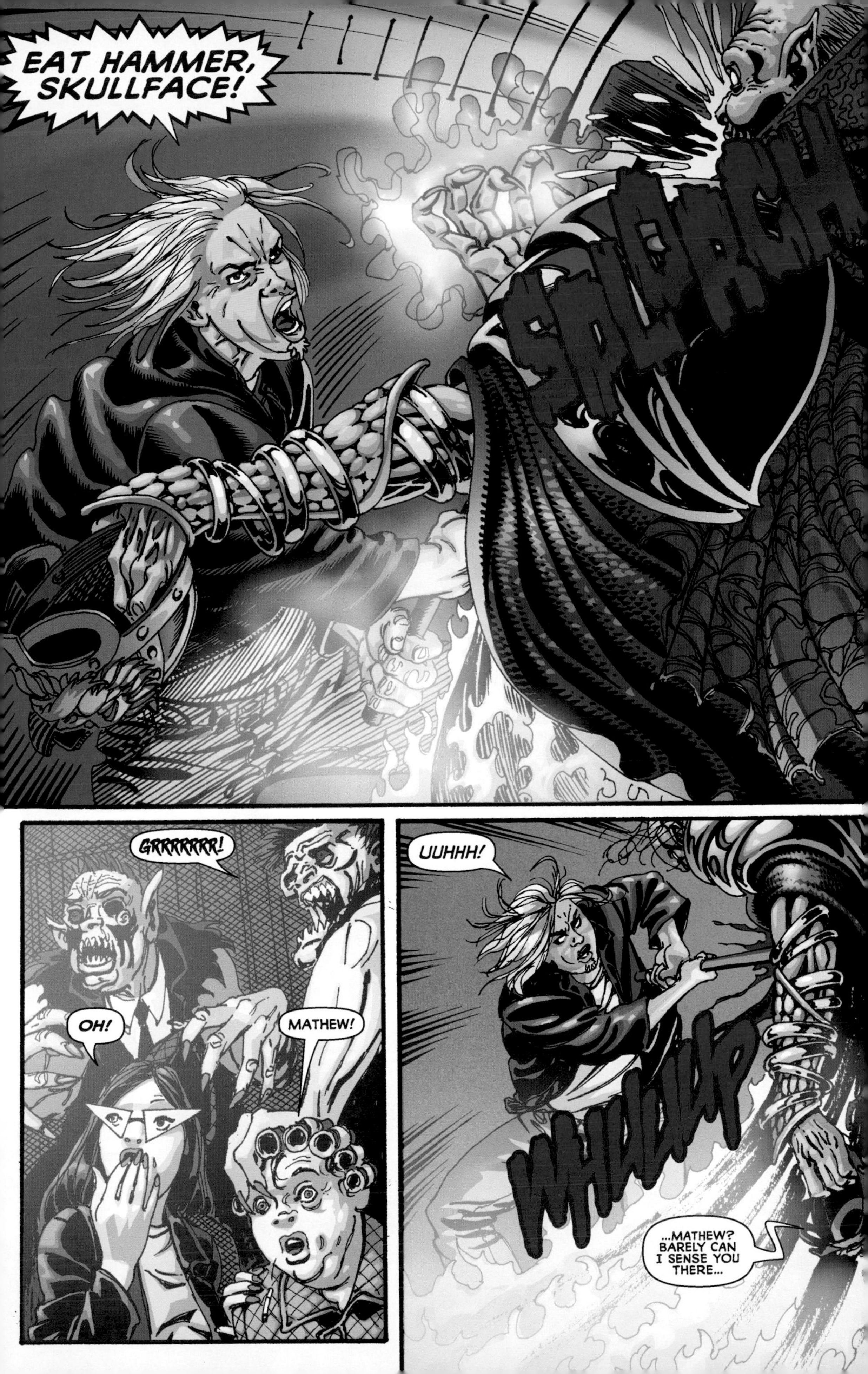
EAT HAMMER, SKULLFACE!
SPLUDARCH!
GRRRRRRR!
OH!
MATHEW!
UUHHH!
WHUUUP
...MATHEW? BARELY CAN I SENSE YOU THERE...

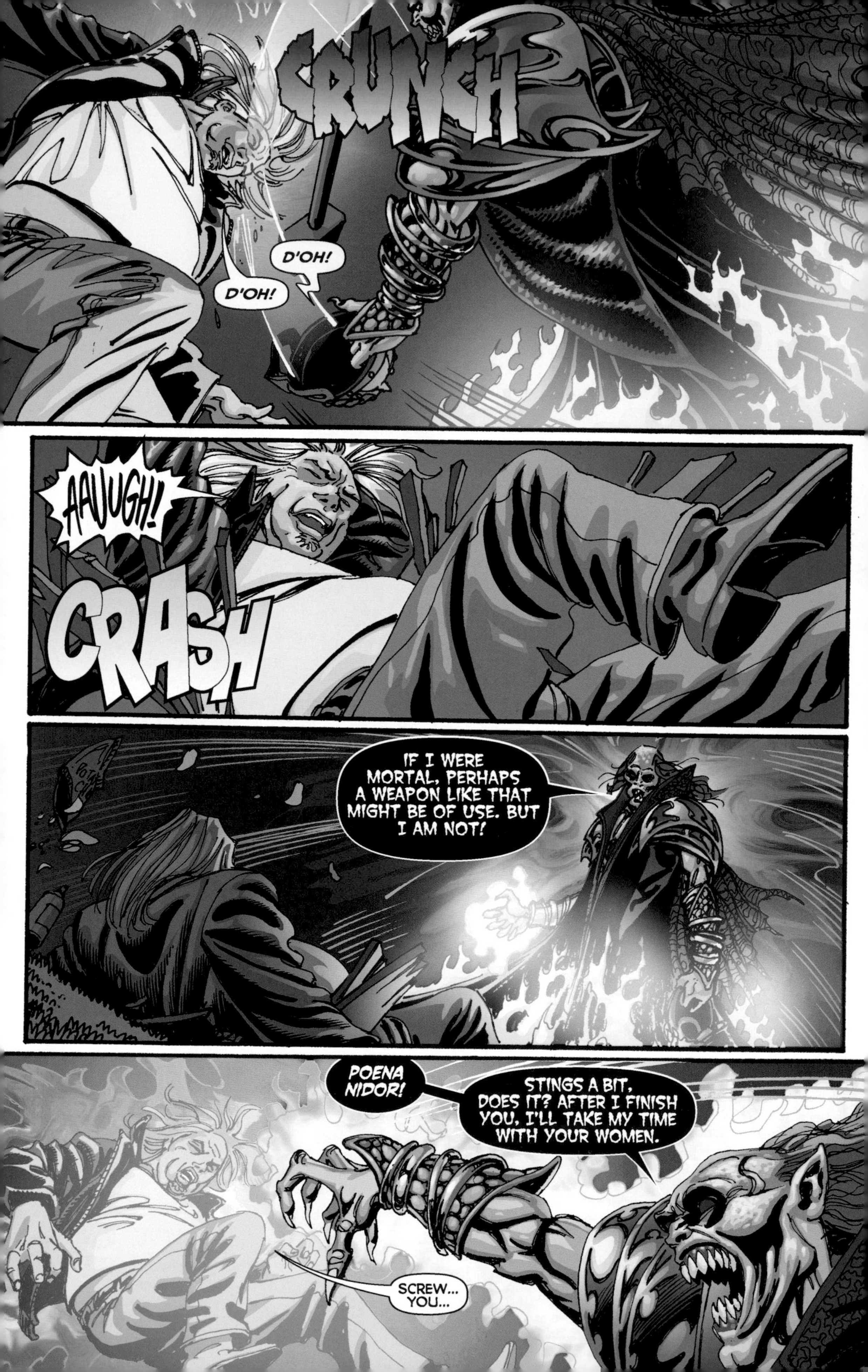
CRUNCH
D'OH!
D'OH!
AAUUGH!
CRASH
IF I WERE MORTAL, PERHAPS A WEAPON LIKE THAT MIGHT BE OF USE. BUT I AM NOT!
POENA NIDOR!
STINGS A BIT, DOES IT? AFTER I FINISH YOU, I'LL TAKE MY TIME WITH YOUR WOMEN.
SCREW... YOU...

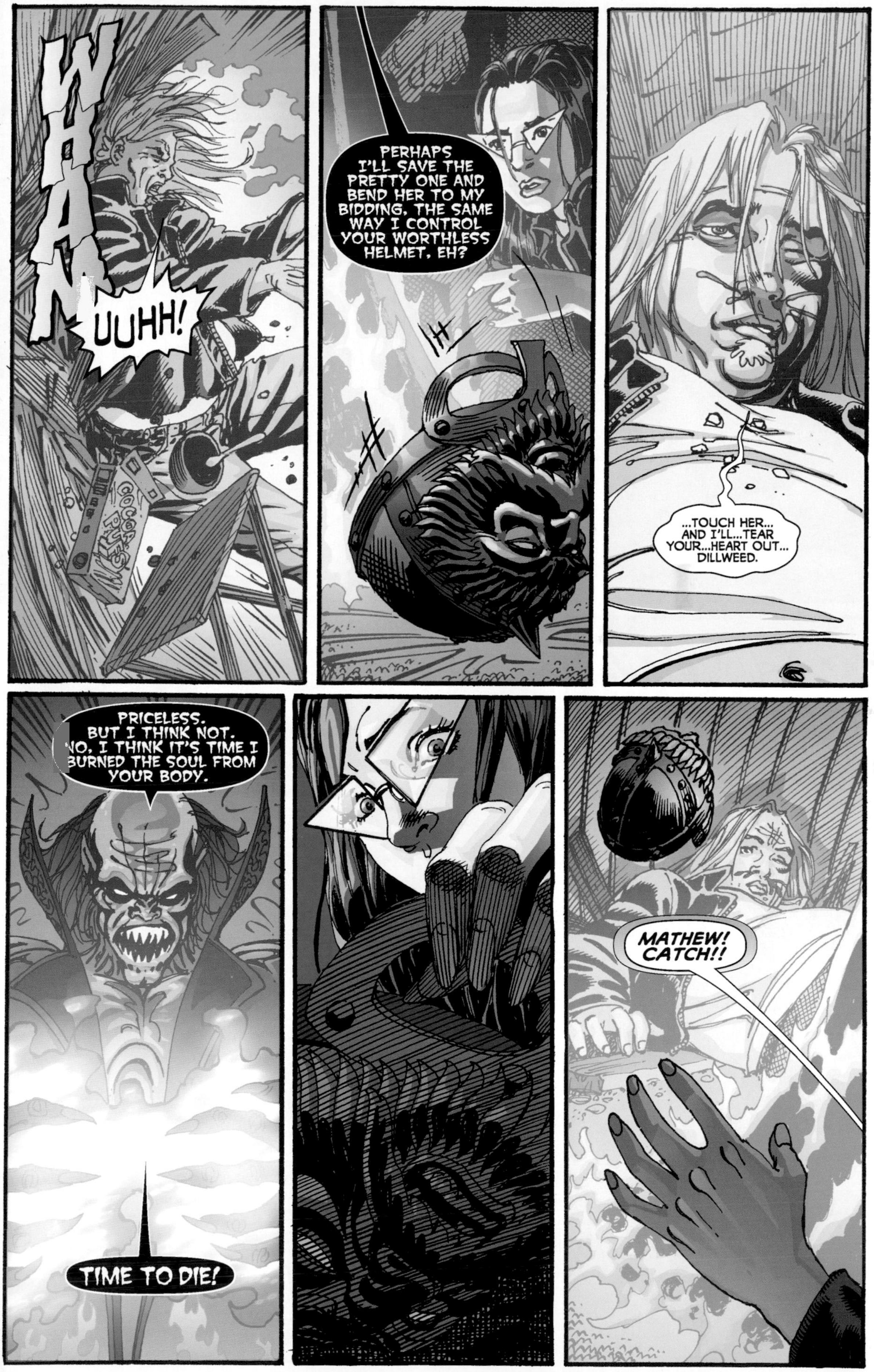
WHAM
UUHH!
PERHAPS I'LL SAVE THE PRETTY ONE AND BEND HER TO MY BIDDING, THE SAME WAY I CONTROL YOUR WORTHLESS HELMET, EH?
...TOUCH HER... AND I'LL...TEAR YOUR...HEART OUT... DILLWEED.
PRICELESS. BUT I THINK NOT. NO, I THINK IT'S TIME I BURNED THE SOUL FROM YOUR BODY.
TIME TO DIE!
MATHEW! CATCH!!

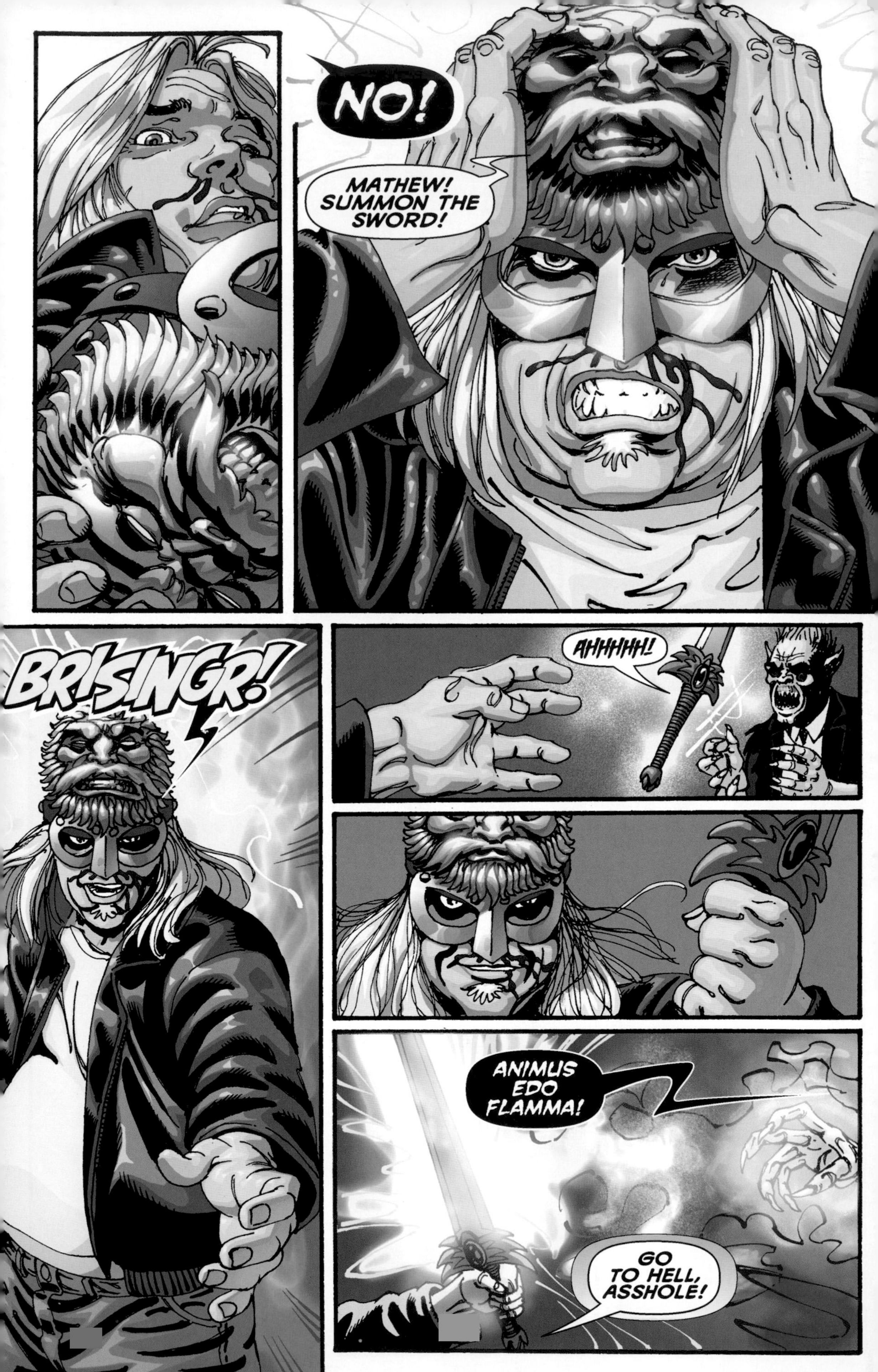
NO!
MATHEW! SUMMON THE SWORD!
BRISINGR!
AHHHHH!
ANIMUS EDO FLAMMA!
GO TO HELL, ASSHOLE!

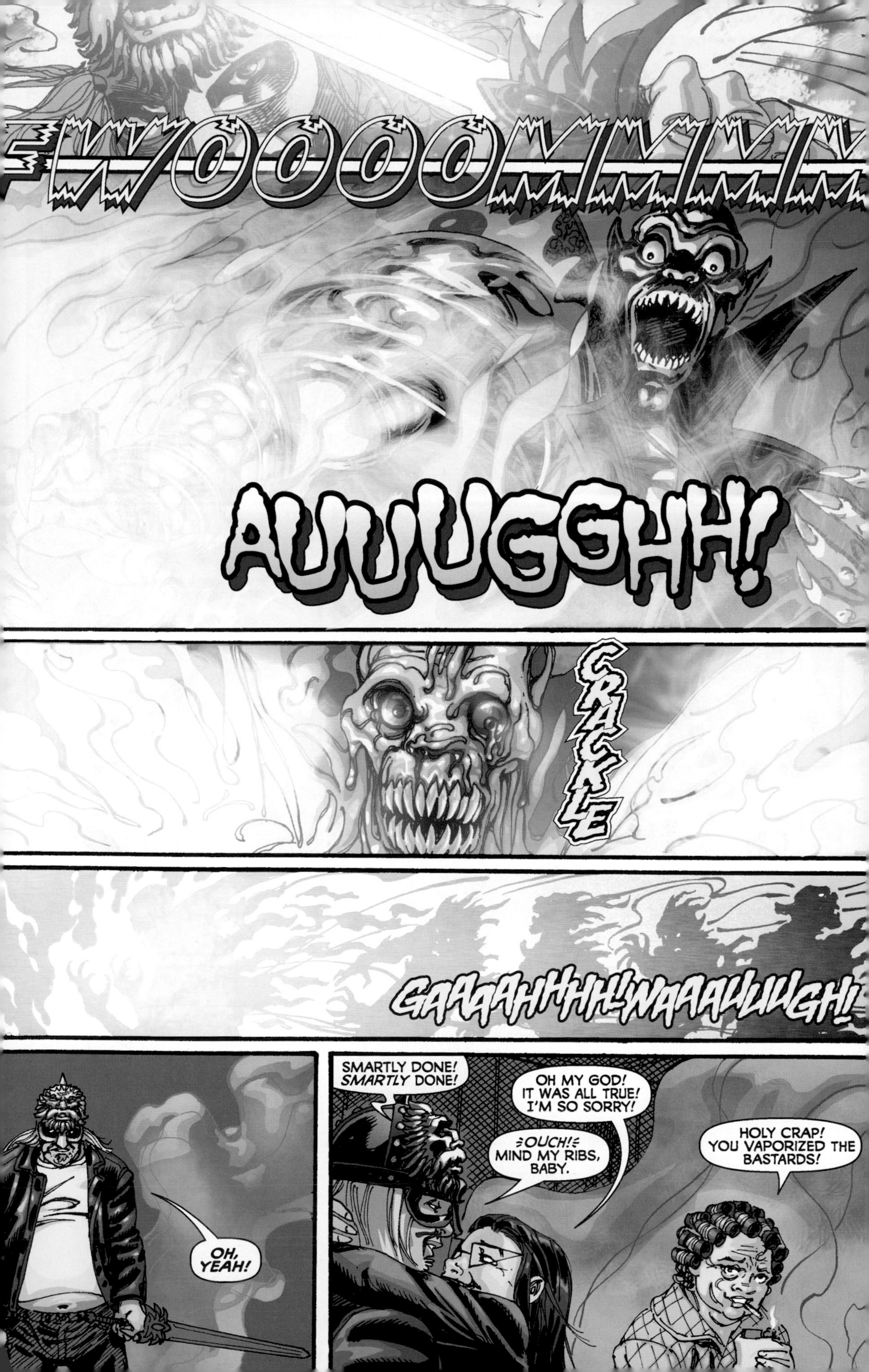
FWOOOOOMMMMM
AUUUGGHH!
CRACKLE
GAAAAHHHH!WAAAAUUUGH!
OH, YEAH!
SMARTLY DONE! *SMARTLY* DONE!
OH MY GOD! IT WAS ALL TRUE! I'M SO SORRY!
OUCH! MIND MY RIBS, BABY.
HOLY CRAP! YOU VAPORIZED THE BASTARDS!

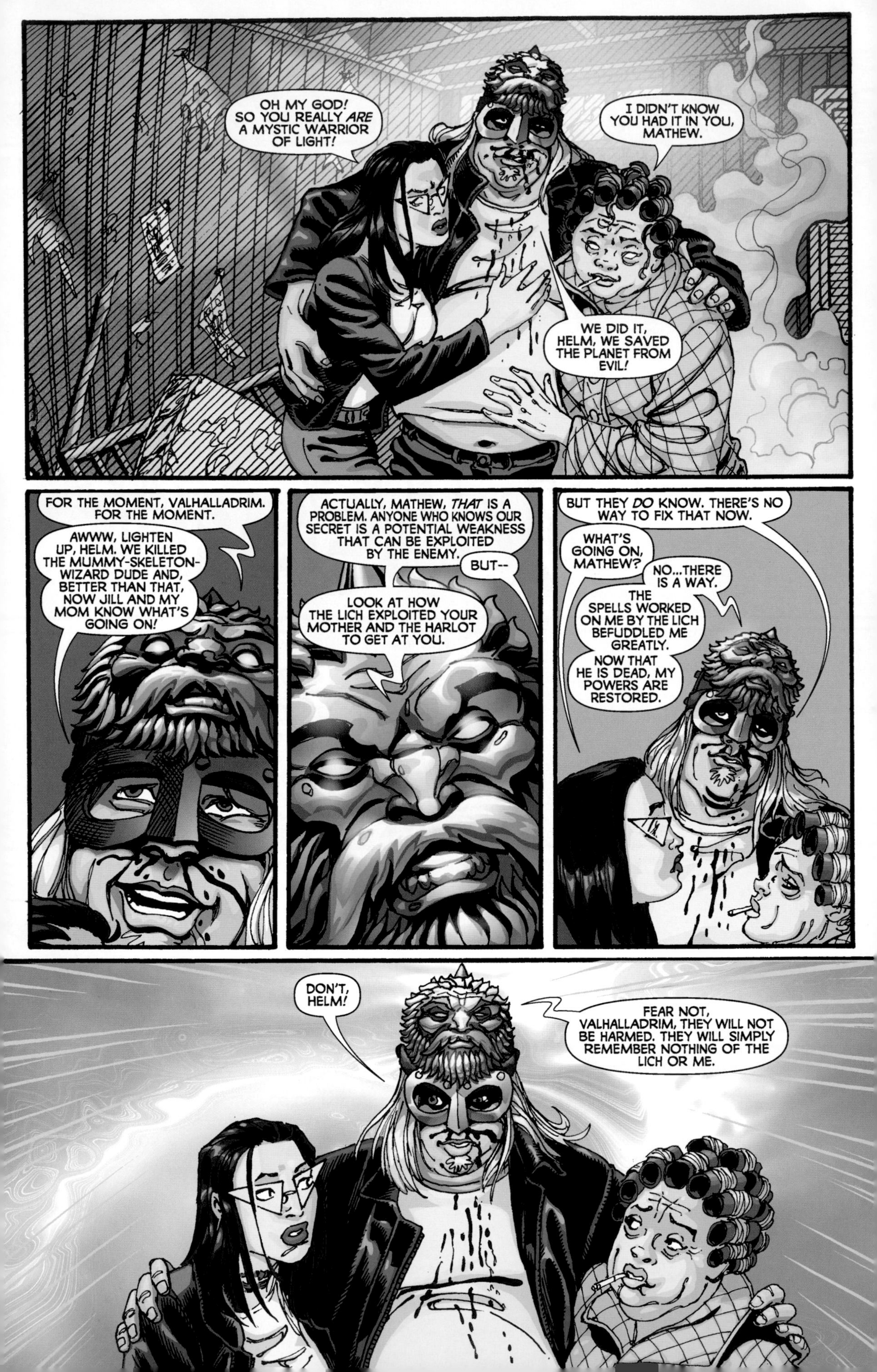
OH MY GOD! SO YOU REALLY *ARE* A MYSTIC WARRIOR OF LIGHT!
I DIDN'T KNOW YOU HAD IT IN YOU, MATHEW.
WE DID IT, HELM, WE SAVED THE PLANET FROM EVIL!
FOR THE MOMENT, VALHALLADRIM. FOR THE MOMENT.
AWWW, LIGHTEN UP, HELM. WE KILLED THE MUMMY-SKELETON-WIZARD DUDE AND, BETTER THAN THAT, NOW JILL AND MY MOM KNOW WHAT'S GOING ON!
ACTUALLY, MATHEW, *THAT* IS A PROBLEM. ANYONE WHO KNOWS OUR SECRET IS A POTENTIAL WEAKNESS THAT CAN BE EXPLOITED BY THE ENEMY.
BUT--
LOOK AT HOW THE LICH EXPLOITED YOUR MOTHER AND THE HARLOT TO GET AT YOU.
BUT THEY *DO* KNOW. THERE'S NO WAY TO FIX THAT NOW.
WHAT'S GOING ON, MATHEW?
NO...THERE IS A WAY.
THE SPELLS WORKED ON ME BY THE LICH BEFUDDLED ME GREATLY.
NOW THAT HE IS DEAD, MY POWERS ARE RESTORED.
DON'T, HELM!
FEAR NOT, VALHALLADRIM, THEY WILL NOT BE HARMED. THEY WILL SIMPLY REMEMBER NOTHING OF THE LICH OR ME.

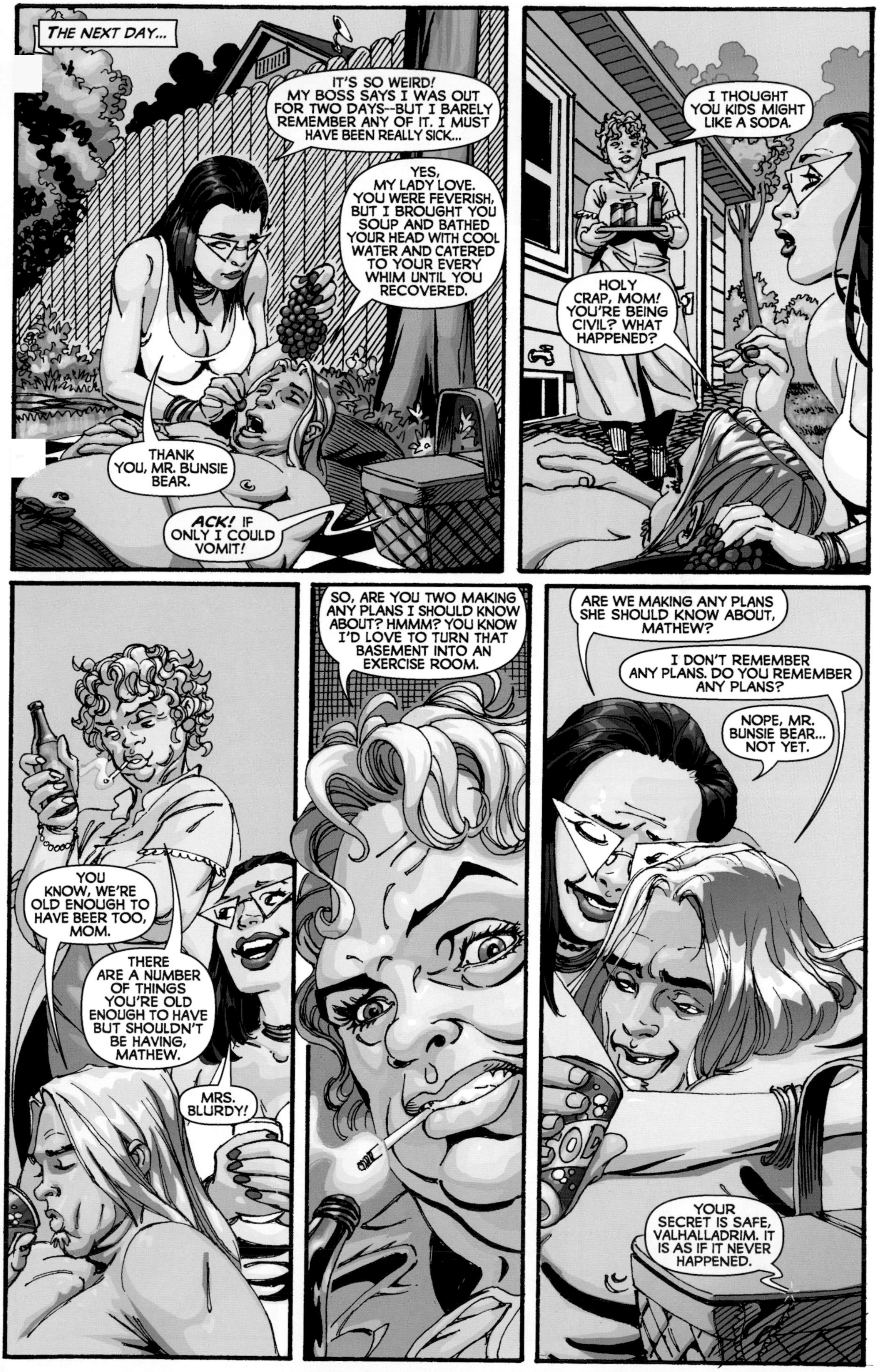
THE NEXT DAY...
IT'S SO WEIRD! MY BOSS SAYS I WAS OUT FOR TWO DAYS--BUT I BARELY REMEMBER ANY OF IT. I MUST HAVE BEEN REALLY SICK...
YES, MY LADY LOVE. YOU WERE FEVERISH, BUT I BROUGHT YOU SOUP AND BATHED YOUR HEAD WITH COOL WATER AND CATERED TO YOUR EVERY WHIM UNTIL YOU RECOVERED.
THANK YOU, MR. BUNSIE BEAR.
ACK! IF ONLY I COULD VOMIT!
I THOUGHT YOU KIDS MIGHT LIKE A SODA.
HOLY CRAP, MOM! YOU'RE BEING CIVIL? WHAT HAPPENED?
YOU KNOW, WE'RE OLD ENOUGH TO HAVE BEER TOO, MOM.
THERE ARE A NUMBER OF THINGS YOU'RE OLD ENOUGH TO HAVE BUT SHOULDN'T BE HAVING, MATHEW.
MRS. BLURDY!
SO, ARE YOU TWO MAKING ANY PLANS I SHOULD KNOW ABOUT? HMMM? YOU KNOW I'D LOVE TO TURN THAT BASEMENT INTO AN EXERCISE ROOM.
ARE WE MAKING ANY PLANS SHE SHOULD KNOW ABOUT, MATHEW?
I DON'T REMEMBER ANY PLANS. DO YOU REMEMBER ANY PLANS?
NOPE, MR. BUNSIE BEAR... NOT YET.
YOUR SECRET IS SAFE, VALHALLADRIM. IT IS AS IF IT NEVER HAPPENED.

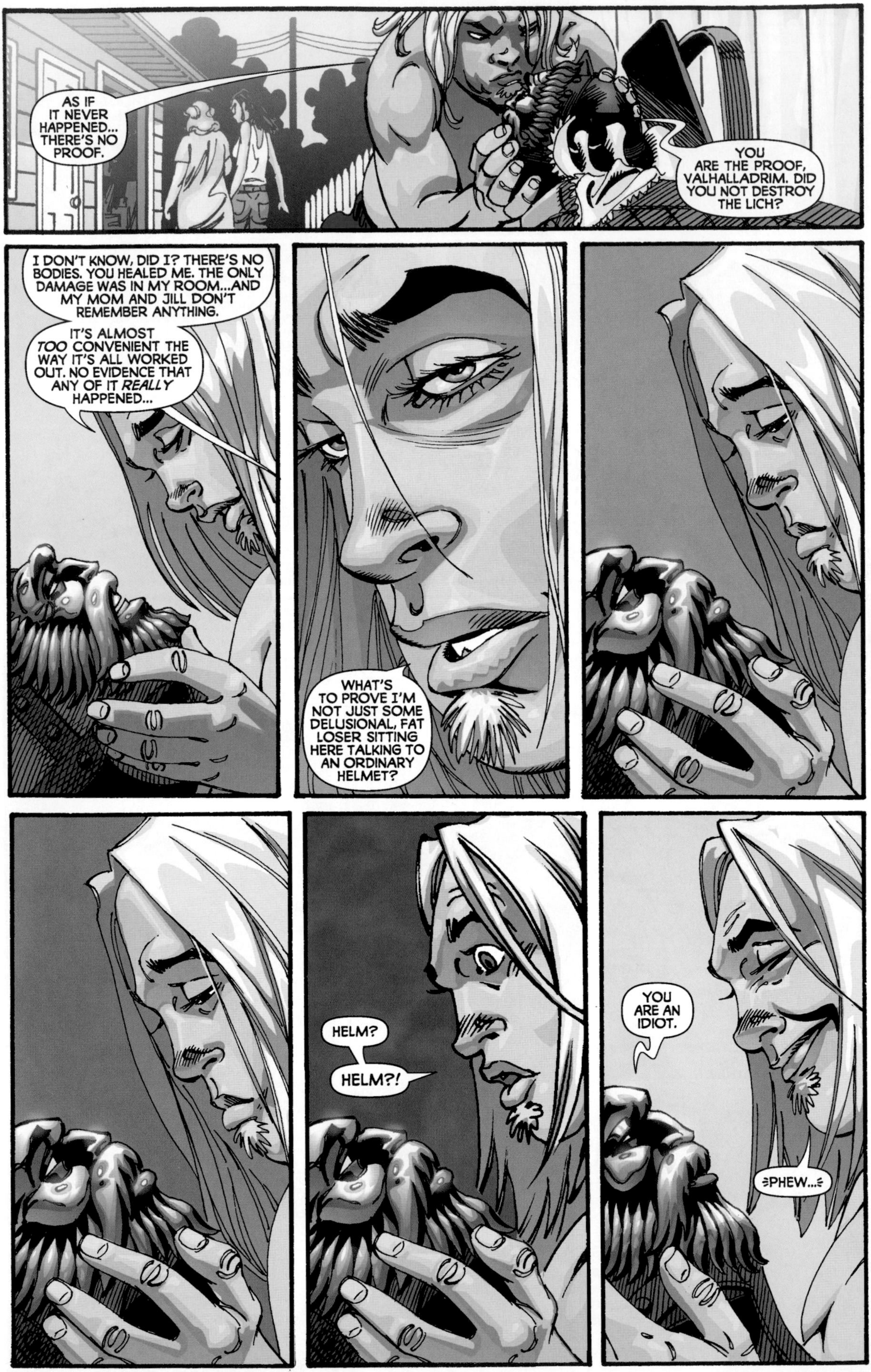
AS IF IT NEVER HAPPENED... THERE'S NO PROOF.
YOU ARE THE PROOF, VALHALLADRIM. DID YOU NOT DESTROY THE LICH?
I DON'T KNOW, DID I? THERE'S NO BODIES. YOU HEALED ME. THE ONLY DAMAGE WAS IN MY ROOM...AND MY MOM AND JILL DON'T REMEMBER ANYTHING.
IT'S ALMOST *TOO* CONVENIENT THE WAY IT'S ALL WORKED OUT. NO EVIDENCE THAT ANY OF IT *REALLY* HAPPENED...
WHAT'S TO PROVE I'M NOT JUST SOME DELUSIONAL, FAT LOSER SITTING HERE TALKING TO AN ORDINARY HELMET?
HELM?
HELM?!
YOU ARE AN IDIOT.
PHEW...

The End